Transactions of the Royal Historical Society

SIXTH SERIES

XVII

CAMBRIDGE
UNIVERSITY PRESS

Published by the Press Syndicate of the University of Cambridge
The Edinburgh Building, Cambridge CB2 8RU, United Kingdom
32 Avenue of the Americas, New York, NY 10013–2473, USA
477 Williamstown Road, Port Melbourne, VIC 3207 Australia
Ruiz de Alarcón 13, 28014 Madrid, Spain

A catalogue record for this book is available from the British Library

First published 2007

ISBN 9780 521 896054 hardback

SUBSCRIPTIONS. The serial publications of the Royal Historical Society, *Royal Historical Society Transactions* (ISSN 0080–4401) and Camden Fifth Series (ISSN 0960–1163) volumes may be purchased together on annual subscription. The 2007 subscription price (which includes print and electronic access) is £91 (US$147 in the USA, Canada and Mexico) and includes Camden Fifth Series, volumes 30 and 31 (published in July and December) and Transactions Sixth Series, volume 17 (published in December). Japanese prices are available from Kinokuniya Company Ltd, PO Box 55, Chitose, Tokyo 156, Japan. EU subscribers (outside the UK) who are not registered for VAT should add VAT at their country's rate. VAT registered subscribers should provide their VAT registration number.

Subscription orders, which must be accompanied by payment, may be sent to a bookseller, subscription agent or direct to the publisher: Cambridge University Press, The Edinburgh Building, Shaftesbury Road, Cambridge CB2 8RU, UK; or in the USA, Canada and Mexico; Cambridge University Press, Journals Fulfillment Department, 100 Brook Hill Drive, West Nyack, New York 10994–2133, USA. Prices include delivery by air.

SINGLE VOLUMES AND BACK VOLUMES. A list of Royal Historical Society volumes available from Cambridge University Press may be obtained from the Humanities Marketing Department at the address above.

Printed and bound in the United Kingdom at the University Press, Cambridge

CONTENTS

Transactions of the RHS 17 (2007), pp. 1–33 © 2007 Royal Historical Society
doi:10.1017/S0080440107000515   Printed in the United Kingdom

TRANSACTIONS OF THE

ROYAL HISTORICAL SOCIETY

PRESIDENTIAL ADDRESS

By Martin Daunton

BRITAIN AND GLOBALISATION SINCE 1850: II. THE RISE OF INSULAR CAPITALISM, 1914–1939

READ 24 NOVEMBER 2006

ABSTRACT. At the end of the First World War, the British government attempted to return to the pre-war policy trade-off of fixed exchanges rates on the gold standard, capital mobility and free trade, which entailed a sacrifice of domestic monetary policy. But the attempt proved difficult between 1919 and 1931 when the pursuit of international economic polices was constrained by a growing concern for their domestic economic and political repercussions. In the 1930s, a new policy trade-off emerged: managed exchange rates, capital controls and protectionism, with a greater concern for domestic monetary policy. The essay explains the reasons for the emergence of constraints and the subsequent abandonment of the pre-1914 policy trade-off in terms of five variables: changes in the performance of the economy and its impact on different actors; the politics of the national debt and the constraints on interest rates; the impact of capital exports on debt repayment and as an alternative to interest rates in influencing the exchanges; an adjustment in assumptions about flexibility of wages and costs; and a breakdown in the political culture of free trade and gold.

In 1933, John Maynard Keynes pondered the virtues of 'National self-sufficiency' compared with the pursuit of an international division of labour and the benefits of comparative advantage. Prior to the First World War, he was a staunch adherent of the world of Richard Cobden: peace and prosperity rested on 'the interdependence and connexion of material well-being throughout the world'; economic nationalism would only lead to 'jealousy and hostility' and hence to war. As Keynes remarked in 1933, he had been brought up to see free trade not only as an economic policy but 'almost as a part of the moral law'.

Keynes still adhered to free trade and comparative advantage after the First World War as a defence against poverty and as a 'principle of international morals', though now separated from *laissez faire*. But Keynes started to move from cosmopolitan to 'insular capitalism'. The insular turn started with *A Tract on Monetary Reform* in 1923, where he argued that British prices and wages should not be forced to adjust to the dictates of the exchange rate. Rather, the exchange rate should be dictated by domestic considerations. In 1924, he developed his thoughts further by questioning the value of foreign investments which he argued arose from institutional biases in the City rather than an efficient use of resources. A default by a foreign borrower left Britain with nothing; a default on a domestic loan still left the asset. He felt that investment should be directed to domestic capital construction in order to create employment – not least through a programme of public works in housing, roads and electrification. What was the point of redeeming the national debt if the funds so released were invested overseas? He denied the common assumption that investment abroad led to demand for British goods and was therefore just as beneficial as investment at home.

By 1930, he was less convinced of the virtues of free trade. It implied flexibility in wages which no longer existed, and 'well-adjusted tariffs' might now reduce unemployment. Britain no longer had such advantages in manufacturing as in the past, and had relatively high wages. He still hesitated on moral grounds, and saw tariffs more as a means of addressing current difficulties than a long-term policy. But in 1933, he departed still further from his earlier Cobdenism. Free movement of goods and capital might actually provoke war rather than guarantee peace by placing countries 'at the mercy of world forces', and preventing the pursuit of domestic economic recovery through investment at home:

> It does not now seem obvious that a great concentration of national effort on the capture of foreign trade, that the penetration of a country's economic structure by the resources and influence of foreign capitalists, that a close dependence of our economic life on the fluctuating economic policies of foreign countries, are safeguards and assurances of international peace. It is easier, in the light of experience and foresight, to argue quite the contrary.

The economy had changed, he argued, so that he was not persuaded that 'the economic advantages of the international division of labour today are at all comparable with what they were'. Most countries could now undertake mass production with virtually the same level of efficiency, and as prosperity increased so a larger proportion of consumption was on services which could not be traded internationally. Hence the economic costs of self-sufficiency did not 'outweigh the other advantages of gradually bringing the producer and the consumer within the ambit of the same national, economic and financial organisation'.

Not only the economic but also the moral benefits of comparative advantage were in abeyance. Far from leading to peace, free trade and capital mobility were more likely to produce conflict, leading to resentment against foreign ownership of assets. Indeed, it was preferable to 'minimise rather than . . . maximise economic entanglement between nations. Ideas, knowledge, art, hospitality, travel – these are the things which should of their nature be international. But let goods be homespun whenever it is reasonably and conveniently possible; and above all let finance be primarily national.' As he argued in 1932, comparative advantage would destroy the identities and cultures of the different parts of Britain which were dedicated to different trades and crafts. Merely counting costs turned the world into an accountants' nightmare, in which beauty and nature had no value and therefore did not matter. Cobdenism was replaced by something closer to John Ruskin's denunciation of the pursuit of material advantage as destructive of all that was best in life.[1]

Keynes had moved far away from the liberal, cosmopolitan economic order which dominated in the half century before the First World War, of free trade, capital mobility and the gold standard. Not everyone was entirely convinced by Keynes's rejection of Cobden and the tradition of Adam Smith. Perhaps, suggested one sceptical writer in the *New Statesman*, the high table at King's College would in future grow witty by consuming Empire wines. More seriously, Lionel Robbins defended the classic case for the comparative advantages of free trade, and J. A. Hobson argued for internationalism as a resolution of the problems of the economy.[2] But it was Keynes who was more representative of changes in the economic culture of interwar liberalism. Even in the opinion of its honorary secretary, Wedgwood Benn, the Cobden Club – the home of true believers in free trade and liberal economics – was an irrelevance. George Paish, the adviser to Lloyd George as chancellor of the Exchequer before 1914 and a leading member of the Club, was dismissed as 'a bit of a laughing stock'.[3]

Keynes's loss of his Cobdenite faith led to a new trade-off between the constituent elements of the 'inconsistent trinity' which I discussed in the previous address. As we saw, it is possible to have two but not three of fixed exchange rates; capital movements; and an active domestic monetary policy. Prior to the First World War, the British government – in line with most other advanced economies – was firmly committed to

---

[1] R. Skidelsky, *John Maynard Keynes*, II: *The Economist as Saviour, 1920–1937* (1992), 183–6, 191, 476–8. The lecture was delivered in Dublin on 17 Apr. 1933 and published in *New Statesman*, 8 and 15 July 1933. See also D. Markwell, *John Maynard Keynes and International Relations: Economic Paths to War and Peace* (Oxford, 2006), 7–19, 152–65.

[2] Skidelsky, *John Maynard Keynes*, II, note on 478, quoting G. L. Schwartz, *New Statesman*, 22 July 1933; Markwell, *John Maynard Keynes and International Relations*, 156–8.

[3] F. Trentmann, 'The Resurrection and Decomposition of Cobden in Britain and the West: An Essay in the Politics of Reputation', in *Rethinking Nineteenth-Century Liberalism: Richard Cobden Bicentenary Essays*, ed. A. Howe and S. Morgan (Aldershot, 2006), 273, quoting House of Lords Record Office, Stansgate Papers ST28614.

a fixed exchange rate on the gold standard. It followed that if the value of the pound started to appreciate (say in response to a strong balance of payments or an inflow of funds), interest rates would be reduced in order to make the London money market less attractive and so hold down the value of the pound. The lower cost of borrowing might stimulate the domestic economy by boosting demand and investment – but in the absence of controls on capital mobility, investors were likely to seek outlets overseas. Conversely, if the value of the pound started to depreciate, interest rates would be raised in order to attract funds into London. Higher domestic interest rates would retain funds in Britain, but the additional cost might well depress the domestic economy. As a result of the need to protect the exchange rate, and the lack of any controls on capital movements, the government could do little to stimulate the British economy through an active domestic monetary policy. This particular trade-off in the 'inconsistent trinity' was complemented by a commitment to free trade up to 1914.[4]

Between the wars, the policy trade-off changed in two phases. The first phase covered post-war preparations for the return to gold in 1925 up to its abandonment in 1931. The aim was to restore the pre-war trade-off, a strategy which faced greater difficulties. The British government was committed to returning to fixed exchanges at the pre-war parity and prepared the ground by adjusting British prices to the dictates of £1 = $4.86. At the same time, capital mobility was desired but the level of overseas investment was now considerably lower and constrained by a variety of considerations. The logic of the international economy could no longer be pursued to its conclusion at the expense of domestic considerations which now started to play a larger, though still subordinate, role. Finally, free trade was the norm but was coming under greater pressure. In other words, the late Victorian and Edwardian policy mix was still pursued within a new set of constraints and limitations which rendered it less stable, with greater difficulties in sacrificing domestic considerations to international issues.

The second phase ran from the economic crisis of 1931 to the outbreak of the Second World War. Fixed exchanges were abandoned and the pound could now be managed with a modest under-valuation in order to encourage exports and limit imports. Capital mobility fell to low levels with much tighter controls on the market, and Britain became a net importer of capital. It followed that an active domestic monetary policy could now be pursued to hold down the value of the pound, to permit a reduction in the cost of servicing the national debt and to stimulate the housing market. At the same time, free trade was abandoned and

⁴ See M. Daunton, 'Britain and Globalisation since 1850: I. Creating a Global Order, 1850–1914', *Transactions of the Royal Historical Society*, 16 (2006), 6–8.

imperial preference introduced. The result was a move from globalisation to 'insular capitalism', the abandonment of international considerations for a greater concern for domestic stability. Economic adjustment was now externalised (devaluation and protection) rather than internalised (deflation to reduce costs).

Why did the trade-off change so radically from the globalised economy of the period prior to the First World War? The international economy before 1914 certainly experienced tensions, with a growing demand for trade protection and limits on migration by those who were suffering from globalisation. In the late nineteenth century, the level of per capita income in the Atlantic economies converged as labour left some parts of Europe (so forcing up wages) and moved to the new world (so moderating the impact of scarcity). The movement of labour also had distributional consequences within each area of the Atlantic economy, with a rise in income inequality in the rich, labour-scarce countries of the new world (Argentina, USA, Canada) as immigration eroded the bargaining position of workers, and a fall in inequality in poor, labour-abundant countries of the old world (Italy, Ireland) as the bargaining position of workers improved. These outcomes produced a nationalist backlash against globalisation: workers in the new world resented the inflow of migrants and demanded restriction on immigration; farmers and landowners in the old world resented the influx of cheap grain from across the Atlantic and demanded tariffs. Thus the inequalities created by globalisation were leading to a backlash even before the war in order to defend the poor in the labour-scarce countries, and to protect both the landed poor and the landed rich in much of Europe. Britain was somewhere between these two groups of countries which helps to explain the muted resistance to globalisation before 1914: emigration increased the bargaining power of workers; and farmers and landowners who lost from competition with imports from the new world had much less political clout than their counterparts in France or Germany. The backlash was therefore weak compared with other countries where, as O'Rourke and Williamson argue, globalisation planted the seeds of its own destruction in the 1870s which sprouted in the 1880s, grew at the turn of the century and reached maturity after the First World War.[5]

As Harold James points out, globalisation both depended on the nation state and provoked nationalism – an uneasy relationship. The nation state was a response to threats from outside, seeking 'to externalize the costs

---

[5] P. Aghion and J. G. Williamson, *Growth, Inequality and Globalization: Theory, Inequality and Policy* (Cambridge, 1998), Part II;these lectures summarise and bring out some of the implications of K. H. O'Rourke and J. G. Williamson, *Globalization and History: The Evolution of a Nineteenth-Century Atlantic Economy* (Cambridge, MA, 1999) – see 93 for the metaphor of plants.

of economic adjustment... on those outside the national community. The state's duty lay in protecting its citizens and in ensuring that the inhabitants of other national communities suffered as much as possible.' Globalisation would be threatened if politicians in nation states succumbed to domestic political pressures and were not constrained by commitment mechanisms and international organisations. The post-war institutions were too weak and the forces of nationalism too strong.[6]

Why did the forces of economic nationalism prove so powerful? Eichengreen points to three factors. First, those who stood to suffer from the pursuit of fixed exchanges now gained voice with the coming of manhood suffrage. He argues that the credibility of the commitment to gold before 1914 'depended on a unique constellation of political and economic factors' which insulated central bankers and governments from pressures to adopt other policies, both because 'the connections between monetary policy and unemployment were only vaguely understood' and because 'those most concerned about the domestic consequences of international monetary policies had as yet acquired only limited political influence'. Between the wars, this insulation was breached as groups and interests affected by restrictive monetary policies gained voice. Second, central bank cooperation was now much weaker and less able to handle tensions in the international financial system, for central bankers were constrained by rules designed to prevent a repeat of hyperinflation and instability after the war, so removing their flexibility to offer mutual support in times of crisis and making for more instability. At the same time, the post-war settlement failed to create new institutions which could offer a different approach to international cooperation and make commitment to fixed exchanges credible. The so-called 'Geneva consensus' failed to prevent the pursuit of nationalistic interest, for international conferences and institutions such as the Bank of International Settlements were permeated with the tensions of reparations and debts, and weakened by the isolationism of the United States. Thirdly, Eichengreen suggests that the 'self-equilibrating tendencies of the market' did not come into operation after the initial shock of 1929 and the restrictive monetary policy of the Federal Reserve. Many observers argued that wages were more 'sticky' between the wars, and Eichengreen suggests that the same problem arose with respect to other variables so that costs did not fall in order to moderate the reduction in sales and employment. He points out that mortgages and rents were set in nominal terms for long periods, and that bonds similarly offered fixed payments. The problem, he argues, was that each recipient of income – *rentiers*, capitalists and workers – would have accepted a cut if everyone else did the same. However, 'without a

---

[6] H. James, *The End of Globalization: Lessons from the Great Depression* (Cambridge, MA, 2001), 13, 197.

mechanism to coordinate their actions, no one group was prepared to be the first to offer concessions'.[7]

The implication of last year's address is that the first two points were not crucial. Before 1914, the gold standard was widely seen as beneficial so that the key change was not that workers gained voice to express an existing, disregarded hostility; rather, hostility to the gold standard developed anew. Furthermore, cooperation of central banks was not crucial to the maintenance of the gold standard before the First World War; rather, adherence to the gold standard and its norms rested on an assessment of self-interest. After the war, the issue was not so much a weakness of international rules and regulations as a reassessment of self-interest which meant they became less willing or able to pursue internationalism.[8] What exactly changed to alter the pre-1914 trade-off so that the attempt to return to the apparently golden age of Edwardian Britain was no longer feasible? I will suggest that the answer lies, in the first place, in significant changes in the performance of the economy which affected calculations of self-interest by a number of major actors.

I

A major shift in the performance of the British economy led to an objective change in the welfare benefits of the pre-war trade-off for workers, industrialists, bankers and the state. Although economic historians have spent much time and effort in debating the timing of the so-called 'climacteric' in economic growth in the later nineteenth century, the most striking feature in the statistics is the low growth rate of the transwar period (see Table 1). The shock of war pushed the economy from equilibrium, and in the words of Matthews, Feinstein and Odling-Smee 'the absolute fall in GDP across the war, not made good until the late 1920s, is one of the most spectacular features of recent British economic history'. The explanation for this poor growth performance was in part a drop in labour input and hours of work: growth of labour input (adjusted for quality) fell from 1.7 per cent per annum in the period 1873–1913 to −0.4 per cent per annum between 1913 and 1924 before rising to 2.1 per cent per annum between 1924 and 1937. At the end of the war, hours of work fell from fifty-four to forty-seven per week or a drop of 13 per cent without a cut in wages. During the final stages of the war and the post-war boom, wages rose as a result of the increased bargaining power of labour which led to a surge of union membership, increased militancy and a spate of strikes. Wage-push inflation, as well as the pressures of war finance and the heavy

[7] B. Eichengreen, *Golden Fetters: The Gold Standard and the Great Depression, 1919–1939* (New York and Oxford, 1992), 4 21, 31, 391 4; on the problems of international institutions, see James, *End of Globalization*, 33–7.

[8] Daunton, 'Britain and Globalisation: I', 1–38.

Table 1 *Growth of GDP and GDP per man-year in the United Kingdom and Great Britain and Northern Ireland, 1856–1951, annual percentage growth rates*

	United Kingdom		GB and N Ireland	
	GDP	GDP per man-year	GDP	GDP per man-year
Peace-time phase				
1856–73	2.2	1.3	2.4	1.2
1873–1913	1.8	0.9	2.0	0.9
Transwar phase				
1913–24	−0.1	0.3	−0.1	0.3
Peace-time phase				
1924–37	2.2	1.0	2.2	1.0
Transwar phase				
1937–51	1.8	1.0	1.8	1.0
Peace-time phase				
1951–73	2.8	2.4	2.8	2.4

Source: Matthews, Feinstein and Odling-Smee, *British Economic Growth*, table 2.1, 22.

reliance on loans, resulted in high levels of inflation during the war and post-war boom compared with the USA.[9]

These trends had very serious consequences for the British economy after the war. The increased price of British goods meant that overseas markets were lost, so exacerbating the erosion of markets as a result of the imperative of the war effort; the emergence of competition from India, Japan and the USA in Latin America and Asia; and the shift from coal to oil which hit the export trade from south Wales and the north-east of England. Furthermore, foreign firms entered British markets in 1920–2 when their goods were particularly cheap; and once they created distribution networks and established a reputation, they were not easily displaced until the development of protection in the 1930s. The import ratio increased in the early 1920s and remained high for the rest of the decade.[10] The loss of overseas markets led to high unemployment

[9] R. C. O. Matthews, C. H. Feinstein and J. C. Odling-Smee, *British Economic Growth, 1856–1973* (Oxford, 1982), 501, 503, 543; also J. R. Dowie, '1919–20 Is in Need of Attention', *Economic History Review*, 28 (1975), 429–50.

[10] S. N. Broadberry, 'The Emergence of Mass Unemployment: Explaining Macroeconmic Trends in Britain during the Trans-World War I Period', *Economic History Review*, 43 (1990), 271–82; S. Solomou, *Themes in Macroeconomic History: The UK Economy, 1919–1939* (Cambridge,

Table 2 *Multilateral real effective exchange rate for £ (1913 = 100)*

	Deflating by	
	Wholesale prices (trade weighted, 19 countries)	Retail prices (trade weighted, 16 countries)
1924	95.2	83.4
1925	94.8	79.6
1926	92.0	73.8
1927	97.3	81.5
1928	98.5	81.9
1929	101.3	84.9
1930	103.5	87.2

Below 100 for overvaluation, above 100 for under-valuation.
Source: Redmond, 'Sterling Overvaluation', table 3, 529.

in the staple export industries of cotton, coal, shipbuilding and heavy engineering, and the slack was not taken up by the domestic market.

As a result of British inflation, the pre-war parity of the pound sterling was too high at the end of the war, and the decision to return to the gold standard exacerbated the problems in export markets. Keynes claimed that the pound was over-valued by 10 per cent against the dollar at the time of the return to gold, and his estimate has been disputed and refined by a number of scholars. Of course, Britain traded with many other countries than the United States, so that the best measure of over-valuation is to weight the exchange rate by trade with various partners. On this measure, sterling was overvalued by at least 5 and possibly as much as 20 per cent in 1925 compared with 1913 (see Table 2). Of course, British prices were reduced in preparation for the return to gold, so that the over-valuation of sterling was still greater before 1925.[11] Although historians have focused on the impact of the return to gold in 1925 and the conflict over cost-cutting which resulted in the miners' lock-out and general strike in 1926, these policies had their greatest impact before 1925 when the British government adopted deflationary monetary policy and high real interest rates in the early 1920s which hit the domestic economy. In the words of Stephen Broadberry, 'It was the unfortunate combination of the scale of the hours reduction, the maintenance of the weekly wage,

1996), 47; M. Kitson and S. Solomou, *Protectionism and Economic Revival: The British Interwar Economy* (Cambridge, 1980), 51–3, 83.
[11] J. Redmond, 'The Sterling Overvaluation in 1925: A Multilateral Approach', *Economic History Review*, 37 (1984), 520–32; and K. G. P. Matthews, 'Was Sterling Overvalued in 1925?', *Economic History Review*, 39 (1986), 572–87.

and the appreciation of the exchange rate which was so devastating for British industry in the aftermath of World War I.'[12]

The deflationary policies of the government are well known, but the problems of the British economy were further exacerbated by the behaviour of businessmen. During the post-war boom, firms in a number of leading export sectors – above all cotton, shipping and steel – incurred high debts for what soon turned out to be inappropriate ventures or flotations at excessive prices. The boom was transitory, reflecting the need to build up stocks on the return to peace rather than a high level of demand in normal conditions. Ships were under-utilised as a result of the convoy system, and at the end of the war needed to relocate to meet the demand for restocking. In this interlude, freight rates were very high, and both second-hand and new ships changed hands or were constructed at inflated prices. In reality, there was a glut of tonnage, and freight rates and shipping prices soon fell, so leaving ship-owners heavily burdened with debt and British shipyards without orders. The ship-owners had to focus on writing down their loans and capital rather than investing in new, efficient ships using new technology, and they fell behind their competitors. In the past, British ship-owners were able to compete by purchasing new, efficient vessels with low running and maintenance costs so offsetting their higher labour costs; now, their competitors were able to buy new ships with low maintenance costs as well as benefiting from low wages. The outcome was similar in cotton and steel, and contributed to the difficulties of these leading export industries.[13]

As a result, the debt–income ratio in Britain rose from 1.6 in 1913 to 2.8 in 1929: British industrialists were burdened with a higher cost of servicing loans out of narrower profit margins. By contrast, the debt ratio in France fell from 2.8 to 2.1. Of course, a lower debt ratio was not always desirable, for Germany's low debt–income ratio was a result of hyperinflation which weakened the financial system.[14] Although Britain avoided such a harmful and destructive outcome, the high level of debt created dangers for British banks which had lent unwisely to industry, and contributed to a shift in the policies of the Bank of England: domestic considerations were now much more relevant, for a collapse of British businesses would threaten the stability of the banking sector. These new circumstances contributed to a reassessment in the trade-off between domestic and international concerns. Of course, the industries most seriously affected were in export

---

[12] Broadberry, 'Emergence of Mass Unemployment', 282; Solomou, *Themes*, 39–40.

[13] C. E. Fayle, *The War and the Shipping Industry* (1927); S. G. Sturmey, *British Shipping and World Competition* (1962); G. W. Daniels and J. Jewkes, 'The Post-War Depression in the Lancashire Cotton Industry', *Journal of the Royal Statistical Society*, 91 (1928), 170–7; S. Tolliday, *Business, Banking and Politics: The Case of British Steel, 1918–1939* (Cambridge, MA, 1987), 177–8.

[14] Solomou, *Themes*, 47.

Table 3 *Profits' share in trading income and rate*

| | Gross | | Net | |
	Share	Rate	Share	Rate
1856	35.6	13.2	32.7	15.6
1873	38.1	14.0	35.1	17.3
1913	33.8	11.8	29.8	14.9
1924	24.9	8.7	20.5	11.2
1937	27.0	10.6	23.0	14.2
1951	23.8	7.7	18.2	9.3

Source: Matthews, Feinstein and Odling-Smee, *British Economic Growth*, tables 6.12 and 6.13, 186.

trades, so international considerations remained important, but in a more complex way, mediated by a concern for the industrial structure and performance.

Above all, changes in the interest rate had a serious impact on industry. The cost of servicing loans was particularly onerous because profit margins were squeezed over the transwar period. An excess profits tax was introduced in 1915 to tax increases in profits above a prescribed level, and it was continued after the war as part of a trade-off with other interests in response to the political difficulty of dealing with 'profiteers' and *rentiers*. However, taxation and inflation meant that the real return to equity capital fell from 10.0 per cent in 1910–14 to 8.7 per cent in 1915–20 and 3.1 per cent in 1920–4. The share of net profits in trading income fell from 29.8 per cent in 1913 to 20.5 per cent in 1924 (see Table 3).[15] Not surprisingly, industrialists were aggrieved and complained that their competitors in other countries were less burdened by the costs of the war as a result of a different fiscal regime, as well as the use of post-war inflation to reduce the burden of national and corporate debt. The British government was aware of the issue but leading officials at the Treasury and Inland Revenue argued that higher taxes would redeem the national debt and so benefit industry by returning money to bondholders for investment in productive enterprise. As we will see, the government's

[15] A. J. Arnold, 'Profitability and Capital Accumulation in British Industry during the Transwar Period, 1913–24', *Economic History Review*, 52 (1999), table 3; S. N. Broadberry, 'The Impact of the World Wars on the Long-Run Performance of the British Economy', *Oxford Review of Economic Policy*, 4 (1988), 25–37; Matthews, Feinstein and Odling-Smee, *British Economic Growth*, 186.

Table 4 *Average unemployment rates (%) in major industrial economies,*
1921–9

	Industrial unemployment	Total unemployment
France	3.8	—
Germany	9.2	4.0
UK	12.0	6.8
USA	7.7	4.9

Source: Solomou, *Themes*, 55.

concern with the politics of the national debt marked a major change in its approach to interest rates.[16]

The economic shock of the war was arguably worse in Britain than in other countries, with a long-term impact on equilibrium (see Table 4). Before 1914, unemployment was around 4.5 per cent and casual under-employment was in decline; after the war, the level of unemployment was never less than 10 per cent, and countries such as Britain that returned to gold at 1913 parities did worse than those which devalued.[17] The changed attitude to the gold standard and its need for higher interest rates was less the result of workers securing voice for a pre-existing and long-standing grievance than a change in economic conditions which created an objective justification for growing hostility to the previous trade-off between international and domestic policies. The link between fixed exchange rates and unemployment and the need to defend wage rates was much more apparent than it had been before 1914.

II

The war not only led to increased costs and a loss of competitiveness; it also increased the national debt and the costs of servicing it. The politics of debt collided with the imperative of the return to gold and the need to preserve the exchange rate through high interest rates. But there were reasons why the state could not pursue this policy as far as might be needed. The explanation was not only the political repercussions of high interest rates on different groups of the electorate, though that was undoubtedly a consideration. The state also had its own reasons to be wary, for servicing the post-war debt was a crucial political issue: in 1920/1, it took 22.4 per cent of budget receipts, and in 1925/6 36.4 per cent. The scale of the national debt at the end of the war, and the need to

---

[16] M. J. Daunton, 'How to Pay for the War: State, Society and Taxation in Britain, 1917–24', *English Historical Review*, 111 (1996), 896–903, 912; Daunton, *Just Taxes: The Politics of Taxation in Britain, 1914–1979* (Cambridge, 2002), 83–94.

[17] Solomou, *Themes*, 44–5, 53.

issue new long-term loans to replace short-term or floating debt, meant that high interest rates would increase the costs of debt service and hence the tax burden. The short-term bills reached a peak of £1,570m in 1919 and needed to be funded or paid off; otherwise, as Basil Blackett of the Treasury pointed out, there would be a vicious circle of new credit created by the government, followed by rises in prices and wages. By 1920, he was very concerned that 'the vicious circle will go on spinning and the crash will come'.

The treatment of the national debt was a central theme in post-war politics. Labour was pressing for a one-off capital levy on personal wealth to redeem the debt – a proposal that alienated property owners as the thin end of a wedge leading to further assaults on private capital. But a sales tax, on the lines adopted in France, would alienate workers as a blatant attack on distribution, a means of reducing taxes on *rentiers* and profiteers which might only strengthen support for the capital levy. Although some bankers argued for a higher income tax in order to reduce the debt as a threat to economic stability, the Treasury was more realistic in its assessment, fearing that it would alienate the middle class who had suffered from an erosion of their standard of living during the war, and so play into the hands of the critics of 'waste'. Of course, there were also dangers in responding to the attack on 'waste' by cutting welfare, so once again strengthening Labour support for the capital levy as a means of funding social spending rather than debt redemption. In the end, the best option was to retain a tax on industry on the grounds that it was the only interest with the capacity to pay. As the Treasury argued, it would probably bear the incidence of higher taxes. If a tax were imposed on sales, workers would demand higher wages: if they succeeded, industry would pay; if they failed, there would be strikes and disputes which would also increase costs. Would it not be better for industry to accept a tax which was only paid after a profit was earned? Furthermore, by repaying the debt, money would be returned to lenders who could then invest in industry.[18]

An increase in interest rates was closely connected with this debate over the redemption of the post-war debt. In considering taxation, one important strand in the Treasury's thinking was the need for neutrality between interests – and similar sentiments were held on interest rates which affected the relationships between debtors and creditors. Any increase in interest rates would intensify the political problems of handling the debt and resolving the dispute over the relative treatment of *rentiers* and taxpayers. At the Treasury, Winston Churchill, chancellor of the Exchequer from 1924 to 1929, believed that the debt should be paid off as soon as possible, for large payments of interest 'will not be allowed

---

[18] This and the previous paragraph are based on Daunton, 'How to Pay for the War', 882–919.

to continue indefinitely in a country based on an adult suffrage'. But debt redemption also meant high taxes, and he worried about their impact on production alongside the post-war policy of deflation. What was the merit of strengthening the exchange rate to support the gold standard at the expense of 'bad trade, hard times, an immense increase in unemployment'? As prices fell, so the real burden of debts rose, and taxes and the *rentier* class 'lie like a vast wet blanket across the whole process of creating new wealth by new enterprise'. He feared that he would be criticised for favouring the City and *rentiers* over production. At the end of 1924, he accordingly asked the Treasury to consider conversion of the national debt to a lower interest rate or to suspend the sinking fund. The Treasury had no objection to conversion which had been done before (most recently by George Goschen in 1888), and was compatible with fiscal orthodoxy. But how to do it? Otto Niemeyer, controller of finance at the Treasury, advised against dramatic measures to induce bondholders to convert; rather, he recommended occasional conversions in the market which would be made possible by following a cautious policy of balanced budgets, sinking funds and stable spending. Indeed, Niemeyer proposed a larger sinking fund paid for by a tax on *rentiers* with the right to bonds paying lower interest which would be free of this additional tax. Nothing came of the proposal and the government maintained its policy of steady redemption through sinking funds and controls over spending. But Churchill remained aware of the dangers and used all of his creative imagination to rebalance the fiscal system in favour of active producers against 'inert' *rentiers*.[19]

Between 1919 and 1931, the government had to balance the role of interest rates in preparing for or maintaining the gold standard and the impact on its own finances and on the politics of debt redemption. When gold was abandoned in 1931, interest rates could obviously be used in a much more active way to hold down the exchange rate, to simulate domestic recovery and to convert the national debt to a lower interest rate. The maintenance of low interest rates in the 1930s and 1940s was to be crucial to holding down the costs of debt service remaining from the First World War and to prevent a repeat of the experience in the Second World War, so ensuring that the politics of debt were much more muted after 1945.[20]

III

The level of interest and the politics of the national debt also connected with capital exports which now became a much more significant feature

[19] Daunton, *Just Taxes*, 123, 125–7.
[20] E. Nevin, *The Mechanism of Cheap Money: A Study of British Monetary Policy, 1931–1939* (Cardiff, 1955); Daunton, *Just Taxes*, 188–9.

of policy debate than before the First World War when, as argued in the previous address, criticism was 'surprisingly muted'.[21] There were some criticisms. Tariff reformers complained that Britain was becoming a *rentier* state, a 'nation of bankers and commission agents, supporting armies of unemployed loafers', a *rentier* state such as Holland.[22] They preferred to see Britain be a productive state through replacing free trade by imperial preference. Some Liberals were also dubious. J. A. Hobson argued that imperialism was a result of over-saving and under-consumption – but he did not argue this position consistently and was often supportive of capital exports. More pertinently, Lloyd George, guided by George Paish, clung to capital exports right up to 1914, arguing that like free trade it led to cheaper food and prosperous markets.[23] Change was apparent after the war. The Bank of England was much more concerned with the plight of the domestic economy as a result of the loans made to industry at the end of the war which created the potential for financial disaster if businesses failed and brought down the banks with them. In seeking to support industry, the Bank could not pursue international considerations so clearly as before the war. In order to raise the value of the pound before 1925 and then to maintain it, the Bank had two options: to raise interest rates or to control capital flows. The first option was politically difficult, and the obvious answer was to restrict capital mobility in order to limit pressure on domestic monetary policy.

A United Nations' survey of interwar capital movements estimated that UK net capital exports between 1911 and 1913 were $1,042m; during the First World War, something like $4,000m of foreign investments were sold. After the war, capital exports at first seemed to return to the earlier pattern, reaching $881m in 1921. But the recovery was temporary, with exports in 1922–8 amounting to only $407m. In the 1930s, the UK became a net importer of capital, amounting to $313m in 1931 and $269m in 1938, or an annual average of -$74m in 1931–5 and -$212m in 1936–8.[24] Before 1914, capital exports were not controlled with the single exception of the Colonial Stocks Acts of 1877–1900 which gave a preference to colonial governments by allowing their bonds to be purchased by trustees. During the war, controls were imposed. In 1915 fresh capital could not be issued without approval of the Capital Issues Committee; in November 1917 the purchase of securities issued abroad was forbidden. These controls were relaxed in 1919, but the CIC was instructed by the Treasury to take into account 'the extent to which the proceeds of the issue will be

[21] Daunton, 'Britain and Globalisation: I', 36.
[22] George Wyndham, quoted in E. H. H. Green, *The Crisis of Conservatism: The Politics, Economics and Ideology of the British Conservative Party, 1880–1914* (1995), 236.
[23] P. F. Clarke, *Liberals and Social Democrats* (Cambridge, 1978), ch. 3; P. Cain, *Hobson and Imperialism: Radicalism, New Liberalism and Finance, 1887–1938* (Oxford, 2002).
[24] United Nations, *International Capital Movements during the Inter-War Period* (Lake Success, New York, 1949), 4, 10, 15.

expended in the United Kingdom, and the assistance which the issue may be expected to give to British trade. Preference should be given *ceteris paribus* to those cases in which the proceeds of the issue are to be applied in the British Dominions overseas.' In November 1919, explicit controls on overseas issues were removed but as the Treasury withdrew, so the Bank used its moral influence in the City to enforce a voluntary 'embargo' on loans through persuasion rather than regulation, in consultation with the Treasury which had no formal role so that it could deny the existence of government control. In 1921, the embargo on imperial borrowers was removed, but limits remained on foreign public authority loans and large fixed interest issues by foreign companies until 1924.[25]

Between 1919 and 1924, the motivation for controlling capital exports was primarily domestic. In 1920, the Bank urged a limit on overseas issues to allow local authorities to borrow for council housing schemes, and established a queue of domestic borrowers followed by dominions and colonies, with foreigners bringing up the rear. This consideration was followed by a desire to exclude foreigners until large government loans were issued in order to convert the short debt into longer-term funded debt and to replace maturing debt. There was less concern about the diversion of capital into domestic industry, which was assumed to have sufficient funds, and protection of the foreign exchanges was a secondary matter.[26]

The embargo came under pressure from merchant banks which were anxious to make loans to foreign governments, and some relaxation was sensible to prevent a collapse of the Bank's moral influence. In 1924, the embargo was withdrawn, but with the prospective return to gold an outflow of capital could no longer be permitted to affect the exchange rate. From this point, the key motive of capital controls was the need to protect the pound. This is not to say that international considerations were dominant: controls over capital movements offered a much more domestically acceptable alternative to the use of the bank rate to protect the exchanges, which was no longer politically feasible. One element of the global economy – capital mobility – was now sacrificed to maintain another – the gold standard. At the end of November 1924, an embargo was reintroduced on foreign loans and was soon extended to dominion and colonial loans.[27]

The embargos led to an extensive debate within the government and City. Did loans stimulate the domestic economy by creating export demand for British goods? At the Treasury, Niemeyer argued in May

[25] J. Atkin, 'Official Regulation of British Overseas Investment, 1914–1931', *Economic History Review*, 23 (1970), 325.
[26] Atkin, 'Official Regulation', 326–8.
[27] *Ibid.*, 329–31.

1925 that Britain was over-lending given its weaker balance of payments and should reduce both foreign and colonial loans. He accepted that foreign or colonial loans offered some benefits: they paid an immediate commission; they offered a future flow of income; and the development of works abroad would provide future customers; and some loans would secure orders in Britain. These were, he remarked 'substantial advantages, if we can afford to acquire them i.e. if our surplus savings, and more particularly our surplus foreign balances are sufficient to meet the loans we make'. If this were not the case, there were serious disadvantages: if loans were spent in Britain, exports were in effect given away for nothing, since Britain provided the funds; and if loans were spent outside Britain, there was not even a temporary benefit of employment at home and instead gold was exported or the exchange deteriorated. In Neimeyer's opinion, 'we should clearly do what we can to discourage borrowers generally, for we do not want bank rate to be put up'. But he felt that there was little to be done beyond the present voluntary constraint: the Colonial Stock Act could not be repealed; and it was not possible for the colonial secretary to hint to the dominions that they should reduce their borrowings. 'I am inclined to believe that we must trust to such persuasion as the Governor can use in the City and to the repercussions of that persuasion on brokers and issuing houses.'[28]

In fact, the Treasury did draft a telegram for Churchill to send to the governor generals of Australia, New Zealand and Canada asking them to urge their premiers to reduce their borrowing in London – an action firmly rejected by Leo Amery, the colonial secretary who threatened to make it a Cabinet matter. F. W. Leith-Ross, the deputy controller of finance at the Treasury, was concerned by Amery's attitude:

> This attitude is somewhat unreasonable. We don't want to stop Colonial borrowings if we can avoid it. But if their amount cannot be restricted by agreement and consent, the restriction will come about automatically through rise in Bank Rate, which, I should imagine, will raise more serious political (not to speak of economic) difficulties than a slowing-down of Dominion Loans.[29]

Norman at the Bank also informed Churchill that Britain was lending more than its current savings or 'savings fund', and he was particularly concerned about demand from the dominions which would endanger the exchanges. Norman pointed to four ways of dealing with the situation. First, the bank rate could be raised; second, the amount available to the dominions and colonies could be reduced by agreement with the prime

[28] The National Archive [hereafter TNA], T176/17, O. Niemeyer, 13 May 1925.

[29] TNA, T176/17, draft telegram to governor generals of Australia, New Zealand and Canada, 27 May 1925, and O. Niemeyer to H. Lambert (Colonial Office), 30 May 1925; Lambert to Niemeyer, 2 June 1925; Lambert to Leith-Ross, 5 June 1925; Leith-Ross to Fergusson, 8 June 1925.

ministers; third, the New York market could provide funds; and finally, joint issues could be made in London and New York. He urged the chancellor to consider the problem so as to avoid a higher bank rate.[30]

For their part, the dominions complained about their difficulties in borrowing in London and they threatened to look to New York. The agent general for New South Wales warned Amery that the embargo would harm development work designed to place settlers on land and would end assisted emigration; it would affect Australian exchanges and hence trade with Britain; and would hit purchases of British goods. The agent general of Western Australia concurred: 'gradually, imperceptibly, but none the less surely, we may be removed from the economic ambit of this country into the economic ambit of the United States of America'. Amery was extremely worried, pressing for the end of the embargo on the dominions: 'we are pledged up to the hilt to a policy of Empire preference and Empire development and yet, whenever we come up against any opportunity of showing that we mean something by our declarations, we are told by the pundits that no differentiation is possible'. Churchill's attitude to Amery and the embargo was pragmatic: 'A rise in the Bank rate – chilling the trade revival – is not a prospect which should be needlessly courted.' The Colonial Office had no option except to explain the predicament to the dominions and hope for their understanding. [31]

Neither was the City entirely happy about the embargo on foreign loans, fearing that 'this branch of the business would be completely atrophied', and complaining at 'the inconsistency of saying we are "anchored to reality" through the Gold Standard when, as a matter of fact, we refused by all sorts of devices to allow a free market'. One possible solution was rationing to keep open each channel of investment. Niemeyer was not impressed by the complaints or by the proposed solution. Rationing was not possible, for he pointed out that

> You can let all in or keep all out; but how are you going to discriminate e.g. for Japan and against Czecho Slovakia. Such discrimination, apart from political troubles, would very probably do more harm to the London market than a temporary exclusion. And you would have further trouble if you excluded some Dominions in order to let in some foreigners.[32]

Industrialists were no more content. In 1925, the Federation of British Industries pointed to 'the important role that the large annual investment of British capital abroad has in the past played in developing exports'.

[30] TNA, T176/17, M. Norman to W. S. Churchill, 9 June 1925.

[31] TNA, T176/17, Commonwealth of Australia to Churchill, 11 June 1925; S. J. Chapman to Niemeyer, 24 June 1925; R. Horne to Churchill, 3 July 1925; Amery to Churchill, 16 Oct 1925; Churchill to Amery, 20 Oct. 1925; cutting from *Morning Post*, 23 Oct. 1925; 'Dominion loans'; T. Coghlan to L. Amery, 27 Oct. 1925; Edgcumbe to Coghlan, 29 Oct. 1925.

[32] TNA, T176/17, Churchill to O. Niemeyer, 21 July 1925; Niemeyer to chancellor, 21 July 1925.

Engineering concerns feared the loss of orders which were now financed by American firms. As one representative of engineering remarked,

> This seems to me a very short-sighted policy for two reasons. First, the whole of the material, plant and stores required for such Works instead of coming from this country comes from America, and, in the next place, the securities which are issued in New York find their way here in very large amounts to the British investors.[33]

The strongest case against the embargo was made by George Paish who continued the same line of reasoning as his pre-war advice to Lloyd George as chancellor to continue capital exports. He argued that the increase in unemployment was not due to the recovery of the pound to par but the stoppage of foreign and colonial capital issues in London. The solution to the problem of unemployment was evident to Paish: 'to reopen the London money market to new issues of capital for Colonial and Foreign Countries'. The result would be additional demand for British goods which would increase employment and keep up wages, but Paish argued that the export of capital would mean that wages elsewhere would rise which would have the same practical effect as a wage cut – a much easier task than reducing domestic wages. His argument attracted a succinct Treasury reply: 'tommy rot'. Niemeyer accepted that foreign lending might well increase exports which would be welcomed by some interests, but he argued that it was not necessarily for the benefit of the country as a whole. Niemeyer argued that Paish failed to notice a major difference from the situation before 1914 when there were large surplus savings for overseas investment. This was no longer the case:

> If, as before the war we have a surplus of savings over internal needs, it pays us to use them to acquire claims on future foreign remittances.
>
> If we have no such surplus, we cannot afford to deal in futures, and we must not be misled by the appearance of an addition in our export figures into thinking that our balance of payments has improved.
>
> If, having no such balance of savings, we yet make loans we give the foreign borrower a claim on London which he takes in goods. But those goods we are for the moment giving away for nothing. We are consequently making our balance of payment less favourable, not more favourable; and to remedy this we shall be forced to apply the recognised methods of correcting an unfavourable exchange position (i.e. export goods and increase money rates in London to deter borrowers and attract lenders). Higher money rates will then react not only on our external trade but also on our whole internal trade.[34]

[33] Atkin, 'Official Regulation', 333; TNA, T176/17, R. W. Perks to comptroller-general, Department of Overseas Trade, 28 July 1925.

[34] TNA, T176/17, G. W. Paish to Montagu Norman, 29 Sept. 1925, with marginal comments by the Treasury; see also article by Paish, 'World Commerce and Credit, No. 1, The Treasury Embargo on Foreign Loans', *Westminster Gazette*, 31 July 1925; O. Niemeyer, 19 Sept. 1925

Whilst these debates were proceeding, the Cabinet set up a secret Overseas Loans Committee in June 1925 to consider 'the question of the capacity of this country to meet the demands for capital at home and abroad, with particular regard to the requirements of Empire development and to the maintenance of our export trade'. When the committee reported later in the year it argued that the removal of the embargo might lead to an export of capital beyond the capacity of the country, but admitted that it was being evaded by purchases of securities in New York. Churchill ended the embargo in November 1925, but it was clear that policy towards capital mobility had now changed from passive acceptance prior to 1914 to a careful estimation of the benefits for the economy as a whole, and an assessment of its political ramifications.[35]

By the late 1920s, the Treasury was more sympathetic to capital export as a means of stimulating trade, and was wary of Liberal plans of diverting investment to domestic public works. As Leith-Ross pointed out in 1928, 'what we invest in foreign loans must, sooner or later, be exported; and insofar as it is sunk in development schemes for the Empire, it is probably exported almost at once in the form of capital goods'. Additional spending at home on bridges and similar public works was a 'poor substitute' for building entire railways overseas. The Treasury contribution to the White Paper on the Liberal plan of public works accordingly stressed the dangers of diverting funds to domestic public works:

> On the ordinary view there is an intimate relation between the export of capital and of goods. If the plan were successful in diverting money from investment abroad that change would be accompanied by a great decrease in our exports or increase in imports, either of these things being highly prejudicial to important branches of industry.

However, opposition to Liberal schemes for public works did not mean that the Treasury supported Conservative proposals for imperial development in 1929. In estimating the impact of development loans on domestic employment, the Treasury concluded that rather more than half the money went on colonial land, labour and materials (so turning exchanges against Britain) and only part was spent on British goods with very modest benefits for exports. As P. F. Clarke argues, the Treasury remained committed to overseas investment on theoretical grounds but adjusted its views for pragmatic reasons and was more concerned to block state expenditure wherever it came from – Liberal domestic public works or Conservative Empire development.[36]

---

[35] Atkin, 'Official Regulation', 330–1.

[36] P. F. Clarke, 'The Treasury's Analytical Model of the British Economy between the Wars', in *The State and Economic Knowledge: The American and British Experiences*, ed. M. O. Furner and B. Supple (Cambridge, 1990), 180–3, citing TNA, T172/2095, Leith-Ross memo., 9 Aug. 1928; CP 53(29); *Memorandum on Certain Proposals relating to Unemployment* (1929), 51.

Although Niemeyer informed the Macmillan Committee in 1931 that 'I believe, in spite of recent criticism, that the vast majority of foreign borrowing does bring orders to industry in this country', the Treasury was willing to abandon capital exports in order to hold down domestic interest rates, and the benefits were assessed against the political and economic costs at home and in the colonies.[37] The Board of Trade was more cautious or realistic, arguing that overseas lending had no effect either way on total employment: high levels would boost employment in exports; low levels would stimulate employment for domestic consumption. The important point was the impact on industrial structure: capital exports in the past influenced the structure of industry and a cut now would harm employment in these sectors. 'The serious thing is the shock of a sudden change.' Henry Clay, an economist at the University of Manchester who became an increasingly influential adviser to the Bank of England, made a similar point, arguing that unemployment was concentrated in industries specialising in exports, and that the spending that had to be stimulated was export demand:

> To relieve unemployment, therefore, by stimulating the complete spending of income, either on commodities or investments, it is necessary to ensure that the allocation of expenditure will not diverge too much from the allocation to which industry is adjusted. Any sudden or large transfers of means of payment from home to foreign account, or vice versa, or from one class of purchasers to another, is likely to dislocate employment, and cause, not a general increase in employment, but overtime and rapid expansion in one part of the industrial field balanced by increased unemployment in another part.[38]

Despite these concerns of the Treasury and Board of Trade, the embargo on foreign loans was reintroduced in 1929. Certainly, the emphasis changed in the 1930s. Although the embargo was relaxed for a short time in 1930, it was re-imposed later in the year and extended to the Empire in 1931. The embargo helped create liquidity for conversion of government stock to a lower rate of interest in 1932. The establishment of the sterling area in 1934 meant that controls were reduced for member countries in order to support the stability of their exchange rates; and loans were also tied to the purchase of goods in order to create domestic employment. In 1936 a special committee was appointed to advise the chancellor on the general principles of lending as well as to consider specific loans. The war led to stricter controls, and the return to peace did nothing to remove the constraints which were embedded in the Exchange Control Act, 1947.[39]

---

[37] Atkin, 'Official Regulation', 333.

[38] Clarke, 'Analytical Model', 191–3, citing TNA, T175/26, 'Note on Mr Keynes's Exposition', 'The Assumptions of Mr Keynes'; TNA, T200/1, 'Effects of Lending Abroad'; Clay, 'Remedies', in Clay to Osborne, 18 May 1930, Bank of England Archives, S44/1 (1).

[39] Atkin, 'Official Regulation', 331, 334; UN, International Capital Movements, 54.

IV

In the absence of variation in the exchange rate, international competitiveness and maintenance of the balance of payments was only possible by adjusting costs. The successful operation of the gold standard therefore depended on flexibility in costs and above all wages. The issue was much debated by contemporary economists who generally assumed that wages were more sticky after the war, and that this failure of adjustment contributed to higher costs, unemployment and the collapse of the gold standard.

The distinction between pre- and post-war experience may be exaggerated, for as we noted in the previous lecture, wages were sticky before 1914 and did not follow prices down between 1873 and 1896 to the extent assumed by post-war commentators. But it was certainly believed by most economists that wages before the First World War could not rise higher than the market could bear. As Alfred Marshall remarked, 'the power of Unions to raise general wages by direct means is never great; it is never sufficient to contend successfully with the general economic forces of the age, when their drift is against a rise in wages'.[40] However, the situation was different in the 1920s, for wages had risen in the final stages of the war and during the post-war inflation above the ability of the market to sustain, and the success of gold would require a greater degree of flexibility in order to restore competitiveness at pre-war parities.

At the time of the return to gold in 1925, Keynes warned of the consequences of attempting to adjust wages and costs to the international situation. He pointed to a clash between two theories of economic society:

> The one theory maintains that wages should be fixed by reference to what is 'fair' and 'reasonable' as between classes. The other theory – the theory of the economic juggernaut – is...that our vast machine should crash along, with regard only to its equilibrium as a whole, and without attention to the chance consequences of the journey to individual groups.

Under this second theory,

> the object of credit restriction...is to withdraw from employers the financial means to employ labour at the existing level of prices and wages. The policy can only attain its end by intensifying unemployment without limit, until the workers are ready to accept the necessary reduction of money wages under the pressure of hard facts.

But why should they accept these 'hard facts'? 'The gold standard, with its dependence on pure chance, its faith in "automatic adjustments", and its general regardlessness of social detail', argued Keynes,

> is an essential emblem and idol of those who sit in the top tier of the machine. I think that they are immensely rash in their regardlessness, in their vague optimism and comfortable belief that nothing really serious ever happens. Nine times out of ten, nothing

---

[40] A. Marshall, *Elements of the Economics of Industry* (1892), 19, cited in E. H. Phelps Brown, *The Origins of Trade Union Power* (Oxford, 1983), 27.

really serious does happen – merely a little distress to individuals or to groups. But we run a risk of the tenth time (and are stupid into the bargain), if we continue to apply the principles of an economics which was worked out on the hypotheses of *laissez-faire* and free competition to a society which is rapidly abandoning these hypotheses.[41]

Keynes's answer was simple: 'in modern conditions wages in this country are, for various reasons, so rigid over short periods, that it is impracticable to adjust them to the ebb and flow of international gold-credit, and I would deliberately utilize fluctuations in the exchange as the shock-absorber'.[42] Not all economists accepted Keynes's policy conclusion but most accepted that wages were now more sticky. As A. C. Pigou argued in 1927:

Before the Great War there can be little doubt that wage-rates in Great Britain were adjusted in a broad way to the conditions of supply and demand . . . It was nowhere suggested that the general body of wage-rates had been forced up too high relatively to the openings for employment . . . In the post-war period, however, there is strong reason to believe that an important change has taken place in this respect . . . wage-rates have, over a wide area, been set at a level which is too high in the above sense.[43]

Why were wages sticky both at the end of the post-war boom and in response to the crisis of 1931? Eichengreen points out that the initial deflationary shock of monetary contraction in the depression would soon come to an end and 'at this point the self-equilibrating tendencies of the market would come into play. Wages and other costs should have fallen along with prices to limit the rise in unemployment and the decline in sales. They did so only modestly.'[44] Empirical studies of ten industrial countries in 1935 by Eichengreen and Sachs and of twenty-two countries in 1931–6 by Bernanke and Carey both indicate that wages were sticky despite the monetary shock. In the words of Bernanke and Carey, 'the inverse relationship of output and real wages reflects largely the effects of incomplete nominal wage adjustment in the presence of aggregate demand shock'. Bernanke and Carey are puzzled by the slowness of adjustment in the 1930s, for they argue that the forces that might be expected to lead to stickiness were weak: union membership had declined since the peak at the end of the war; the government's role in the economy was limited; price declines were too large to lead to monetary illusion; and there were many unemployed workers. As they say, 'the solution to the aggregate supply puzzle of the Depression remains very much an open issue'.[45]

[41] J. M. Keynes, *The Economic Consequences of Mr Churchill* (1925), in *Collected Writings of John Maynard Keynes*, XIX: *Activities 1922–1929: The Return to Gold and Industrial Policy* (1981), 218, 224, 233–4.
[42] Quoted in Skidelsky, *John Maynard Keynes*, II, 205.
[43] A. C. Pigou, 'Wage Policy and Unemployment', *Economic Journal*, 37 (1927), 355.
[44] Eichengreen, *Golden Fetters*, 15–16.
[45] B. Bernanke and K. Carey, 'Nominal Wage Stickiness and Aggregate Supply in the Great Depression', *Quarterly Journal of Economics*, 111 (1996), 872; B. Eichengreen and J. Sachs,

Various reasons were proposed at the time and by historians more recently. Eichengreen suggests that there was a coordination problem. He points out that certain variables were fixed in nominal terms for some time – mortgages, rents, bonds – and

> claimants to these sources of income – rentiers, capitalists, and workers – each would have accepted a reduction in their incomes had they been assured that others were prepared to do the same. Without a mechanism to coordinate their actions, no one group was prepared to be the first to offer concession.[46]

But is he entirely correct? Any attempt to make rents and mortgages more flexible was difficult as a result of restrictions imposed in 1915 in response to political unrest. The issue was not how to create flexibility in a downwards direction; it was how to permit rents to rise to a remunerative level.[47] For their part, bondholders *did* accept a reduction in their interest in the conversion of 1932 – a change which was only possible because interest rates in general were held down, which was in turn only possible as a result of abandoning the gold standard. In other words, a degree of flexibility was possible after 1931 because fixed exchange rates were dropped.

The inflexibility of wages is often blamed on welfare benefits, both at the time and since. Lionel Robbins remarked in 1934 that 'the post-war rigidity of wages is a by-product of Unemployment Insurance'.[48] His view was reaffirmed more recently by Benjamin and Kochin.[49] However, the case against welfare benefits is somewhat implausible, as suggested by data from the *New Survey of London Life and Labour.* Male heads of household were not likely to opt for benefits in preference to work; the old were more likely to leave the labour market, but the overall effect was modest.[50] More realistically, the nature of production institutions limited flexibility. To reduce wages would be to call into question the institutions of collective bargaining underwritten by the state since the 1870s and especially 1906. In 1926, the Conservative government preferred to maintain these institutions rather than creating flexibility.

Clay estimated that 2.4m working people were covered by collective agreements in 1910, and probably around 8m in 1929 out of a workforce

---

'Exchange Rates and Economic Recovery in the 1930s', *Journal of Economic History*, 45 (1985), 925–46.

[46] Eichengreen, *Golden Fetters*, 16; see also R. Cooper, 'Predetermined Wages and Prices and the Impact of Expansionary Government Policy', *Review of Economic Studies*, 57 (1990), 205–14.

[47] M. Daunton, *A Property Owning Democracy? Housing in Britain* (1987), 28–31.

[48] See James, *End of Globalization*, 170, citing L. Robbins, *The Great Depression* (1934), 60–1.

[49] D. K. Benjamin and L. A. Kochin, 'Searching for an Explanation of Unemployment in Interwar Britain', *Journal of Political Economy*, 87 (1979).

[50] B. Eichengreen, 'Unemployment in Interwar Britain: Dole or Doldrums?', *Oxford Economic Papers*, 39 (1987), 597–623.

(excluding domestic service) of 14m – and he argued that the influence of the agreements extended beyond those formally covered so that 'we may safely conclude that there are few important gaps left in the provision for the settlement of wages by collective bargaining in Great Britain'. The adjustment of wages to changes in prices or prosperity no longer rested on the individual action of employers, for 'the process of general wage-changes has . . . been constitutionalised'. Clay expressed some concerns about the outcome. Was it really the case that collective bargaining led to efficiency (as was strongly argued by the Webbs), given productivity gains in America in the absence of powerful unions, and given the possibility that higher wages might be at the expense of unemployment? The extension of collective bargaining, he argued, had destroyed 'plasticity' of wages in the light of opportunities of employment. Collective agreements prevented 'nibbling' at wages by 'hard-pressed or unscrupulous employers' and set rates by the larger and better organised firms. Above all, non-economic factors intruded:

> The mere fact of publicity, or organised discussion, invites appeal to social and ethical standards of 'fair' and 'living' wages, to pseudo-principles such as the sanctity of pre war real wages, to the unpopularity of reducing rates of wages to lower-paid workers, none of which have any bearing on the capacity of industry to pay wages and provide employment.

As he pointed out, economists could argue for lower wages in private, 'but directors of large companies, who may be candidates for Parliament, will not commit themselves publicly to such unpopular opinions'. Further, wage-earners were more inclined to resist reductions than before the war when they realised that the result would be unemployment; now, relief meant that unemployment did not cause the same level of distress. In Clay's opinion, the influence of unemployment relief was not a direct refusal of work which was policed by the Labour Exchanges; it was indirect in making union leaders less inclined to take account of unemployment – a much more significant change than the spread of collective bargaining. Pigou concurred: if the unemployed were supported by the union's fund, the costs of unemployment would check demand for higher real wages; a state system removed this constraint.[51]

Consequently, a number of economists argued that the statistical relationship between wage movements and unemployment had been reversed. Before the war, the movement of wage rates was closely connected with unemployment; after the war, unemployment ceased to influence wage negotiations which Clay argued was 'the principal and direct explanation of the loss of plasticity in wage-rates'. The French economist Jacques Rueff produced data to show that real wages and

---

[51] H. Clay, 'The Public Regulation of Wages in Great Britain', *Economic Journal*, 39 (1929), 323–43; A. C. Pigou, *The Theory of Unemployment* (1933), 254.

unemployment were negatively correlated before the war, and positively after the war. Josiah Stamp calculated that the correlation was as high as +0.95. Pigou himself was sceptical of Rueff's statistical techniques and worried whether correlation was the same as causation, but warned that 'if it be true that wage-rates are set at a level involving a permanent addition of 5 per cent to the numbers of the unemployed, the position is a grave one'.[52]

Clay found that other influences worked in the same direction. The depth of depression meant that unions argued that no reduction in wages would help. Further, wages were a lower proportion of total costs: loan charges, taxes and social insurance contributions were heavier, and any reduction in wages would be seen less as a way of reviving trade than benefiting these other interests. Clay concluded that an open reduction of wages was not possible, and a reduction by inflation undesirable. He had two recommendations. First, the problem of the 'loss of plasticity' in wages required a change in bargaining processes, away from sectional considerations and individual trades to consider industry as a whole – a somewhat difficult task, as he admitted. Second, he urged rationalisation. Clay assumed that new sectors could not expand to take up labour: motor cars, for example, were close to saturation. He accepted that redistribution might take place by 2000 or even 1950, 'but the people engaged in industry to-day, unlike economists, are not able to look at economic problems *sub specie aeternitatis*'. Transfer of labour no longer worked as before 1914, less because of unemployment relief than because wages were sticky. Further, Clay stressed

> the heavy direct taxation of profits, out of which expansion and new enterprise are financed. The growth of industry before the war, which carried with it the redistribution of labour, was effected mainly by successful firms expanding out of profits, and the increased rate of taxation of profits is one of the most obvious and largest economic changes that distinguish the post-war from the pre-war period. It is difficult to see how new openings, at equal or higher rates of pay, can be created for displaced labour as rapidly as they were created before the war.[53]

Clay minimised the possibilities of industrial transformation and instead argued for policies to operate within the existing structure – a somewhat fatalistic view.

Pigou was more sanguine, arguing that there was no need to reverse the shift from capital to labour or to reduce real wages: the problem would solve itself if wages did not rise every time there was an increase in demand for labour.[54] His position was close to Keynes in *The General*

[52] Pigou, 'Wage Policy and Unemployment', 355–68, citing Rueff and Stamp.

[53] H. Clay, *The Post-War Unemployment Problem* (1929); Clay, 'Public Regulation', 323–43; H. Clay, 'Dr Cannan's Views on Unemployment', *Economic Journal*, 40 (1930), 331–5.

[54] Pigou, 'Wage Policy and Unemployment'.

Theory where he stressed that nominal wage stickiness depended on the protection of relative wages: 'Any individual or group of individuals, who consent to a reduction in money wages relative to others, will suffer a relative reduction in real wages, which is a sufficient justification for them to resist it.' However, a reduction caused by inflation could not be resisted for it affected everyone. Keynes also argued that real wages were not necessarily responsive to employment. Cutting money wages would not affect the real wage: in a competitive economy, the price of a commodity equalled its cost of production; a cut in money wages would therefore reduce the marginal cost and hence the price; and cuts in wages would reduce demand, so reducing prices and leaving the real wage unchanged.[55] By contrast to Clay's stress on rigidity of the industrial structure, Keynes assumed flexibility.

Edwin Cannan took a third position: 'The true remedy for long-term unemployment always applied throughout history, and always effectual, is neither rationalisation nor reduction of wages, but redistribution of labour-force between the different occupations.' Cannan believed that rationalisation was futile as a cure for unemployment in the export industries. Although he doubted the impossibility of wage cuts, he emphasised 'the utter undesirability of a reduction'. Lower wages would only mean more output and hence lower prices. Cannan argued that it was possible to develop different export industries – and even if not possible, no reason for 'obstinate adherence' to exports which ceased to provide as good a living as domestic trades. 'There is, in fact, no reason whatever for supposing that transference of labour from the depressed trades cannot take place': it would take time, but was not impossible and would not necessarily create unemployment in other trades.[56] Unlike Keynes, he did not simply assume flexibility of the industrial structure: it was something to encourage rather than take for granted.

These economists, for all their divergences, accepted two things: wages were more rigid than before the war, for reasons which they analysed; and they should not be forced down in response to the dictates of the gold standard. However, the Treasury was not convinced that wages were so rigid, believing that adjustment was possible and that the return to gold would provide the basis for recovery. At first, they seemed justified in their case. At the time of the return to gold, the official figure of unemployment stood at 10.9 per cent, rising to 12 per cent and then falling back to 9.1 per cent in April 1926. Despite a rise during the general strike, the level of unemployment was down to 8.7 per cent in May 1927. But in 1928 and 1929, the level fluctuated around 10 and 11 per cent, and the economy seemed to be 'jammed'. Initially, the Treasury

---

[55] J. M. Keynes, *The General Theory of Employment, Interest, and Money* (1936), 12–14.
[56] E. Cannan, 'The Post-War Unemployment Problem', *Economic Journal*, 40 (1930), 45–55.

denied Keynes's contention that wage stickiness prevented the necessary adjustment of costs to the gold standard. In 1928, Leith-Ross pondered the problem. Although his colleague at the Treasury, R. G. Hawtrey, the director of financial enquiries, pointed out that the wage data of A. L. Bowley supported Keynes's contention that wages were indeed sticky, Leith-Ross was not convinced. He accepted that political pressures had increased the 'natural resistance of wages to falling prices' but felt that Keynes exaggerated 'stickiness' and that Ministry of Labour data indicated that 'the average wage rates showed a substantial decline during the past 4 years'. The economic problem facing Britain was therefore not sticky wages so much as industrial organisation which could be solved by 'a bold industrial concentration policy'.[57]

In 1929, Leith-Ross shifted his position. Keynes was arguing that, given sticky wages, the solution was public works and tariffs to restore economic prosperity. As we have seen, such proposals alarmed the Treasury which preferred to argue that the solution was to make the gold standard work by restoring flexibility to wage rates. Leith-Ross now accepted that Ministry of Labour data on wage rates confirmed Bowley's claims, and that Keynes and Hawtrey were right. What was the solution? As Leith-Ross said, it was to reduce costs by improvements in the organisation and efficiency of industry, a task that would be made much easier if wages could be cut:

> The remedy is easy enough to find. If our workmen were prepared to accept a reduction of 10 per cent in their wages or increase their efficiency by 10 per cent, a large proportion of our present unemployment could be overcome. But in fact organized labour is so attached to the maintenance of the present standard of wages and hours of labour that they would prefer that a million workers should remain in idleness and be maintained permanently out of the Employment Fund, than accept any sacrifice. The result is to throw on to the capital and managerial side of industry a larger reorganization than would otherwise be necessary: and until labour is prepared to contribute in larger measure to the process of reconstruction, there will inevitably be unemployment.

Leith-Ross's brutal assessment was toned down by the Treasury's memorandum of May 1929 that was written for public consumption. This memorandum pointed out that the time had passed when a reduction in costs could be taken as synonymous with a reduction in wages: what was needed was better organisation, efficiency and rationalisation. The Treasury position was, then, that British costs had failed to respond to the adoption of the gold standard and that they should be made to adjust, if not by cutting wages then by industrial efficiency.[58]

[57] Clarke, 'Analytical Model', 179–80, citing TNA, T172/2095, Leith-Ross to Hawtrey, 1 Aug. 1928, and Leith-Ross memo., 9 Aug. 1928.

[58] Clarke, 'Analytical Model', 184–6, citing TNA, T175/26, Leith-Ross to Hawtrey, 13 Mar. 1929; TNA, T172/2095, Leith-Ross, draft for Churchill, Apr. 1929; *Memorandum on Certain Proposals*.

Attempts to make wages less sticky were severely curtailed, and best avoided in public statements: the implications of the gold standard were now politically dangerous. Most economists devoted their energy to explaining why 'plasticity' had been lost without suggesting how it could be regained. The real question was: what policies should follow from the existence of stickiness and how successful could they be?

V

In the previous lecture, we saw that the gold standard and free trade were integral parts of political culture, linked with notions of peace, prosperity, civilisation and progress which extended far beyond technical matters of monetary and trade policy. The tariff reformers' outright attack on free trade rallied Liberals and Labour to support the principles of Cobden in Edwardian Britain, but in securing victory they also started to divide. Opposition to a shared enemy of protection was not the same as shared beliefs, for free trade was redefined by Labour and new Liberals in order to support regulation of the economy and redistribution of income and wealth. When the Labour party debated imperial preference in 1904, it condemned Chamberlain yet at the same time questioned the benefits of free trade to workers. As Keir Hardie remarked in 1903, 'production is far outstripping effective demand. The wages paid to the worker do not enable him to purchase what the labour of his hands has produced.' Free trade no longer offered an unproblematic balance between production and consumption. The mere pursuit of free trade was not necessarily an agent of civilisation: it might lead to sweated labour at home and abroad.[59] The emphasis shifted from free trade as the guardian of consumption to concern for the circumstances of production and the conditions shaping purchasing power. An individual should not have the freedom to buy in the cheapest market if it meant poverty for others; and the distribution of income should be rectified to ensure that workers received their fair reward.

The result was a shift from free trade as a guardian of consumers to a stress on the circumstances of production and the distribution of purchasing power. Labour support for free trade was therefore linked with redistribution and regulation. As Trentmann argues, the rhetoric of consumption and the consumer was separated from free trade. An open market for the benefit of the consumer was no longer desirable when policies were needed to protect employment and to prevent 'dumping'. The cooperative movement, for example, demanded a ban on sweated imports and the adoption of controls over resources to balance the

[59] F. Trentmann, 'Wealth versus Welfare: The British Left between Free Trade and National Political Economy before the First World War', *Historical Research*, 70 (1997), 77.

needs of producing and consuming countries. Cheap food was no longer an unmitigated blessing if it meant a collapse in export markets and unemployment in the export industries of Lancashire or south Wales, where the cooperative movement was so strong. The emphasis shifted from free trade to organised consumer councils and the socialisation of food trades to weaken the hold of traders and profiteers. The needs of the consumer were to be guaranteed by high wages and welfare benefits, secured by redistributive taxation and nationalisation. The iconic feature moved from Lloyd George's cheap loaf to pure milk, with welfare no longer protected by removing import duties but rather by state regulation.[60]

Did free trade mean peace? The progressive Rainbow Circle expressed doubts in 1915, worrying that 'the peaceful influence of trade is perhaps something of a delusion and . . . trade has in fact been one cause of the present war'. Arthur Greenwood concurred, arguing that the 'policy of non-intervention cuts at the very roots of freedom, because . . . [it] is nothing more than a policy of short-sighted selfishness. It places the weak at the mercy of the strong.' As Trentmann points out, Cobden's internationalism was now seen as a piece with his social *laissez faire* (rather than detached from it as around 1900). The pursuit of Cobdenite pacifism shifted from free trade and the blessings of comparative advantage to what Hobson called 'organised economic internationalism'. Although protectionism remained a sign of hostility and conflict over the scarce resources of the world, the mere imposition of free trade was not enough. A world of peace and prosperity could only be achieved through positive action, by regulation and international cooperation.[61]

The war also marked a shift in attitudes towards trade policy by industrial organisations. Before the war, industrial support for tariffs was largely based on reciprocity or retaliation to force other countries to reduce their duties. Problems were seen as arising from 'unfair' competition rather than any need for internal reform of the structure of industry. This approach changed in the 1920s, when tariffs were designed to 'modernise' or rationalise British industry, encouraging a shift to larger and more efficient units. However, industrialists were not interested in direct state involvement in their affairs or in corporatism: the state should provide tariffs and then leave industry to resolve its own problems. The approach changed in the 1930s with a shift to 'productivism': the invisible

[60] F. Trentmann, 'Civil Society, Commerce, and the "Citizen-Consumer"', in *Paradoxes of Civil Society*, ed. *idem* (Oxford and New York, 2000), 321–2; F. Trentmann, 'Bread, Milk and Democracy: Consumption and Citizenship in Twentieth-Century Britain', in *The Politics of Consumption: Material Culture and Citizenship in Europe and America*, ed. M. Daunton and M. Hilton (Oxford, 2001), 129–63.

[61] Trentmann, 'The Resurrection and Decomposition of Cobden', especially 270–6. Trentmann, Harvard University Center for European Studies Working Paper 66, 28–9.

hand of the market was no longer sufficient for efficiency and rational business structures were needed.[62]

At the same time, expert opinion moved towards protection. In October 1930, the majority of the Committee of Economists of the Economic Advisory Committee decided in favour of protection. They argued that since wages were 'sticky' and could only be reduced at considerable social cost, it was difficult to correct the balance of trade by cutting money costs. The obvious answer was tariffs. Keynes argued that tariffs would increase prices and so reduce the *real* wage more easily than by cutting money wages; the result would be higher profits.[63] Not everyone was convinced: Lionel Robbins and other economists at the LSE questioned whether a reduction in real wages would help exporters who were more concerned with the level of money wages and costs.[64] But in the circumstances of the early 1930s, protection made sense to many politicians and economists. The political culture of free trade dissolved.

Support for gold was closely linked with the political culture of free trade with a common assumption that it was automatic, leading to peace and freedom from special interests. After the war, the attack on gold as a fetish became more assertive in the face of the imminent return to the gold standard. There was a growing feeling that gold was in fact a special interest, linked with deflation that benefited *rentiers* and harmed producers. Critics of the gold standard no longer saw it as a sign of civilisation: on the contrary, in the opinion of G. D. H. Cole in 1924, it was nothing but superstitious idol worship:

There is a Great God named Par who is worshipped daily at the Treasury and in the magnificent temples the big five [banks] are erecting on every street. Par likes unemployment; it is his form of human sacrifice. And on Par's altars the Treasury daily burns incense in the form of currency and credit. Par is a great God and the Treasury is his Prophet.[65]

Keynes took the same line, that 'the gold standard is clearly a barbaric relic'.[66]

Of course, these complaints did not prevent a return to gold in 1925 but support was by no means enthusiastic, even in the temples of the big five clearing banks. L. J. Hume has shown that there was 'persistent criticism' of the gold standard or at least of the use of deflation to prepare for its re-adoption. Both the *Economist* and the Federation of British Industries

[62] F. Trentmann, 'The Transformation of Fiscal Reform: Reciprocity, Modernization, and the Fiscal Debate within the Business Community in Early Twentieth-Century Britain', *Historical Journal*, 39 (1996), 1042–4.

[63] Skidelsky, *John Maynard Keynes*, II, 370–2, 374–6.

[64] In *Tariffs: The Case Examined*, ed. W. H. Beveridge (1932).

[65] Quoted in W. A. Brown, *England and the New Gold Standard, 1919–1926* (New Haven, 1929), 253.

[66] Keynes, *Economic Consequences of Mr Churchill*, 170.

expressed concern about the impact on the domestic economy, but the most serious criticism came from the chairmen of some of the leading domestic banks. Their doubts went back to the Edwardian period. In 1901, Felix Schuster of the Union Bank complained of frequent and severe changes in the bank rate, and argued for 'a return to that condition when our money market was the cheapest in the world'. The problem, it seemed to him, was the smallness of the Bank's gold reserve and (to a much lesser extent) the rigidity of the Bank Charter Act of 1844. Above all, the issue was taken up by Edward Holden (of the London City and Midland Bank) and concern was intensified by the financial crisis of 1907, when the banks argued that the Americans lacked a lender of last resort and that the Bank's reserve was too small. An interest rate of 6 per cent was, they felt, not desirable for domestic reasons and only needed to protect the gold reserve. Subsequently, a number of clearing bankers set up a Gold Reserve Committee to create their own reserves, and in 1914 Holden demanded a Royal Commission to consider the matter. The Bank was not impressed – and neither was the Treasury.[67]

After the war, Holden, Schuster and other bankers continued to argue the case against the Cunliffe Committee's report, stressing that the Bank Charter Act needed more radical reform. As Holden complained, the committee 'have stated in effect that they cannot recommend anything better than the old system. They simply put us back to the old machine which has broken down before and which may break down again.' The need for large and frequent changes in the bank rate was now even more harmful, and for reform even more urgent at a time 'when the country is reconstructing its trade and industry, and when manufacturers and others are requiring increased accommodation'. Holden died in 1920, and his mantle was taken by F. C. Goodenough of Barclays Bank who urged a loosening of the Cunliffe Committee's recommendations on the rigid gold backing of currency. Rather than the Bank Charter Act driving out speculation and imposing prudence (as intended in 1844), it now seemed rigid and harmful. The return to gold was therefore accepted in the context of 'persistent criticism' rather than outright enthusiasm.[68]

The inconsistent trinity or quartet was highly unstable from 1925 to 1931 and fell apart in 1931. The outcome was a managed exchange rate with a degree of under-valuation; a low level of capital mobility with Britain now a net importer; interest rates fixed for domestic reasons to reduce

[67] M. De Cecco, *Money and Empire: The International Gold Standard, 1890–1914* (Oxford, 1974), 102, 132–41; see the Treasury memorandum by Basil Blackett, 25 May 1914 (TNA, T170/19), printed on 173–206; L. J. Hume, 'The Gold Standard and Deflation: Issues and Attitudes in the 1920s', *Ecomomica*, 30 (1963), 226.
[68] Hume, 'Gold Standard and Deflation', 225–42.

the burden of debt and stimulate the economy; and protectionism. The consequences were later seen as deeply harmful, leading to beggar-my-neighbour policies and contributing to war. The outbreak of the Second World War led Keynes and others to reflect on the harm caused by national self-sufficiency and the pursuit of beggar-my-neighbour policies of protectionism and competitive devaluations. His task, culminating in the Bretton Woods agreement of 1944, was to resolve the tensions between economic nationalism and internationalism that had fallen apart between the wars. In the next address, I will consider how the task was attempted, and with what success.

Transactions of the RHS 17 (2007), pp. 35–55 © 2007 Royal Historical Society
doi:10.1017/S0080440107000527   Printed in the United Kingdom

KING HENRY I AND NORTHERN ENGLAND
By Judith Green

READ 31 MARCH 2006 AT THE UNIVERSITY OF HULL

ABSTRACT. England north of the Humber and the Mersey in the early twelfth century has in the past tended to be discussed in the context of the development of the monarchy. The Normans moved into the northern counties later and in fewer numbers than the south, and in the wake of the Norman settlement the north came to be more fully integrated into the southern kingdom. A fresh perspective on the period is gained by comparing Henry I's rule over the north with that in other regions of England, Wales and Normandy. Its keys were old-style dynastic politics and patronage, and his achievement that of bringing peace to the region.

The idea that 'the north' is a far-away part of England whose inhabitants can barely be understood by civilised people is an old one.[1] It may be found in the pages of the early twelfth-century chronicler, William of Malmesbury, who, in the introduction of the section on Northumbria in his *Deeds of the Bishops of England*, described York as 'a large metropolitan city, still exhibiting Roman elegance', but went on to comment on the speech of the Northumbrians, *especially* that of the men of York, that it

> grates so harshly upon the ear it is completely unintelligible to us southerners. The reason for this is their proximity to barbaric tribes and their distance from the kings of the land, who, whether English as once or Norman as now, are known to stay more often in the south than in the north. The king himself [Henry I], who in the south of England is content with an escort from his household, does not set forth without a great company of auxiliary troops whenever he is visiting northern parts.[2]

Thanks to a series of papers by John Gillingham, we have been made aware of the way William sought to refashion English identity in a way which sharpened consciousness of those outside her frontiers as belonging to other, lesser nations.[3] But before we dismiss William's comment as a

---

[1] See, for instance, H. M. Jewell, *The North–South Divide. The Origins of Northern Consciousness in England* (Manchester, 1984); F. Musgrove, *The North of England. A History from Roman Times to the Present* (Oxford, 1999).

[2] *Gesta pontificum, The Deeds of the Bishops of England*, ed. N. E. S. A. Hamilton (Rolls Series, 1870), 209, trans. D. Preest (Woodbridge, 2002), 139.

[3] These have been conveniently collected in J. Gillingham, *The English in the Twelfth Century: Imperialism, National Identity and Political Values* (Woodbridge, 2000).

personal prejudice by a southerner, it is worth asking how far the north in the early twelfth century did correspond to his view, as somewhere distant and dangerous for Henry I.

In his use of the term Northumbria, William was thinking in terms of the old kingdom, consisting of the archdiocese of York, which was made up of the pre-Viking sees of Lindisfarne (Durham), Hexham and Whithorn, which he described as 'at the very end of England next to Scotland'.[4] For the purposes of this discussion, 'the north' is used in a general sense as meaning the region north of the Humber and the Mersey. In the early twelfth century it was composed of peoples of different ethnic stock and political allegiances. The Anglo-Scottish border cut across earlier boundaries, those of Strathclyde in the west and Northumbria in the east.[5] Cumbria south of Solway is thought to have been within the sphere of influence of the Scots' king in 1066.[6] North Lancashire, or 'the honour of Lancaster', had strong ties with south Cumbria, whilst south Lancashire, described in Domesday Book as 'the land between Ribble and Mersey', was more obviously linked with Cheshire, and was part of the diocese of Coventry and Lichfield.[7] North of Yorkshire, in the east, were the lands which historically formed the patrimony of St Cuthbert, concentrated round Durham, but with important estates in Northumberland and beyond the river Tweed, and south, in Yorkshire.[8] 'Northumberland' was the rump of the old earldom of Northumbria, and had been confiscated from Earl Robert de Mowbray in 1095.

William of Malmesbury was obviously correct in one sense, that these regions were far outposts of the realms of the king of the English. Pre-Conquest kings were richest in land in the south, where they mostly spent their time. After 1066 the Norman kings had the duchy to worry about, and the defence of Normandy took them away from England for long spells. Yet from the time of William the Conqueror the kings of England went to the north more often than their predecessors.[9] William the Conqueror had made forays in 1068, 1069 and 1070 to deal with uprisings, and then again in 1072 as he travelled north to exact submission

    4 William of Malmesbury, *Gesta pontificum*, 256.

    5 C. Phythian-Adams, *Land of the Cumbrians. A Study in British Provincial Origins. A.D. 400–1100* (Aldershot, 1996); J. G. Scott, 'The Partition of a Kingdom: Strathclyde 1092–1153', *Transactions of the Dumfries and Galloway Natural History and Antiquarian Society*, 72 (1997), 11–40.

    6 N. J. Higham, *The Kingdom of Northumbria* (Stroud, 1993); D. W. Rollason, *Northumbria, 500–1100: The Creation and Destruction of a Medieval Kingdom* (Cambridge, 2003).

    7 C. P. Lewis, 'Introduction', *Lancashire, Domesday Book* (Alecto County Edition of Domesday Book, 24, 1991), 38–41; N. J. Higham, *A Frontier Landscape. The North West in the Middle Ages* (Lancaster, 2004).

    8 R. A. Lomas, *North-East England in the Middle Ages* (Edinburgh, 1992).

    9 G. W. S. Barrow, 'Northern English Society in the Twelfth and Thirteenth Centuries', *Northern History*, 4 (1969), 26.

from King Malcolm III.[10] Rufus had taken armies north in 1091, 1092 and again in 1095.[11] According to tradition, Henry may actually have been born in Yorkshire, though this seems unlikely given the volatile situation there in 1068 and 1069.[12] Henry I marched to Tickhill to secure the castle's surrender in 1102.[13] He returned to the north in 1105,[14] again in 1109,[15] possibly in 1113 (the evidence is circumstantial)[16] and in 1122.[17]

Why then were the Norman kings so much more in evidence in the north than most of their predecessors? William the Conqueror knew right from the start that the north could not simply be left to its own devices.[18] Not only was there the danger of northerners rising up against the Normans, but there was the possibility of invasion by the Scots or the arrival of fleets from Norway and Denmark in the Humber. The few Normans stationed in the north were dangerously isolated, and it was only after the harrying of the north in 1069–70 that a framework of lordships took shape, with great compact lordships forming a protective shield for the rich lands of lowland Yorkshire.[19] Settlement proceeded slowly and was substantially altered in the wake of Norman opposition to the rule of William Rufus and Henry I. The departure of some of the greatest of the first wave of new lords provided Rufus and even more, Henry I, with a great reservoir of land with which to reward their followers.

Henry's dealings with the north were what might be called reactive: his visits were made at times of concern about security, whether this was about the loyalty of the northern magnates, relations with successive kings of Scots or the security of Carlisle. He was driven above all by the need to

[10] *Regesta Regum Anglo-Normannorum. The Acta of William I (1066–1087)*, ed. D. Bates (Oxford, 1998), itinerary, 75–84.

[11] F. Barlow, *William Rufus* (1983), itinerary, 449–52.

[12] For discussion see J. A. Green, *Henry I King of England Duke of Normandy* (Cambridge, 2006), 20 n. 4.

[13] *The Chronicle of John of Worcester* [hereafter *JW*], III, ed. P. McGurk (Oxford, 1998), 100–1.

[14] *Regesta Regum Anglo-Normannorum, 1066–1154* [hereafter *RRAN*], II: *Regesta Henrici Primi 1100–1135*, ed. C. Johnson and H. A. Cronne (Oxford, 1956), nos. 709–15.

[15] *Ibid.*, nos. 925–7.

[16] This depends on the confused details surrounding the foundation of Nostell priory which include the story of Henry going to Scotland with an army, possibly after his return to England in 1113. The evidence is reviewed by A. A. M. Duncan, *The Kingship of the Scots 842–1292. Succession and Independence* (Edinburgh, 2002), 64.

[17] Symeon of Durham, *Historia Regum*, in *Opera Omnia*, ed. T. Arnold (2 vols., Rolls Series, 1882–5), II, 267.

[18] For background, see D. Whitelock, 'The Dealings of the Kings of England with Northumbria in the Tenth and Eleventh Centuries', in *The Anglo-Saxons. Studies in Some Aspects of their History and Culture Presented to Bruce Dickins*, ed. Peter Clemoes (London, 1959), 70–88; W. E. Kapelle, *The Norman Conquest of the North* (1979); R. Oram, *The Lordship of Galloway* (Edinburgh, 2000), 39–44.

[19] For these see P. Dalton, *Conquest, Anarchy and Lordship. Yorkshire 1066–1154* (Cambridge Studies in Medieval Life and Thought, fourth series, 27, Cambridge, 1994), ch. 2.

secure the totality of the legacy of his father, William the Conqueror: not just to keep the English throne he had won, but also to take Normandy from his elder brother Robert, and to ensure that both passed to his heir. The defence of Normandy against rebellious lords and hostile neighbours, only too ready to promote the claim of Duke Robert's son William, was Henry's priority, and necessitated frequent and sometimes protracted absences from England. On his return there were flurries of activity as decisions about patronage and preferment were made. His attention on northern England thus could only be intermittent, and the driving force, here as elsewhere, it will be suggested, was dynastic politics rather than administrative innovation.

The character of Henry's rule over northern England has been assessed very differently by historians. Some have argued that it was a final, somewhat crude phase in the passing of the old English state. According to this line of argument, in the early middle ages, kings had little power outside their own estates and in regions they did not visit. Their authority had to be upheld by forming alliances with those who did exercise power in the localities: their influence was thus exercised at one remove. It was only when kings could deal directly with local communities, or still more, with individuals, that a further stage of development was reached.[20] English kingship had already made this breakthrough before 1066. Shires, hundreds, and their courts, sheriffs and writs, were the mechanisms by which Anglo-Saxon kings could reach out to the localities.[21] The arrival of the Norman kings did not assist the further development of these mechanisms, rather they may instead have put them under severe strain, leading to collapse under Stephen and refashioning under Henry II.[22]

The north of England of course did not fit neatly into this model of an advanced old English state. Southern kings had visited less often and had fewer estates there. There were fewer points of entry for royal authority in the form of dioceses and religious houses. The north-west, or Cumbria, was for most of the eleventh century in the orbit if not the control of the kings of Scots.[23] The politics of Northumberland and Durham seem to have belonged to an earlier, more violent era, to judge from the famous

[20] J. Campbell, 'The Significance of the Anglo-Norman State in the Administrative History of Western Europe', *Transactions of the Royal Historical Society*, fifth series, 25 (1975), 39–54, reprinted in *Essays in Anglo-Saxon History*, ed. J. Campbell (London, 1986); W. L. Warren, 'The Myth of Norman Administrative Efficiency', *Transactions of the Royal Historical Society*, fifth series, 34 (1984), 113–32.

[21] The work of James Campbell is particularly important here, especially the essays collected in *The Anglo-Saxon State* (London, 2000), of which 'The Late Anglo-Saxon State: A Maximum View' and 'Some Agents and Agencies of the Late Anglo-Saxon State' are particularly relevant.

[22] Warren, 'Myth of Norman Administrative Efficiency', 124, 130–2.

[23] For the evidence relating to the Scots and Cumbria see Duncan, *Kingship of the Scots*, 23–4, 40–1, 61.

bloodfeud recorded at Durham.[24] William the Conqueror had faced
major opposition in the north, especially in Yorkshire, and resorted to the
infamous harrying during the winter of 1069–70.[25] This further conjures
up an image of a region more violent and less orderly than the south. If
we are to believe William of Malmesbury, a wide swathe of the north was
still desolate some half century or more later.[26] For those who subscribe
to the view that the Norman kings crushed opposition and made use of
the resources they inherited rather than developed new ways of ruling,
the harrying simply underscores the impression that this was part of the
passing of the old order.

By the reign of Henry II, however, the north seems to be a much
more settled and orderly place, with sheriffs and justices, castellans
and forest officials.[27] It is the world of the great religious houses and
landed families whose lives and lands can be traced in the volumes of
Early Yorkshire Charters.[28] In this process of transformation from violence
and self-help to law and order, other historians have seen the reign of
Henry I as part of the new world, where England was governed by
a centralised administrative system emanating from the king's court.
The term 'administrative kingship' was coined to sum up its essential
characteristics.[29] At first sight there is a certain amount going for this
point of view. More royal writs and charters dealing with northern
affairs survive, and the 1130 pipe roll, the earliest original record from
the medieval exchequer, has entries which deal with all parts of the
north. Nor do contemporary narratives composed in the north support

---

[24] C. J. Morris, *Marriage and Murder in Eleventh-Century Northumbria: A Study of De Obsessione
Dunelmi* (University of York Borthwick Paper, no. 82, York, 1992); R. Fletcher, *Bloodfeud.
Murder and Revenge in Anglo-Saxon England* (2002).

[25] *The Anglo-Saxon Chronicle: A Revised Translation* [hereafter *ASC*], ed. D. Whitelock, D. C.
Douglas and S. I. Tucker (1961), E 1068, 1069; *JW*, III, 10; Symeon of Durham, *Historia
Regum*, in *Opera Omnia*, II, 188; *The Ecclesiastical History of Orderic Vitalis* [hereafter *OV*], ed.
M. Chibnall (6 vols., Oxford, 1969–80), II, 228–32; D. Palliser, 'Domesday Book and the
"Harrying of the North"', *Northern History*, 29 (1993), 1–23; J. Palmer, 'War and Domesday
Waste', in *Armies, Chivalry and Warfare in Medieval Britain and France. Proceedings of the 1995
Harlaxton Conference*, ed. M. Strickland (Stamford, 1998), 256–75.

[26] William of Malmesbury, *Gesta pontificum*, 208.

[27] J. C. Holt, *The Northerners. A Study in the Reign of King John* (Oxford, 1961), ch. 11; P. Dalton,
'The Governmental Integration of the Far North, 1066–1199', in *Government, Religion and
Society in Northern England 1000–1700*, ed. J. C. Appleby and P. Dalton (Stroud, 1997), 14–26;
Fletcher, *Bloodfeud*, ch. 10.

[28] *Early Yorkshire Charters*, I–III, ed. W. Farrer (Edinburgh, 1914–16); IV–XII, ed. C. T. Clay
(Yorkshire Archaeological Society Record Series, extra series, I–III, V–X, 1935–65; extra
series vol. IV is index to first three vols. ed. C. T. Clay and E. M. Clay, 1942).

[29] J. W. Baldwin and C. Warren Hollister, 'The Rise of Administrative Kingship',
American Historical Review, 83 (1978), 868–91. The section on Henry I was reprinted in
Hollister, *Monarchy, Magnates and Institutions* (1986). See in this reprinted version 'Henry's new
administrative machine' 231, 'judicial system' 238, 'eyre system' 239; cf. Warren, 'Myth of
Norman Administrative Efficiency', 114 'central institutions operating for all England'.

an idea of a political and cultural world separate from the kingdom of the English.

Yet if the north was becoming more fully integrated into the rest of the kingdom, the extent and character of that integration have to be considered. The north beyond the Tees and the Ribble was not shired in the same way as the south, and there were great jurisdictional liberties which meant that many of the duties of justice and police were in the hands of local lords rather than the sheriffs.[30] It has been suggested that the Normans seemed indifferent to the idea of shiring the north.[31] By comparison with tenth-century kings, their approach to regional administration seemed almost crudely pragmatic.

One dimension of the rise of modern states which has attracted much attention in recent years has been the establishment of settled frontiers. Recent work on medieval frontiers has distinguished between linear boundaries and frontier zones, where society had special characteristics different from regions closer to the centres of political authority, and local inhabitants sometimes had strong links with those living across a political frontier.[32] Linear frontiers were often traced by reference to physical features such as rivers, or, in the case of the north, Hadrian's Wall. The location of the Anglo-Scottish border in this era may be identified, as Professor Barrow demonstrated, but questions remain about its permanence, and about society and allegiances of those living to its north and south.[33] The border came to mean a linear boundary between two kingdoms, but was this quite the case in the early twelfth century? The kings of Scots had territorial claims south of the border, to Cumbria and to Northumberland, which had formerly been united with Lothian north of the border.

Our perception of the status of the Anglo-Scottish border is sharpened by comparison with the Anglo-Welsh border or with the frontiers of Normandy in the early twelfth century. In the case of the border with Wales, it is abundantly clear that the Normans did not regard its location in 1066 as an obstacle to further conquest.[34] Henry reinforced existing Norman lordships in Wales by making sure those who held them had

[30] Holt, *Northerners*, 194–201, provides a brief survey; see also B. English, 'The Government of Thirteenth-Century Yorkshire', in *Government, Religion and Society in Northern England 1000–1700*, ed. Appleby and Dalton, 90–103.

[31] Warren, 'Myth of Norman Administrative Efficiency', 123.

[32] *Frontiers in Question: Eurasian Borderlands, 700–1700*, ed. D. Power and N. Standen (Houndmills, 1999); *Medieval Frontier Societies*, ed. R. Bartlett and A. Mackay (Oxford, 1992).

[33] G. W. S. Barrow, 'The Anglo-Scottish Border', in *The Kingdom of the Scots*, ed. G. W. S. Barrow (1973), 21–42; W. M. Aird, 'Northern England or Southern Scotland? The Anglo-Scottish Border in the Eleventh and Twelfth Centuries and the Problem of Perspective', in *Government, Religion and Society in Northern England 1000–1700*, ed. Appleby and Dalton, 27–39.

[34] R. R. Davies, *Age of Conquest. Wales 1063–1415* (paperback edn, Oxford, 1987), 4, 7.

resources both for their defence and for the consolidation of their power.[35] There was even some opportunity to push the boundaries further forward, for Henry granted Ceredigion (Cardigan) to Gilbert FitzRichard de Clare.[36] When there were attacks on estates held by the Normans, Henry was prepared to make a show of strength. In both 1114 and 1121 he marched into Wales and exacted submissions from the Welsh princes and exploited their differences.[37]

The status of the frontiers of Normandy was different again, for these separated a duchy from its neighbours, and from the French royal demesne.[38] Henry could not simply incorporate neighbouring territories within the duchy. Some sectors of the frontier were 'hot', to use Daniel Power's phrase, especially in the Vexin, and in south-east Normandy.[39] Here warfare was frequent, and local families often rebellious. Henry's reaction was to strengthen the border castles. In some ways his legacy to Normandy was the many stone-built castles which came by the end of his life to encircle the frontier.[40] In southern Normandy the downfall successively of the count of Mortain (1106) and of Robert de Bellême (1112) provided opportunities for reshaping local society. The confiscated county of Mortain was entrusted to the king's nephew Stephen of Blois.[41] Those whose families had been rivals of Robert de Bellême benefited. Robert Giroie recovered Montreuil and Echauffour.[42] Rotrou, count of Perche, Henry's son-in-law, was granted the confiscated lordship of Bellême.[43] Although Henry restored Robert de Bellême's lands to his son, he retained the castles. Security along the southern frontier remained problematic and trouble erupted again in 1135, but after 1112 Henry did not have to face

[35] Green, *Henry I*, 192–3.

[36] *Brut y Tywysogyon or the Chronicle of the Princes. Red Book of Hergest Version*, ed. and trans. T. Jones (Cardiff, 1955), 71–3; *Brut y Tywysogyon or the Chronicle of the Princes. Peniarth MS. 20 Version*, trans. T. Jones (Cardiff, 1952), 34.

[37] *Brut (Red Book of Hergest Version)*, 78–83, 105–9; *Brut (Peniarth)*, 37–8, 47–8.

[38] P. Bauduin, *La première Normandie (Xe–XIe siècles). Sur les frontières de la haute Normandie: identité et construction d'une principauté* (Caen, 2004); D. Power, 'French and Norman Frontiers in the Middle Ages', in *Frontiers in Question*, ed. Power and Standen, 105–37; idem, *The Norman Frontier in the Twelfth and Thirteenth Centuries* (Cambridge Studies in Medieval Life and Thought, fourth series, 62, Cambridge, 2004), part 1.

[39] Power, *Norman Frontier*, 10.

[40] *The Gesta Normannorum Ducum of William of Jumièges, Orderic Vitalis and Robert of Torigni*, ed. E. M. C. Van Houts (2 vols., Oxford, 1992, 1995), II, 250–2.

[41] *OV*, VI, 42. The date of the grant of Mortain is not made clear by Orderic. For the suggestion that it might have been not long before Henry's visit to Saint-Evroult in 1113 in the company of Theobald and Stephen, see E. King, 'Stephen of Blois, Count of Mortain and Boulogne', *English Historical Review*, 115 (2000), 274.

[42] *OV*, VI, 224. For the family see P. Bauduin, 'Une famille châtelaine sur les confins normanno-manceaux: les Géré (Xe–XIIIe s.)', *Archéologie médiévale*, 22 (1992), 309–56.

[43] *Gesta Normannorum Ducum*, II, 264; K. Thompson, *Power and Border Lordship in Medieval France* (Royal Historical Society, Studies in History, new series, Woodbridge, 2002), ch. 3.

such a powerful presence in the south. Some frontiers were thus treated with more respect than others by Henry.

The status of the frontiers of England and Normandy raises a further question as to how far Henry intended them to limit his power. It has been suggested that he, unlike his father and brother, was content with the lands he had inherited, and 'rejected Norman imperialism'.[44] A variant on this view is that, whether Henry wished it or not, the opportunity for further expansion had disappeared, and that it took all his resources simply to defend what he had.[45] Yet views such as these are hard to reconcile with the suggestion that Henry sought to assert rights of 'overkingship' which the Normans had inherited from their Anglo-Saxon predecessors, and which formed the justification for imperialistic claims towards their neighbours in the British Isles.[46] The terms 'overkingship' and 'imperialism' in the context of Henry's relations with the Scots thus need careful consideration.

Finally, there are the questions of identities and allegiances of those living in northern England. The numbers of Normans settled north of the Humber and the Mersey were fewer and later to arrive, and a higher proportion of native landholders survived in the local aristocracy and gentry. The processes of accommodation and co-existence were neither simple nor straightforwardly bilateral.[47] As well as relations between natives and newcomers, those between Normans in northern England, their kin elsewhere in the Anglo-Norman world, and in Scotland, have to be taken into account. Some families belonged to great Anglo-Norman families, whilst others possessed little or nothing outside the north. Ties of kinship and lordship soon helped to link northern families with those across the border in Scotland.[48]

The political allegiances of both laymen and ecclesiastics thus had to take account of multiple social ties. By the early twelfth century, the desire of Scottish kings and their bishops to be independent, and the pretensions of both York and Canterbury to primacy over the Scottish church raised

[44] C. Warren Hollister (with T. K. Keefe), 'The Making of the Angevin Empire', in Hollister, *Monarchy, Magnates and Institutions*, 248.

[45] K. Stringer, *The Reign of Stephen. Kingship, Warfare and Government in Twelfth-Century England* (1993), 10.

[46] R. R. Davies, *The First English Empire. Power and Identities in the British Isles 1093–1343* (Oxford, 2000), ch. 1, see especially 10.

[47] A. Williams, *The English and the Norman Conquest* (Woodbridge, 1995); H. M. Thomas, *The English and the Normans. Ethnic Hostility, Assimilation, and Identity 1066 – c. 1220* (Oxford, 2003).

[48] J. A. Green, 'Aristocratic Loyalties on the Northern Frontier of England, c. 1100–1174', in *England in the Twelfth Century*, ed. D. Williams (Woodbridge, 1990), 83–100; K. Stringer, 'Identities in Thirteenth-Century England: Frontier Society in the Far North', in *Social and Political Identities in Western History*, ed. C. Bjørn, A. Grant and K. J. Stringer (Copenhagen, 1994), 28–66.

the potential for conflict between the northern and southern kings.[49] In Henry's lifetime, good relations with David eased points of tension.[50] After Henry's death a conflict of loyalty could not be avoided. It was at its most acute in 1138 at the battle of the Standard, when David's army faced that of the northern magnates, and the combatants were forced to choose sides.[51]

In brief, recent historiography has tended to view northern England in the reign of Henry I as a period of peace and incorporation within the kingdom, and to see it as ruled by administrative techniques and officials rather than by punitive expedition. This essay is concerned to explore the bases on which these assumptions rest. It is suggested that we should not treat the north in isolation from other areas of Henry's realms, and that his methods were much the same there as elsewhere. Peace he certainly brought to the north, but the keys were dynastic politics, patronage and the judicious application of pressure. The second part of this essay is thus concerned with both the politics and the administration of the north.

Crucial to peace in northern England was the *modus vivendi* which Rufus and then Henry were to establish with the successors (bar one, Domnall) of King Malcolm III.[52] Duncan, Edgar, Alexander and David each benefited from the Norman kings' support in their efforts to secure the Scottish throne, but that support came at a price. Malcolm had been prepared to perform an act of submission to the Conqueror, but Rufus's insistence on treating him as a vassal had led to a quarrel and, finally, to the death of Malcolm and his son Edward.[53] Rufus was then able to use

---

[49] For the former see Hugh the Chanter, *The History of the Church of York 1066–1127*, ed. and trans. C. Johnson, revised by M. Brett, C. N. L. Brooke and M. Winterbottom (Oxford, 1990); for Canterbury Eadmer, *Historia Novorum*, ed. M. Rule (Rolls Series, 1884). M. Brett, *The English Church under Henry I* (Oxford, 1975), 14–28; N. F. Shead, 'The Origins of the Medieval Diocese of Glasgow', *Scottish Historical Review*, 47 (1969), 220–5; for Turgot at St Andrews see Symeon of Durham, *Historia Regum*, in *Opera Omnia*, II, 202–5.

[50] J. A. Green, 'Anglo-Scottish Relations 1066–1174', in *England and her Neighbours 1066–1453. Essays in Honour of Pierre Chaplais*, ed. M. Jones and M. Vale (1986), 61–3.

[51] Ailred of Rievaulx, 'De Standardo', in *Chronicles of the Reigns of Stephen, Henry II and Richard I*, ed. R. Howlett (4 vols., Rolls Series, 1894–9), III, 181–99.

[52] See Green, 'Anglo-Scottish Relations 1066–1174'; Duncan, *Kingship of the Scots*, 53–65.

[53] On this quarrel the language of the Worcester chronicler is particularly interesting as suggesting that Malcolm was claiming that he only owed 'hommage en marche', whereas William intended to treat him as a vassal in his court: 'Nam Malcolmum uidere aut cum eo colloqui, pre nimia superbia et potentia, Wilelmus despexit, insuper etiam illum ut, secundum iudicium tantum suorum baronum, in curia sua rectitudinem ei faceret, constringere uoluit, sed id agere, nisi in regnorum suorum confiniis, ubi reges Scottorum erant soliti rectitudinem facere regibus Anglorum, et secundum iudicium primatum utriusque regni, nullo modo Malcolmus uoluit', *JW*, III, 64. In fact the submission Malcolm had made to the Conqueror in 1072 had not been on the frontier between their realms but at Abernethy. The language of the Anglo-Saxon Chronicle at this point differs:

the ensuing power struggle to assert his authority over Duncan, Malcolm's son by his first wife, and then Edgar, his son by Queen Margaret. Edgar seems to have acknowledged that superiority in a form more explicitly subordinate than his father had done.[54] In 1100 Henry married Edgar's sister Edith, and her brother David soon joined Henry's court.[55] In 1107 Alexander succeeded Edgar, and, if we are to accept the Anglo-Saxon Chronicle at face value, this was 'with King Henry's consent'.[56] In 1113 David was permitted to marry a widow, Matilda de Senlis, and to hold her English lands in custody. He was further enriched when, according to the testimony of Ailred of Rievaulx, his brother King Alexander was persuaded to hand over land which his predecessor had bequeathed to David.[57] Alexander himself married an illegitimate daughter of King Henry,[58] and in 1114 led a contingent in the army which King Henry took to Scotland.[59] Alexander thus had to deal not only with Henry's assertion of superior rights, but also with a younger brother, David, who between 1113 and 1124 ruled a great swathe of southern Scotland and was a loyal ally of King Henry.[60] That territory is thought to have comprised

'When he [Malcolm] came to the king, he could not be granted speech with our king nor the fulfilment of the terms that had been promised him, and so they parted with great dissension', *ASC*, E 1093.

[54] At issue here is, first of all, the authenticity of the charter which Edgar granted to Durham which referred to his possession of 'the whole land of Lothian and the kingship of Scotland by gift of King William and by paternal heritage', *Early Scottish Charters prior to 1153*, ed. A. C. Lawrie (Glasgow, 1905), no. 5. The authenticity of this charter has been debated: queried by J. Donnelly, 'The Earliest Scottish Charters?', *Scottish Historical Review*, 68 (1989), 1–22, its authenticity was reaffirmed by A. A. M. Duncan, 'Yes, the Earliest Scottish Charters', *Scottish Historical Review*, 78 (1999), 1–35; and most recently by Duncan, *Kingship of the Scots*, 56–7. The language used in the charter in any event may be assumed to reflect Rufus's view of his superior authority over Edgar. Secondly, according to Gaimar, writing in the 1130s, Rufus promised Edgar a daily allowance when he visited the English court, and further claimed that Edgar carried a sword at the great court held in the new hall at Westminster in 1099, *L'estoire*, ed. A. Bell (Oxford, 1960), ll. 6176–83, 5975–6020; Duncan, *Kingship of the Scots*, 58.

[55] For the marriage see Green, *Henry I*, 53–9; Lois. L. Huneycutt, *Matilda of Scotland. A Study in Medieval Queenship* (Woodbridge, 2003), 26–30. David was at Henry's court by Whitsuntide 1103, *RRAN*, II, no. 648. It is significant that this text concerns an exchange of lands for Robert de Brus.

[56] *ASC*, E 1107.

[57] Ailred of Rievaulx, 'De Standardo', in *Chronicles of the Reigns of Stephen, Henry II and Richard I*, ed. Howlett, III, 193.

[58] G. H. White suggested that Sibyl's mother may have been Sibyl Corbet, but K. Thompson pointed out there are chronological difficulties with this, *Complete Peerage*, by G. E. C. (13 vols. in 12, 1910–59), XI, Appendix D, 118; K. Thompson, 'Affairs of State: The Illegitimate Children of Henry I,' *Journal of Medieval History*, 29 (2003), 149.

[59] *Brut (Red Book of Hergest)*, 79–83; *Brut (Peniarth)*, 37–8.

[60] R. Oram, *David I. The King Who Made Scotland* (Stroud, 2004), ch. 4.

a considerable part of south-west Scotland, and, in south-east Scotland, Teviotdale and Tweeddale.[61]

David's northern lordship was only one of a whole series which formed a *cordon sanitaire* in the north and north-west. Carlisle may have been granted in the first instance to Ivo Taillebois and, after his death and the death of Lucy's second husband, to her third, Ranulf Meschin. Ranulf served Henry loyally and was one of his commanders at the battle of Tinchebray in 1106.[62] He seems to have enjoyed wide-ranging authority in the north-west. As well as founding a Benedictine priory at Wetheral near Carlisle,[63] he seems to have been responsible for the establishment of Robert de Trivers at Burgh by Sands, Richer de Boiville at Kirklinton and Turgis Brundos at Liddel. These lordships were all beyond Hadrian's Wall, and as such springboards for further advance.[64] Lordships in the remainder of Cumbria took shape.[65] Some were held by native families, and the daughter of one lord, Forne son of Sigulf, was one of Henry I's mistresses.[66] Westmorland consisted of two great lordships, one in the north centred on Appleby,[67] the other in the south at Kendal. Appleby was in the king's hands in 1130, whilst it seems that Kendal had passed to Nigel d'Aubigny.[68] South of the river Duddon, the two portions of the

[61] For Teviotdale where the monks of Durham had claims to land see W. M. Aird, *St Cuthbert and the Normans* (Woodbridge, 1998), 230 and n. 12. David founded the abbey of Selkirk in Tweeddale: Symeon of Durham, *Historia Regum*, in *Opera Omnia*, II, 247.

[62] E. King, 'Ranulf (I), third earl of Chester (d. 1129), *Oxford Dictionary of National Biography* (Oxford, 2004), http://www.oxforddnb.com/view/article/23127. For Ranulf at Tinchebray see *OV*, VI, 84.

[63] *Register of Wetheral Priory*, ed. J. E. Prescott (Cumberland and Westmorland Antiquarian and Archaeological Society [hereafter CWAAS], Record Series I, 1897), no. 1.

[64] For Robert see I. J. Sanders, *English Baronies* (Oxford, 1961), 23; for Richer, G. W. S. Barrow, *The Anglo-Norman Era in Scottish History* (Oxford, 1980), 176; and for Turgis Brundos, T. H. B. Graham, 'Turgis Brundos', *CWAAS*, *Transactions*, new series, 29 (1929), 49–56. For the 'debateable land' see J. Todd, 'The West March on the Anglo-Scottish Border in the Twelfth Century, and the Origins of the Western Debateable Land', *Northern History*, 43 (2006), 11–19. For a recent discussion of these lordships see G. W. S. Barrow, 'King David I, Earl Henry and Cumbria', *CWAAS*, *Transactions*, 99 (1999), 117–29, at 120.

[65] A. J. L. Winchester, *Landscape and Society in Medieval Cumbria* (Edinburgh, 1987), ch. 2; Phythian-Adams, *Land of the Cumbrians*, 170.

[66] For Forne see *Early Yorkshire Charters*, ed. Farrer, II, 505; R. Sharpe, *Norman Rule in Cumbria 1092–1136*, CWAAS, Tract Series XXI (2006), 41.

[67] Ranulf gave the church of St Lawrence 'of my castle of Appleby' to Wetheral: *Register of Wetheral Priory*, ed. Prescott, no. 3.

[68] For Kendal see W. Farrer, *Records relating to the Barony of Kendale*, ed. J. F. Curwen (CWAAS, Record Series, IV–VI, 1923–6), IV, xi. As indicated, there is no evidence to illustrate Nigel's possession of Kendal. On the other hand, Burton in Lonsdale, which had also been held by Ivo, had passed by 1130 to Nigel's son, Roger de Mowbray: *Magnum Rotuli Scaccarii, vel magnum rotulum pipae, anno tricesimo primo regni Henrici primi, ut videtur, quem plurimi hactenus laudarunt pro rotulo quinti anni Stephani regis* [hereafter *PR 31 Henry I*], ed. J. Hunter for Record Commission (1833), 138.

later county of Lancashire, previously held by Roger the Poitevin, passed to Stephen of Blois, probably in 1113.[69]

In the north-east, Henry made no attempt to appoint a new earl of Northumberland in succession to Robert de Mowbray, who had forfeited his lands in 1095. Instead a patchwork of lesser lordships emerged, some of which were in the hands of native families like Gospatric, earl of Lothian (Dunbar) and lord of Beanley in Northumberland.[70] In the Inquest of Feudal Service of 1166 a number of the new lordships were said to have been 'of the old enfeoffment', that is, they were created before 1135, and most of these were thought to have dated from the reign of Henry I.[71] The bishopric of Durham by contrast was another great compact lordship, this time in the hands of a bishop. The historic lands belonging to St Cuthbert straddled the Anglo-Scottish border, and the first bishop after 1066, William of Saint-Calais, had to tread carefully between the courts of the Scottish and English kings.[72] His successor, Ranulf Flambard (1099–1128), suffered a period of imprisonment and exile after Henry's accession, as the minister who had effected the fiscal exploitation of the English church for Rufus. After Ranulf's return to Durham, however, he strengthened the defences of Durham and built a castle at Norham on the river Tweed.[73] Not only that, but, here, as elsewhere, lordships took shape with members of Ranulf's own family strongly represented in the local aristocracy.[74]

The wreck of the White Ship and with it the death of the king's only (legitimate) son together with over 300 hundred members of the

[69] Roger the Poitevin's land in Lincolnshire had passed to Stephen by the time of the Lindsey survey, now dated between 1115 and 1116; J. A. Green, 'Ranulf II and Lancashire', in *The Earldom of Chester and Its Charters*, ed. A. T. Thacker, *Journal of the Chester Archaeological Society*, 71 (1991), 97–108; King, 'Stephen of Blois, Count of Mortain and Boulogne', 274–5.

[70] A. McDonald, 'Gospatric, first earl of Lothian (d. 1138)', *Oxford Dictionary of National Biography*, http://www.oxforddnb.com/view/article/50322.

[71] When the nineteen Northumberland tenants-in-chief reported their enfeoffments in 1166, only three did not specifically say that they held 'of the old enfeoffment', that is, that they had been enfeoffed before 1135: *Red Book of the Exchequer*, ed. H. Hall (3 vols., Rolls Series, 1896), I, 436–44. When the Northumberland baronies were surveyed in 1212, their holders reported variously on the date their ancestors had received the lands. No fewer than nine said that the grants had been made by Henry I, and several others '*post conquestum*' or '*de veteri feoffamento*', *Liber Feodorum. The Book of Fees Commonly Called Testa de Nevill Reformed from the Earliest MSS. by the Deputy Keeper of the Records* (3 vols., 1920–31), I, 200–5; for discussion of these lordships see W. Percy Hedley, *Northumberland Families* (2 vols., Newcastle upon Tyne, 1968–70).

[72] See the essays by G. W. S. Barrow, 'The Kings of Scotland and Durham', and V. Wall, 'Malcolm III and the Foundation of Durham Cathedral', in *Anglo-Norman Durham 1093–1193*, ed. D. Rollason, M. Harvey and M. Prestwich (Woodbridge, 1994), 311–38.

[73] Symeon of Durham, *Libellus de Exordio atque Procursu istius hoc est Dunhelmensis Ecclesie*, ed. D. Rollason (Oxford, 2000), 276.

[74] *Durham Episcopal Charters*, ed. H. S. Offler (Surtees Society, CLXXIX, 1968), no. 20; Aird, *St Cuthbert and the Normans*, 208–9.

court was a seismic shock which had repercussions in every quarter of Henry's realms, northern England included. His immediate priority was remarriage with the hope of fathering another son as quickly as possible, but he also had to reassert his authority in England after a long absence, and to take decisions about a series of honours whose lords had died. One of these was the earldom of Chester, as the young earl of Chester was one of those who had drowned. Henry decided to allow his kinsman, Ranulf Meschin, to succeed to the earldom and the vast estates, but a price was exacted, in that Ranulf surrendered the lordship of Carlisle, and Henry chose not to appoint a successor of similar status and powers.[75]

There are other indications of Henry's concern about the north. In 1121 a great gathering of northern magnates at Durham is mentioned,[76] and we know that castles were built at Norham, by the bishop of Durham, and Wark, by Walter Espec, on the Tweed frontier.[77] Henry himself travelled north late in 1122, proceeding from York as far as Carlisle, where he ordered the strengthening of the town's defences.[78] A possible explanation for Henry's concern suggested recently is that he was exercised about the prospects for the succession to the Scottish throne.[79] Alexander's marriage to Henry's daughter Sibyl is not known to have produced children, and in July 1122 she died. Henry presumably felt that his interests would be best served if Alexander were to be succeeded by his younger brother David, but Alexander may have needed some persuasion.[80] This may well have been the case, but the strengthening of defences along the Solway–Tweed frontier may have been prompted by other considerations.

It may also have been around this time that Henry allied with Fergus, lord of Galloway, who married yet another of Henry's illegitimate daughters.[81] Galloway was a region largely independent of the power of the king of Scots and of David as prince in south-west Scotland. Fergus, it has been suggested, was keen to keep it so.[82] When a bishop was appointed for the ancient see of Whithorn, in about 1128, he professed obedience to Archbishop Thurstan of York, an act which, it may be presumed, would not have been welcome to David, who had succeeded to the Scottish

---

[75] Sharpe, *Norman Rule in Cumbria*, 11–16.

[76] Symeon of Durham, *Historia Regum*, in *Opera Omnia*, II, 259–60.

[77] For Norham, see n. 73 above. Walter had come into possession of Wark by about 1122 when he gave the church there to Kirkham priory in Yorkshire at its foundation, W. Dugdale, *Monasticon Anglicanum*, new edn (6 vols. in 8, London, 1817–30), VI, 208–9.

[78] Symeon of Durham, *Historia Regum*, in *Opera Omnia*, II, 267. For the city see H. Summerson, *Medieval Carlisle. The City and the Borders from the Late Eleventh to the Mid-Sixteenth Century*, CWAAS, extra series 25 (1993), I, 18–54.

[79] Oram, *David I*, 71–2.

[80] *Ibid.*

[81] For the marriage see Oram, *Lordship of Galloway*, 51–62.

[82] *Ibid.*, 61.

throne in 1124.[83] Between Galloway and Carlisle lay Annandale, where Robert de Brus was established.[84] Robert seems to have owed great estates in northern England to Henry, but he was and remained a close associate of David.[85]

Another piece of evidence pointing towards concern about the north around 1122 was the foundation by Stephen of Blois, as lord of Lancaster, of an abbey established first at Tulketh and then at Furness.[86] Stephen seems to have held his great estates in the north-west for some years before taking any steps to assert his lordship there, and the timing may be explained if he had accompanied his uncle the king to Carlisle in 1122.[87] Savigny, the mother house of Tulketh, had close links with Stephen as count of Mortain. The monks soon moved to Furness, where they enjoyed easy access to the sea and sent out colonies, to Erenagh near Downpatrick in northern Ireland, and to Rushen on the Isle of Man.[88] These foundations are a salutary reminder that links between northern England and the Isle of Man and Ireland remained very important, though reported in less detail than affairs in southern England and Normandy. Man retained its strategic important in the Irish Sea zone, and its ruler, Olaf, was said to have been brought up at Henry's court.[89]

A map of northern England in this era thus shows a great arc of large, compact lordships from Chester north to Carlisle, and across to Northumberland and Durham in the north-east, with David's lands to the north forming an outer shield. The final piece of the jigsaw was Yorkshire, and here there was considerable reorganisation of lordships in the early twelfth century. As Paul Dalton demonstrated, the harrying of 1069–70 had been followed up by the construction of lordships centred on castles, but confiscations and deaths ensued, and by 1135 the composition

---

[83] Evidence for the consecration is contained in a letter of Archbishop William: *British Library Harleian Manuscript 433*, ed. R. Horrox and P. W. Hammond (4 vols., Gloucester, 1979–83), III, 93–4; R. Oram, 'In Obedience and Reverence: Whithorn and York *c.* 1128 – *c.* 1250', *Innes Review*, 42 (1991), 83–100; *idem*, *Lordship of Galloway*, 164–74; P. Hill, *Whithorn and St Ninian. The Excavation of a Monastic Town 1984–91* (Stroud, 1997), 23.

[84] *The Charters of David I*, ed. G. W. S. Barrow (Woodbridge, 1999), no. 16.

[85] R. Blakely, *The Brus Family in England and Scotland 1100–1295* (Woodbridge, 2005), ch. 1. A. A. M. Duncan, 'Brus, Robert (I) de, lord of Annandale (d. 1142)', *Oxford Dictionary of National Biography*, http://www.oxforddnb.com/view/article/3748.

[86] Symeon of Durham, *Historia Regum*, in *Opera Omnia*, II, 267 (1123, but 1124 is the more usually accepted date); *RRAN*, II, nos. 1545–6 (after removal to Furness). King, 'Stephen of Blois, Count of Mortain and Boulogne', *English Historical Review*, 65 (2000), 279.

[87] *Ibid.*

[88] A. Gwynn and R. N. Hadcock, *Medieval Religious Houses. Ireland* (1970), 132, 135 (Erenagh and Inch, its successor); D. Easson, *Medieval Religious Houses. Scotland* (1976), 237 (Rushen). Olaf of Man gave land on Man to Furness, *Chronicon Manniae et Insularum. The Chronicle of Man and the Sudreys from the Manuscript Codex in the British Museum, with Historical Notes by P. A. Munch*, revised by Dr Goss (2 vols., Manx Society, XXII, XXIII, 1874), XXII, 62–3.

[89] *Ibid.*, XXII, 60–1; D. Nicholl, *Thurstan Archbishop of York (1114–40)* (York, 1964), 139.

and structure of many Yorkshire lordships was very different from the start of Henry's reign.[90] Holderness was restored to Stephen count of Aumale,[91] Pontefract was granted first to Hugh de Laval and then to William Maltravers,[92] and Blyth was accounted for at the exchequer in 1130.[93] Meanwhile new lordships were constructed for Henry's men, like Nigel d'Aubigny and Robert de Brus;[94] later Walter Espec and Eustace FitzJohn were granted lands both in Yorkshire and Northumberland.[95]

To this point, therefore, we have seen little that is new about Henry's rule in northern England. He was concerned above all with peace and security. To that end he upheld the alliance with three successive kings of Scots. He asserted his influence at the accession of Alexander, persuaded Alexander to hand over land to David and, it appears, had a hand in securing David's succession in 1124. His methods were distinctly old-fashioned: the assertion of overkingship, the use of marriage alliances and the hint that force would be used if needed. This was much the same as his approach elsewhere, with regard to the Welsh, for instance, or in Normandy. As we have seen, he took care that Norman lordships in Wales were in the hands of men of substance, but, when he felt a show of force was necessary, he took armies to Wales, in 1114 and 1121. He exacted obedience and tribute from the Welsh princes, and those who were prepared to be loyal were left alone. However, he did not turn his back on further advances, as when he allowed Gilbert FitzRichard to take over Ceredigion.

If there were opportunities for military conquest in Wales, it was not the same situation in Normandy. Here the mechanism for an extension of power had to be through oaths of allegiance, marriage and succession, the custody of castles and the occasional show of force. To the south, Maine, long an object of Norman ambition, could not be conquered. Instead Henry cultivated the friendship of Helias of La Flèche and the lords of northern Maine.[96] He had held the castle of Domfront in the Passais

---

[90] Dalton, *Conquest, Anarchy and Lordship*, chs. 2, 3.

[91] B. English, *The Lords of Holderness 1086–1260* (Oxford, 1979), 15.

[92] W. E. Wightman, *The Lacy Family in England and Normandy 1066–1194* (Oxford, 1966), 66–72.

[93] *PR 31 Henry I*, 9–10, 36.

[94] *Charters of the Honour of Mowbray 1107–1191*, ed. D. E. Greenway (Oxford, 1972), xvii–xxiv; Blakely, *Brus Family*, appendix 1.

[95] For Walter Espec see J. A. Green, *The Government of England under Henry I* (Cambridge Studies in Medieval Life and Thought, fourth series, 11, Cambridge, 1986), 245–6; for Eustace, P. Dalton, 'Eustace FitzJohn and the Politics of Anglo-Norman England: The Rise and Survival of a Twelfth-Century Royal Servant', *Speculum*, 71 (1996), 358–83.

[96] R. E. Barton, 'Henry I, Helias of Maine, and the Battle of Tinchebray', in *Henry I and the Anglo-Norman World*, ed. D. Fleming, J. M. Pope and R. Babcock, *Haskins Society Journal*, XVIII (Boydell, 2007), 63–90. For feudal society in Maine see D. Pichot, *Le Bas-Maine du Xe au XIIIe siècle: étude d'une société* (Laval, 1995). The lords of Beaumont and Laval married Henry's

since 1092, and not only ensured that it did not return to the lords of Bellême, but strengthened his hold over the territory south of Domfront with its key castles.[97]

In all quarters of his realms, the marriages of his illegitimate daughters were used to build alliances. His wealth paid for the strengthening of castles, whether at Carlisle or Domfront, and the wages of the men who garrisoned them. Bishops were essential figures: a bishop for Carlisle was one way of separating off Strathclyde south of Solway from the north, which became the bishopric of Glasgow.[98] Territorial bishoprics in Wales were an important element in the 'Normanization' of the Welsh church.[99] In southern Normandy the bishopric of Sées had suffered from the activities of Robert de Bellême, and after the appointment of a new bishop in 1124 steps were taken to reorganise the see in which Henry played a prominent role.[100] He was present at the consecration of the new cathedral in 1126, and granted charters to the bishop. Sées like Carlisle was a cathedral church which was staffed by Augustinian canons. The patronage of religious houses provided opportunities for the assertion of his influence, and again there are parallels between northern England and, for instance, southern Normandy, where he showed favour to the abbey of Saint-Evroult.[101] The foundation of Savigny, within Normandy but very close to the frontiers of Brittany and Maine, gave him the opportunity to extend his patronage in a region authority in a remote area of the duchy.[102]

The evidence relating to royal administration supplies a different perspective on Henry's rule in the north. At first sight our impression, based on the surviving numbers of writs and charters and of the coverage in the 1130 pipe roll, is of growing vigour. A study of writs and charters

daughters; Patrick of Sourches received the English estates of Ernulf de Hesdin, Hamelin de Mayenne received land in England in return for handing over the castle of Ambrières, and Hamelin's brother Juhel received a gold cup. For details, see C. Warren Hollister, *Henry I* (New Haven and London, 2001), 228–9.

[97] *OV*, IV, 258; the key castles were Ambrières (see preceding note), Gorron and Châteauneuf-sur-Colmont: Power, *Norman Frontier*, 72–4.

[98] For Michael, appointed before the death of Archbishop Thomas II in February 1114, and his successor John, see: Hugh the Chanter, *The History of the Church of York 1066–1127*, 52–3, 212–17; Shead, 'Origins of the Medieval Diocese of Glasgow', 220–5; Oram, *David I*, 63; *Charters of David I*, ed. Barrow, nos. 9, 10.

[99] Davies, *Age of Conquest*, ch. 7.

[100] *OV*, VI, 340, 366; *Les clercs au service de la réforme. Etudes et documents sur les chanoines réguliers de la province de Rouen*, dir. M. Arnoux, Bibliotheca Victorina, XI (2000), 120, 142–4, 215–20.

[101] Henry visited the abbey in 1113, granted the monks a charter and received the privilege of confraternity, *OV*, VI, 174–6; *RRAN*, II, no. 1019. For other royal documents for the abbey see *RRAN*, II, nos. 533, 1235, 1337, 1553, 1572, *1594–5.

[102] For Henry's charters see J. Van Moolenbroek, *Vital l'ermite, prédicateur itinérant, fondateur de l'abbaye normande de Savigny*, trans. Anne-Marie Nambet, *Revue de l'Avranchin*, 68 (1991), nos. 1, 3; *RRAN*, II, nos. 1016, 1183, 1212, 1433, 1588, 1973.

must be postponed until the new edition of Henry I's acts appears,[103] but a closer look at the pipe roll is illuminating. Yorkshire was most like the rest of England in terms of royal administration, but even here the crown estates were much less valuable than in southern England, and there were a number of great jurisdictional liberties. The 1130 pipe roll provides a snapshot of the character of royal administration towards the end of Henry's reign. Yorkshire was a full county with a sheriff, Bertram de Bulmer. He was the son of a former sheriff, from a local family, not a magnate of the first rank.[104] There was recurrent annual revenue from land, from at least one royal forest, and from the city of York, but perhaps the most striking feature of the 1130 account was the number of debts rising from agreements with individual magnates. Already, then, the crown was able to deal with individuals as well as communities, the hallmark, it has been suggested, of a new style of ruling.[105] Many of these agreements had doubtless arisen from the activity of royal justices, namely, Eustace FitzJohn and Walter Espec, and the royal chamberlain Geoffrey de Clinton.[106] References are made to those involved in judicial activity, the *judices* and *juratores* of the county.[107] There were possibilities for extending royal influence as the city of York began to prosper. There was a merchant gild,[108] and a mint,[109] as well as two castles.[110] Archbishop Thurstan's refusal to make a profession of obedience to Canterbury had delayed his arrival in his see, but from 1120 he proved to be an active archbishop, promoting the foundation of religious houses, which then sought confirmation charters from the king.[111] Henry gave churches for prebends at York Minster, and he granted the canons privileges.[112] He was a benefactor of the hospital of St Leonard's where, incidentally, he may have spent his birthday in 1122.[113] He was a patron, too, of the Benedictine

---

[103] The edition is under the direction of Richard Sharpe, whose study of the north-west in *Norman Rule in Cumbria* is based on a close examination of the documentary evidence for the north-west, and for Northumberland.

[104] Green, *Government of England*, 238–9.

[105] Warren, 'Myth of Norman Administrative Efficiency', 131.

[106] *PR 31 Henry I*, 27, 33.

[107] *Ibid.*, 24–35. The *judices* are thought to have been the lawmen who delivered judgements and the *juratores*, jurors: H. G. Richardson and G. O. Sayles, *The Governance of Mediaeval England* (Edinburgh, 1963), 181–5.

[108] *Ibid.*, 34.

[109] Two of the moneyers were the archbishops: M. Allen, 'The Archbishop of York's Mint after the Norman Conquest', *Northern History*, 41 (2004), 25–38.

[110] For the castles see D. J. Cathcart King, *Castellarium Anglicanum* (2 vols., London, New York, and Niedeln), II, 528–9.

[111] Nicholl, *Thurstan*, ch. 5.

[112] *Early Yorkshire Charters*, ed. Farrer, I, nos. 128, 130, 132, 426–30, 500.

[113] *Ibid.*, nos. 167–9; *The Historians of the Church of York and its Archbishops*, ed. J. Raine (3 vols., Rolls Series, 1879–84), II, 266.

abbey of St Mary's at York,[114] and confirmed the endowments of the priory of Holy Trinity.[115]

It is instructive to pursue the treatment of different regions of the north in the pipe roll a little further. The heading 'Between Ribble and Mersey' is inserted into the account for Yorkshire. So far as the barons of the exchequer were concerned, the king's rights in south Lancashire had to be maintained, but no revenue was forthcoming, only a record of debts owed for a concord with the count (that is, Stephen count of Mortain), and no reference was made to north Lancashire, the honour of Lancashire, which was entirely in Stephen's hands.[116] Northumberland follows the account for Yorkshire; no pleas are specifically distinguished as 'New', and the account is relatively short: the sheriff, Odard of Bamburgh, accounted for a farm and also for danegeld, levied at the round figure of one hundred pounds.[117]

In 1130 the bishopric of Durham was in the king's hands. Ranulf Flambard had died in September 1128 and as yet the king had not nominated a successor. The royal chamberlain, William de Pont de l'Arche, had visited the bishopric to make arrangements for its custody,[118] and Walter Espec and Eustace FitzJohn had been about the king's business, and been hearing pleas.[119] One of the barons of the bishopric, a man named Geoffrey Escolland, accounted for its revenues.[120] Finally, Carlisle and Westmorland occur on a roll which includes various miscellaneous accounts. The revenues of Carlisle were in the hands of a man named Hildret, and a man named Richard the knight accounted for a geld of animals (no danegeld here).[121] There are signs of change: money had been spent on the wall round the city of Carlisle, and a gift had been made to the Augustinian canons of St Mary for the building of their church.[122] Three years later, the first bishop was consecrated by Archbishop Thurstan and St Mary's became the cathedral church.[123]

---

[114] *Early Yorkshire Charters*, ed. Farrer, I, nos. 351–3; for discussion see J. Burton, *The Monastic Order in Yorkshire 1069–1135* (Cambridge, 1999), 39–43.

[115] *Early Yorkshire Charters*, ed. Clay, VII, nos. 2–4.

[116] *PR 31 Henry I*, 33–4.

[117] *Ibid.*, 35–6.

[118] *Ibid.*, 130–3.

[119] *Ibid.*, 131–2.

[120] Aird, *St Cuthbert and the Normans*, 209.

[121] *PR 31 Henry I*, 140–2.

[122] *Ibid.*, 140–1.

[123] J. C. Dickinson, 'The Origins of the Cathedral of Carlisle', *CWAAS, Transactions*, second series, 45 (1946), 133–43; *idem*, 'Walter the Priest and St Mary's Carlisle', *CWAAS, Transactions*, second series, 69 (1969), 102–14; H. R. T. Summerson, 'Old and New Bishoprics: Durham and Carlisle', in *Anglo-Norman Durham*, ed. Rollason, Harvey and Prestwich, 369–80; *idem*, 'Athelwold the Bishop and Walter the Priest: A New Source for the Early History of Carlisle Priory', *CWAAS, Transactions*, 95 (1995), 85–91; Sharpe, *Norman Rule in Cumbria*, 56–62.

The silver mines at Alston, which had been opened up recently, had been at farm to the burgesses of Carlisle, but in the year just ended the farm was accounted for by a man named William, together with Hildret, presumably the same man who accounted for the king's farm.[124] The revenue from Westmorland was accounted for by a man named Richard son of Gerard of Appleby. This included a farm for the king's lands and rights in the region, and a payment for the geld of animals. Once again, there are references to the pleas of Walter Espec and Eustace FitzJohn.[125]

The pipe roll evidence thus demonstrates that, although it was wide-ranging, royal administration was a relatively thin veneer over northern society. No attempt had been made to shire the northern regions: Carlisle was not a county but a *potestas*,[126] and Northumberland, administered first by the sheriffs based at Corbridge and Bamburgh, was in the later years of the reign administered from Bamburgh alone.[127] Durham was only in royal custody temporarily. Relatively little revenue was coming in from the northern counties in comparison with Berkshire, and none at all from the land between Ribble and Mersey.[128] A good deal of local policing was in the hands of local lords, rather than the sheriff.[129]

On the other hand, the references to the pleas of Walter Espec and Eustace FitzJohn's activities throughout much of the north are striking. They were regionally based justices with a remit to safeguard the king's interests. They supervised restocking of royal manors and work on castles, and imposed fines on local lawmen. Their role possibly derived from that of earlier commissions, including that which had overseen the Domesday Inquest in 1086, and was different from the later general

[124] Robert of Torigny, *Chronique suivi de divers opuscules historiques de cet auteur*, ed. L. Delisle (2 vols., Société de l'Histoire de Normandie, Rouen, 1872–3), I, 191–2; *PR 31 Henry I*, 142; I. Blanchard, "'Lothian and Beyond': The Economy of the "English Empire" of David I', in *Progress and Problems in Medieval England. Essays in Honour of Edward Miller*, ed. J. Hatcher and R. Britnell (Cambridge, 1996), 23–45.

[125] *PR 31 Henry I*, 142–3; Sharpe, *Norman Rule in Cumbria*, 13–14.

[126] For this term see Ranulf's charter for Wetheral, *Register of Wetheral Priory*, ed. Prescott, no. 1.

[127] For the sheriffs see J. A. Green, *English Sheriffs to 1154*, Public Record Office Handbooks, no. 24 (1990), 65–6. To judge from his name, Aluric of Corbridge may have been English. Corbridge had been a Roman fort near the bank of the river Tyne and seems to have been a centre for south Northumberland: H. H. E. Craster, *A History of Northumberland*, X (Newcastle and London, 1914), 38–40. Aluric's son held Dilston as a barony: *Red Book of the Exchequer*, ed. Hall, I, 441. For Odard of Bamburgh, see Green, *Government of England*, 264.

[128] For a table of farms see G. H. White, *Restoration and Reform 1153–1165* (Cambridge Studies in Medieval Life and Thought, fourth series, XLVI, Cambridge, 2000), 220–6: Carlisle accounted for some £56, Northumberland £139, Yorkshire £444. Berkshire by comparison accounted for £521.

[129] For the system of policing known as frankpledge see W. A. Morris, *The Frankpledge System* (Cambridge, MA, 1910).

eyre.[130] References to the pleas of Geoffrey de Clinton at Blyth and the visit of William de Pont de l'Arche to Durham are more significant.[131] They were members of the royal court and inner circle, chamberlains with special responsibility for finance, the link men between the itinerant royal household and the royal treasury. The fact that royal agents in the north were answerable at the exchequer meeting in the south is a further sign of incorporation within the realm. Administrative innovations were incremental, however, superimposed on the old rather than sweeping them aside, and they form only part of the story, and perhaps not its most important part.

In northern England Henry's aims and methods were much the same as elsewhere, whether in England, Wales or Normandy. Old-fashioned dynastic politics were at its heart: the shrewd appreciation of possibilities to be gained by marrying off a daughter, raising a young prince in his household, punishing his enemies and rewarding his friends, as William of Malmesbury noted.[132] What differed in the different parts of his realms were the contexts and therefore the consequences of his actions. In Normandy he had to fight to defend the duchy and its future, and to the south the county of Maine was only secured at a high price and as part of a bigger package, the marriage of his only daughter into the comital house of Anjou. In Wales there was resistance to the Normans but also some opportunity for advance, and the 'Normanisation' of the Welsh church created opportunities for influence. The idea of a superior kingship over the Welsh and Scots was exploited, and, if this is to be defined as imperialism, then Henry was as imperialistic as his predecessors. Yet the Welsh and the Scots were treated differently, for the Anglo-Scots border as a political divide was respected and even reinforced by the creation of the diocese of Carlisle. The dividing line between the English and Scottish kingdoms was not fixed for good, of course, because after 1135 David took over Cumbria, and Northumberland, and sought to place his own nominee as bishop of Durham.[133]

In retrospect Henry's greatest achievement in the north as in the rest of England was to bring peace. It was a stern peace, with winners and losers, and it depended less on administration than on alliances and patronage. This created conditions in which the new lordships could take shape, and for that great flowering of monasticism of the early twelfth century. The northern chroniclers understood this very clearly. One with first hand

[130] Warren, 'Myth of Norman Administrative Efficiency', 124.

[131] *PR 31 Henry I*, 27, 131.

[132] William of Malmesbury, *Gesta Regum Anglorum*, I, ed. R. A. B. Mynors, R. M. Thomson and M. Winterbottom (Oxford, 1998), 742.

[133] K. J. Stringer, 'State-Building in Twelfth-Century Britain: David I, King of Scots, and Northern England', in *Government, Religion and Society in Northern England*, ed. Appleby and Dalton, 40–62; Oram, *David I*, ch. 10.

experience was Richard, prior of Hexham, who wrote a history of the deeds of King Stephen and of the battle of the Standard in 1138. He began by reviewing the achievements of Henry I, the peace of his reign and the religious houses he had founded. He described the terrible effects of the Scots' invasions after 1135, their defeat at the Standard in 1138 and the peace concluded in the following year at Durham. It was agreed at that time that David's son Henry would become earl of Northumbria. The barons performed homage to him, and swore allegiance. The Scots handed over hostages and swore to keep the laws, customs and statutes which King Henry had decreed to be observed in the earldom. Just in case readers were unsure exactly what these laws were, the author thoughtfully included a text of Henry's Charter of Liberties in his chronicle.[134] Peace and the observance of law were no mean legacy.

---

[134] Richard of Hexham, 'De Gestis Regis Stephani et de Bello Standardi', in *Chronicles of the Reigns of Stephen, Henry II and Richard I*, ed. Howlett, III, 139–78. The terms of the treaty are at 177–8.

Transactions of the RHS 17 (2007), pp. 57–82 © 2007 Royal Historical Society
doi:10.1017/S0080440107000539   Printed in the United Kingdom

ARISTOCRATIC WIDOWS AND THE MEDIEVAL WELSH FRONTIER: THE SHROPSHIRE EVIDENCE*
The Rees Davies Prize Essay
By Emma Cavell

ABSTRACT. This article builds upon the work of the late Professor Sir Rees Davies and other scholars interested in the medieval March of Wales, and draws attention to the place, roles and experiences of the noblewomen in a region usually considered the preserve of the warrior lord. In focusing on the aristocratic widow, for whom records are relatively abundant, it examines the widows' experience of dower assignment and of estate and castle management on a frontier district. It contends that, among other things, those who allocated dower to the widows of the region deliberately eschewed the frontier hotspots, and that the normative relationship between female lord and castle was at once improved and restricted by the warlike nature of the region. A final section examines the life and career of the often overlooked Isabel de Mortimer (daughter of Roger de Mortimer of Wigmore and sometime wife of John FitzAlan III), revealing her critical part in holding the Shropshire frontline on the eve of the final conquest of Wales (1282–3). The case is made that we cannot fully understand the aristocratic Marcher society without including women in our histories.

Historians have long been attentive to the male world of the Welsh Marches and English frontier shires – to the activities of frontier barons, to military institutions and lordship, and even to the evolution of a Marcher identity in the aftermath of the Norman Conquest of England. The unsurpassed work of Rees Davies, and indeed the writings of many of his students and mentees in Oxford, has revolutionised our understanding of medieval Wales, and of the frontier between the monolithic kingdom of England and the several smaller kingdoms or principalities that made

* I owe a debt of thanks to those whose expertise and assistance contributed to the research contained in this essay, in particular to Professor Sir Rees Davies, who was my mentor and doctoral supervisor until his untimely passing in May 2005, and to Dr Benjamin Thompson and Mrs Henrietta Leyser who kindly agreed to step into the breach. Thanks must also go to Janet Burton for her tireless editorial assistance, and to my dear friend Frances Flanagan without whose suggestions at the outset this essay would not have been completed, let alone successful. This essay is dedicated to the memory of Rees Davies.

up what is now the nation of Wales.[1] In particular, the Welsh March (or Marches), that congeries of largely autonomous, and by no means static, lordships wedged between the English kingdom and Wales proper, or *pura Wallia*, has traditionally been seen as a man's world – shaped by men, for men: the barons, kings and Welsh princes. The historiographical March is a world in which women, if they feature at all, are cursorily skimmed over as adjuncts to the border lords who occupy centre stage, or as passive conduits for the transfer of land and alliance between men.

The prevailing model of the Welsh frontier is overdue for re-evaluation. It is time that historians of the March of Wales, or indeed of British frontier societies generally (for the expertise of Davies was by no means wholly confined to Wales and the Welsh frontier) engaged in closer scrutiny of the female place in, and contribution to, border societies in Britain during the central medieval period.[2] By the same token, historians interested in the medieval woman (and here particularly in the *noble*woman) ought not only to examine the impact of frontier existence on the propertied females whose lives were played out along the March before, and immediately after, the Edwardian Conquest of Wales (1282–3), but also to consider what the results of this examination might add to our understanding of the English noblewoman more generally, an area of research that, as far as lowland England is concerned, has made considerable headway in recent decades.

Of course, there can be little doubt that in many ways the Welsh March *was* a man's world. Medieval western society, as Margaret Howell has noted, was one 'structured on patriarchy and male dominance'. Although historians disagree over whether the twelfth century or the thirteenth century was more hostile to women, western Christendom was 'a society in which misogyny, at the level of theory, image and crude practice was rife'.[3] Add to this the overt warrior mentality of a military frontier, such as that between England and Wales, and one is looking at a world that was,

---

[1] R. R. Davies, *Lordship and Society in the March of Wales, 1282–1400* (Oxford, 1978); idem, *Conquest, Coexistence and Change: Wales 1063–1415* (Oxford, 1987); Brock Holden, 'The Aristocracy of Western Herefordshire and the Middle March, 1166–1246' (D.Phil. thesis, University of Oxford, 2000); Max Lieberman, 'Shropshire and the March of Wales, ca. 1070–1283: The Creation of Separate Identities' (D.Phil. thesis, University of Oxford, 2004). See also C. P. Lewis, 'English and Norman Government and Lordship in the Welsh Borders, 1039–1087' (D.Phil. thesis, University of Oxford, 1985).

[2] Davies himself recognised the importance of approaching a society through an examination of 'the status of women and the character and consequences of the marriage bond' in his 1980 article 'The Status of Women and the Practice of Marriage in Late-Medieval Wales', in *The Welsh Law of Women*, ed. Dafydd Jenkins and Morfydd E. Owen (Cardiff, 1980), 93–114.

[3] Margaret Howell, 'Royal Women of England and France in the Mid-Thirteenth Century: A Gendered Perspective', in *England and Europe in the Reign of Henry III (1216–1272)*, ed. Björn K. U. Weiler with Ifor W. Rowlands (Aldershot, 2002), 163–81, at 165.

ostensibly, more male-oriented than ever. The medieval March of Wales was a land of hard-bitten and competitive border men, whose castles were truly the *caputs* of their lordships, who championed their immunities from the common law of England and waged private warfare at will, and who might sooner force a royal messenger to eat his writ – parchment, seal and all – than take orders from the king.[4] Here, where the Marcher sword was rarely still, the feudal ethos took far longer to break down than in lowland England and contemporaries shuddered at the lawless reputation of the region and its inhabitants.[5] Little wonder, then, that modern historians of the Welsh frontier have tended to overlook the women of the March in favour of a focus on the barons, knights and castles that likewise fascinated and horrified the chroniclers of the time.

This essay proposes not so much to remedy the near-complete neglect (with one or two exceptions)[6] of the topic of women of the Welsh frontier, as to examine evidence relating to the greater noblewomen of the county and borderlands of Shropshire and, more specifically, to the widows of the barons and lords of the Shropshire frontier. By definition a landed woman, the English dowager (provided she was of full age) graduated from the tutelage of her husband, and came to the fore as a *femme sole* largely operating on a level with men: she was an estate administrator and manager of family affairs, she was prominent in the public sphere, she was highly visible in a broad cross-section of contemporary records and, most importantly, she has been the subject of extensive research by scholars interested in a range of issues including her dower rights and dower-related litigation at common law, the rise of jointure, the place of the noble widow in society and her family, and much more.[7] As this essay will

---

[4] It is recorded that in Jan. 1250 Walter Clifford, lord of Clifford, Glasbury and Cantrefselyf, offended by the tone of a royal letter conveyed to him, forced the hapless messenger to eat the lot: Matthew Paris, *Chronica Majora*, ed. H. R. Luard (7 vols., Rolls Series, 1872–83), V, 95.

[5] Davies, *Lordship and Society*, i; *Chronicles of the Reigns of Stephen, Henry II and Richard I*, ed. R. Howlett (4 vols., Rolls Series, 1884–9), IV, 184; *Anglo-Norman Political Songs*, ed. I. Aspley (1953), 16–19; F. M. Powicke, *King Henry III and the Lord Edward* (Oxford, 1947), 530.

[6] Linda E. Mitchell, *Portraits of Medieval Women: Family, Marriage and Politics in England, 1225–1350* (New York, 2003); idem, 'Widowhood in Medieval England: Baronial Dowagers of the Thirteenth-Century Welsh Marches' (Ph.D. thesis, Indiana University, 1991); idem, 'Noble Widowhood in the Thirteenth Century: Three Generations of Mortimer Widows, 1246–1334', in *Upon my Husband's Death. Widows in the Literature and Histories of Medieval Europe*, ed. Louise Mirrer (Ann Arbor, 1992), 169–90. Although very readable, Mitchell's work does not engage with the dynamic relationship between the women's careers and the locality in which they operated.

[7] E.g. Janet Senderowitz Loengard, ' "Of the Gift of her Husband": English Dower and its Consequences in the Year 1200', in *Women of the Medieval World*, ed. Julius Kirshner and Suzanne F. Wemple (Oxford, 1985), 215–55; idem, '*Rationabilis Dos*: Magna Carta and the Widow's "Fair Share" in the Earlier Thirteenth Century', in *Wife and Widow in Medieval England*, ed. Sue Sheridan Walker (Ann Arbor, 1993), 33–80; Sue Sheridan Walker, 'Litigation

show, despite the large body of excellent scholarship on the subject, the richness of the contemporary materials relating to the English medieval widow means that there is still more to be written. An examination of the activities and experiences of frontier dowagers is part of that process. This essay argues for very specific experiences attached to noble widowhood on the Welsh frontier, and for a unique relationship between widow and locality that highlights both the importance of women to a region often painted as 'men only', and the grave error made by scholars who fail to include women in their histories of the March of Wales.

Dower

The pattern and nature of dower assignment tells us something of the expectations of the socio-familial milieu in which the widow lived, and about contemporary attitudes toward the widow's provisioning. The priorities of the late husband and his family are perhaps especially evident when the arrangement was for pre-ordained dower (*dos nominata*), in the early days typically set out before the door of the church on the wedding-day itself; it might then be less than a third and need not be in land.[8] Such 'church-door' dower probably formed the basis of the arrangements made by William FitzAlan I (d. *c.* 1160), baron of Oswestry, at the time of his marriage to Isabel de Say around 1155, for Isabel subsequently acquiesced in the grant of her predetermined dower in Downton manor to Haughmond Abbey.[9] In return, her husband compensated her with several items of domestic use or ornament. It is unclear whether an interest in Downton was to have been Isabel's only dower land on the death of William FitzAlan, but by the mid-twelfth century it seems to have been typical of FitzAlan dower estates in the region. As a member of the important demesne manor of Upton Magna, Downton was located in the heart of central, lowland Shropshire, in the fertile lower Tern valley. It was also situated away from both the volatile Welsh border and the heavily fortified *caput* of the barony of Oswestry, itself located at the eastern edge of Shropshire's rugged north-west uplands.[10]

From the combined governmental records of the dower allotted by the Crown to the widows of John FitzAlan I (d. 1240), John FitzAlan II (d. 1267) and John FitzAlan III (d. 1272) arises further information on the nature and location of Shropshire widows' dower and, above all, a

as Personal Quest: Suing for Dower in the Royal Courts, circa 1272–1350', in *Wife and Widow*, ed. Walker, 81–108.

[8] Loengard, 'English Dower in the Year 1200', 220; *idem*, '*Rationabilis Dos*', 63.

[9] *The Cartulary of Haughmond Abbey*, ed. Una Rees (Cardiff, 1985), no. 288.

[10] *Victoria History of the County of Shropshire*, IV, ed. G. C. Baugh (1989), 26; Dorothy Sylvester, *The Rural Landscapes of the Welsh Borderland: A Study in Historical Geography* (1969), generally; Trevor Rowley, *The Shropshire Landscape* (1972), generally.

sense that the greater border dowager's lands were seldom situated in the principal estates of the barony – in line with *Bracton*[11] – or in the most turbulent regions of district. Certain manors were also re-assigned to FitzAlan widows in successive generations. Upton Magna, to which Isabel de Say's Downton interest had belonged, together with Cound, Acton Round and the ancient Roman centre of Wroxeter, each members of the barony of Oswestry, were allocated first to Hawise de Blancminster (d. 1242), widow of John FitzAlan I, and then to Maude de Verdun (d. 1284), widow of John FitzAlan II.[12] Evidently earmarked for widows' upkeep, these four demesne manors lay roughly in a sixteen-mile, north–south line from the northern plain to the edge of the Clee Hills plateau, and encompassed some of Shropshire's most fertile lowland ground.[13]

Most notably none of these estates was situated within fifteen kilometres of Offa's Dyke. Nor did the two widows' demesne interests detract from the principal estates of the baronies of Clun and Oswestry. The matter was made explicit at the end of March 1240, when John Lestrange of Knockin, then sheriff of Shropshire and Staffordshire and custodian of the FitzAlan Marcher territories, was instructed to oversee the assignment of a reasonable dower to Hawise de Blancminster from 'anywhere in the late baron's lands, *except* in Oswestry, Clun and Shrawardine' – the three hubs of FitzAlan frontier power: 'Mandatum est Johanni Extraneo quod assignari faciat Hawisie, que fuit uxor Johannis filii Alani, rationabilem dotem suam alibi in terris que fuerunt ipsius Johannis, exceptis terris que fuerunt ipsius Johannis de Albo Monasterio [Oswestry], Clun et Shrawurthin.'[14]

For much of the thirteenth century, the strategic and heavily fortified manors of Oswestry, Clun and Shrawardine represented the principal foci of FitzAlan influence, and critically important staging posts along the northern and upper middle Marches, at a time when the Marcher lords were hunkering down to defend their footholds on the edge of *pura Wallia*. Oswestry and Clun, abutting the eastern flanks of Powys, Cedewain, Ceri and Maelienydd, had been hewn from the county proper by the beginning of the thirteenth century, while Shrawardine, probably still within the purview of royal administration, belonged to an interior line of defence against Welsh aggression within Shropshire.[15] At all

[11] *Bracton on the Laws and Customs of England*, ed. and trans. Samuel E. Thorne (4 vols., Cambridge, MA, 1968–77), II, 269.

[12] *Close Rolls of the Reign of Henry III* (14 vols., HMSO, 1902–38) [hereafter *CR Hen. III*], 1237–42, 197–8; *Calendar of Inquisitions post mortem* (20 vols., HMSO, 1904–95) [hereafter *Inq. p.m.*], II, no. 536.

[13] *Inq. p.m.*, II, no. 536, IV, no. 90; *Two Estate Surveys of the Fitzalan Earls of Arundel*, ed. Marie Clough (Lewes, 1969), generally.

[14] *CR Hen. III*, 1237–42, 183.

[15] R. W. Eyton, *The Antiquities of Shropshire* (12 vols., 1854–60), X, 95.

three locations the obligations of castle-guard and army-service were immediate and pressing, and each, to varying degree, provided military-supply depots, places of rendez-vous and locations for parley between the English and Welsh. At the time of John FitzAlan I's death in 1240, Shrawardine had a newly re-constructed castle to replace that razed by the Welsh in 1215.[16] Military factors alone presumably rendered the three capital manors of Clun, Oswestry and Shrawardine largely unsuitable, in contemporary eyes, for the introduction of a dowager's interests.

The rationale behind the dower allocations described above cannot have been wholly negative, of course. The widow's third was her maintenance allowance (and sometimes that of her young children) after the death of her husband, a social security buffer which was especially crucial if she had no inheritance of her own or a relatively meagre marriage portion, and if she was disinclined or unable to remarry. There was little sense in allocating the widow properties whose annual yields were low, which were ruined by periodic warfare, or, in the most extreme cases, where the widow's own life might be endangered. As the townspeople of Oswestry were to learn to their cost in 1281, the proximity of an impressive fortress could not spare them from the Welshmen of nearby Nanheudwy, who raided the town and demanded a heavy ransom for their plunder.[17]

By contrast to the cases of Hawise de Blancminster and Maude de Verdun, the pattern of dower allocation to Isabel de Mortimer, widow of John FitzAlan III (d. 1272), differed notably. Although, like Hawise de Blancminster, Isabel received the earmarked demesne estates at Little Ness and nearby Forton in western central Shropshire, and, like both of her predecessors, a host of further interests within and outside Shropshire, the manors of Acton Round, Upton Magna, Wroxeter and Cound were not assigned to her. Instead, contrary to the strictures applied to Hawise de Blancminster's dower assignment in 1240, Isabel was granted the whole of the sizeable, fortified demesne manor of Shrawardine, excepting only its satellite estate at Ensden, which initially fell to the king as (default) guardian of the under-age heir. In addition, Isabel was to have a third part of the wardship of the castle of Clun, as it arose, except in time of war, when dower was said not to apply.[18] In the last condition we have further suggestion that military considerations contributed to the shaping of a widow's dower on the March of Wales.

Several factors contributed to the nature of Isabel's dower assignment and marked it out from her predecessors' portions, the most obvious being that Isabel's mother-in-law Maude de Verdun, was very much alive in the

---

[16] *Ibid.*, x, 97–8.
[17] *The Welsh Assize Roll, 1277–1284*, ed. J. C. Davies (Cardiff, 1940), 352.
[18] *Calendar of Close Rolls* (HMSO, 1900–8) [hereafter *CCR*], 1268–72, 511.

1270s and still holding Acton Round, Upton Magna, Wroxeter and Cound in dower.[19] Moreover, when John FitzAlan III died in 1272, his son and heir Richard was a boy of only five or six, a ward of the Crown, and in no position to contemplate the management of his estates then or in the near future. Richard's extreme youth was a far cry from the relative maturity of his father and grandfather, who, aged eighteen and twenty respectively at the deaths of their own fathers, had presumably been capable of active military service despite their legal minority. With Richard FitzAlan still many years away from full age in 1272 the Crown had more room for manoeuvre when it came to the maintenance or temporary allocation of the FitzAlan estates. Yet the untimely death of John FitzAlan III in early March 1272, followed closely by the demise of Henry III and the absence of Edward I overseas, also left an essentially 'headless' Crown, and an important baronial *familia* with an opportunity to bargain over the widow's dower. In the circumstances of a long minority it arguably made sense for some of the dynasty's main estates to remain in the family rather than defaulting to the king, particularly in a restive frontier district where the authority of a locally aware and interested kinsman or woman might better serve the needs of family, locality and realm than the interference of external administrators or of a Crown-appointed guardian (although the latter could also be chosen from among close kin and neighbours). A widowed kinswoman might also be less exploitative than a royal appointee seeking to profit on his investment.

More importantly, changes were beginning to take place both on the frontier and within the FitzAlan family's own socio-political outlook, which may also have convinced Isabel de Mortimer's contemporaries that a widow's tenure of Shrawardine manor and castle was now a reasonable proposition. As the English kingdom recovered from the damage inflicted by civil war and the resurgent might of Gwynedd under Llywelyn ab Iorwerth (d. 1240), and as the Marcher lords found something more like a common cause in the struggle against Llywelyn ap Gruffudd (d. 1282), Shrawardine may have lost some of the direct strategic significance it had held in the days when the frontier lords more often laboured in their own bailiwicks against disunited Welsh incursions.[20] Perhaps it had also begun to lose its appeal to a dynasty which would soon move its principal seat to Arundel.

From what can be gleaned of dower allocation among the widows of the principal vassals, tenants and neighbours of the FitzAlan family, similar considerations applied: the avoidance of the core estates and the

[19] *Inq. p.m.*, I, no. 812.
[20] T. F. Tout, 'Wales and the March during the Barons' Wars, 1258–1267', in *The Collected Papers of Thomas Frederick Tout* (3 vols., Manchester, 1932–4), II, 77–136; J. B. Smith, 'Llywelyn ap Gruffudd and the March of Wales', *Brycheiniog*, 20 (1982–3), 9–22.

immediate frontier region.[21] The most notable exception was the dower of Alice d'Orreby, the widowed second wife of Peter Corbet I of Caus (d. 1300), for whom the shape and configuration of her late husband's barony necessitated her provisioning almost exclusively in Shropshire and the local March. In contrast to the cases just outlined, Alice held much of her dower close to, or directly on, the western border of Shropshire: her portion even included lands to the west of Offa's Dyke.[22] Particularly notable for its inclusion of territory in the region known as the Gorddwr, which had been the subject of the expansionist aggression of both Gruffudd ap Gwenwynwyn and Llywelyn ap Gruffudd, and was ever a bone of contention between the Corbets and the rulers of southern Powys,[23] Alice's dower in the barony of Caus did not, as I shall presently discuss, sit easy with her stepson Peter Corbet II, who did everything he could to harass his father's widow.

Yet the decision of Peter Corbet senior or his associates to allocate Alice's dower on the frontier is less surprising when it is considered that at the time of Corbet's marriage to Alice, around 1297,[24] the Marcher region had acquired a measure of stability. Edward I's conquest of Wales in 1282–3 had removed the immediate military threat to the border lordships, while the conversion of the native Welsh principality of Powys Wenwynwyn into the Marcher barony of Pool meant that Caus no longer lay hard against *pura Wallia* and its western-most regions were no longer the militarised frontlines they had once been.[25] Perhaps, too, Peter senior had intended that Alice should enjoy a share in those Marcher liberties, significantly free of royal control, which as yet the king was not apt to stifle; and it was probably with an eye to the Marcher lordships' virtual immunity from royal authority that Peter junior showed such patent disregard for his stepmother's common law rights.

---

[21] *Calendar of Patent Rolls, of the Reigns of Henry III–Edward II* (HMSO, 1893–1913) [hereafter *CPR*], 1258–66, 453, 582; *CR Hen. III*, 1264–8, 237; *CPR*, 1292–1301, 46; The National Archives [hereafter TNA], Court of Common Pleas: Plea Rolls [hereafter CP40]/125, m. 226, CP40/150, m. 59d.

[22] *Select Cases in the Court of the King's Bench under Edward I. Vol. III* (Selden Soc. LVIII, 1939) [hereafter *Select Cases, Edward I*], 112; *CPR*, 1301–7, 353, 355; TNA, Special Collections: Ancient Correspondence of the Chancery and Exchequer [hereafter SC1]/28/12.

[23] C. J. Spurgeon, 'Gwyddgrug Castle, Forden and the Gorddwr Dispute', *Montgomeryshire Collections*, 57 (1963 for 1961–2), 125–37; *Welsh Assize Roll*, ed. Davies, 333, 340; *Calendar of Inquisitions Miscellaneous, 1219–1422* (HMSO, 7 vols., 1916–68) [hereafter *Inq. Misc.*], I, no. 1088.

[24] This was the year in which John Corbet, the son of Peter I and Alice, was born and in which the same Peter presented a certain Philip d'Orreby, probably his wife's kinsman, to the church of Worthen: *Inq. p.m.*,VI, no. 318; *Register of Richard de Swinfield, Bishop of Hereford (A. D. 1283–1317)*, ed. William W. Capes (Hereford, 1909), Appendix.

[25] Davies, *Lordship and Society*, 19–20, 23–4.

When it came to dower litigation in the courts of law, Shropshire dowagers certainly fared no better in this matter than their counterparts in other regions of England,[26] and they may even have fared worse against the tough border lords who operated at the furthest reaches of royal power.[27] Alice d'Orreby's feud with Peter Corbet II was bitter and protracted. Cast in the mould of his notorious grandfather, Thomas Corbet of Caus, Peter II harassed and bullied his stepmother, withheld dower, stalled and defaulted on dower suits and interfered in matters between Alice and her own tenants. In 1302 Alice complained that she had not been assigned her full share of the Corbet lands by her stepson, and in 1305 that Peter (with accomplices) had ejected her from certain of her Welsh tenements, stolen goods, usurped her judicial rights or blocked proceedings, broken into one of her parks and stolen beasts, poached large game from her reserve and even assaulted some of her men.[28] On two further occasions, when Alice attempted to distrain tenants for non-payment of services, her stepson armed his own tenants and launched a series of raids on her holdings, destroying property and removing the impounded cattle.[29]

The testiness of Marcher lords likewise contributed to Maude de Verdun's trouble, this time with her own flesh-and-blood. In 1269 Maude, the widow of John FitzAlan II, ran into difficulties with her eldest son John III, who baulked at relinquishing £200 from the settlement of his late father's estate, despite an earlier agreement with the Crown, and played the well-worn Marcher-immunities card to justify his refusal to respond to the king's demands that he pay his mother immediately.[30] With great presumption, the twenty two-year-old baron famously announced that 'in the parts of the March where he now resided, he was obliged to do nothing at the king's mandate and nothing would he do'.[31] Rather than directly seeking to injure his mother, FitzAlan may well simply have been making a show of defiance toward the king. He was not the only Marcher baron to have done so, and he would not be the last.

For all that dower litigation at common law was a drawn out and often emotional experience for the English widow, the further westward one went the more difficult that experience seems to have become. Above and beyond the usual legal processes were questions of Welsh law and

---

[26] See Loengard, 'English Dower in the Year 1200', 232.

[27] See, for example, R. R. Davies, 'Kings, Lords and Liberties in the March of Wales, 1066–1272', *Transactions of the Royal Historical Society*, fifth series, 29 (1979), 41–61, and *idem, Lordship and Society*, generally.

[28] *Select Cases, Edward I*, 112–13; *CPR*, 1301–7, 353, 355; TNA, SC1/28/12.

[29] TNA, CP40/155, m. 99d, CP40/160, mm. 259, 270.

[30] *Excerpta e Rotulis Finium*, ed. Charles Roberts (2 vols, Record Commission, 1835–6) [hereafter *Rot. Fin.*], II, 486.

[31] Eyton, *Antiquities*, VII, 257.

tenure, Marcher franchise or customs in time of war and the realities of cross-cultural fertilisation and hybridisation, which had to be considered before any decision could be handed down. The prickliness and ambition of many border lords, and their recourse to Marcher immunity, cannot have made the process any smoother. The complexities of frontier living were scarcely more evident than in the case of Emma d'Audley, relict of Gruffudd Maelor (d. 1269) of northern Powys, who was compelled to sue her son Llywelyn for the restoration of what appears to have been dower land in the commotes of Cynllaith and Nanheudwy. He had to be summoned twice before he relinquished the property.[32] A conflict of interests between Emma's English-style dower claims and her son's inheritance in Wales may lie at the heart of the dispute, and it is certainly conceivable that Welsh heirs of mixed marriages were reluctant to hand over land to their English mothers and into the purview of an alternative authority. When it came to the widow's common law rights, too, Welsh heirs may have found themselves thinking with fondness upon the old native law of dower which did not permit the widow an automatic share of her late husband's patrimonial lands.[33]

But even as she was suing her son, Emma was seeking reinstatement in two manors in the Maelor district of northern Powys – Overton in Maelor Saesneg (English Maelor) and Eyton in Maelor Gymraeg (Welsh Maelor) – from which she claimed to have been evicted by the powerful Llywelyn ap Gruffudd during the recent warring between England and Wales.[34] The inquiry into the status of Overton conducted by the justice of Chester in July 1277 found that Emma had been granted a life-enfeoffment in the manor by her late husband, in accordance with the 'custom of Wales ... that any Welshman can give his lands to his wife, before or after marriage, at will'.[35] This was perhaps not dower *per se*, but a native Welsh custom that might be used to the same effect as English common law dower.[36] The inquisition further found that when the war broke out in early 1277, Llywelyn ap Gruffudd, prince of Wales, had seized Overton from Emma, who had remained in the king's faith (*ad fidem domini Regis*) through the war of 1276–7, and bestowed it upon his own adherent Madog

[32] *Welsh Assize Roll*, ed. Davies, 238.

[33] Dafydd Jenkins, 'Property Interests in the Classical Welsh Law of Women', in *Welsh Law of Women*, ed. Jenkins and Owen, 69–92, at 85; T. P. Ellis, *Welsh Tribal Law and Custom in the Middle Ages* (2 vols., Oxford, 1926), I, 390. The situation changed under the Statute of Rhuddlan (1284).

[34] *Welsh Assize Roll*, ed. Davies, 244–6.

[35] *Inq. Misc.*, no. 1095. A transcript of Gruffudd's charters, and the charter of confirmation issued by their sons, appears in Frederic Seebohm, *The Tribal System in Wales*, 2nd edn (London and New York, 1904), Appendix D, 101–5.

[36] Cf. J. B. Smith, 'Dower in Thirteenth-Century Wales: A Grant of the Commote of Anhuniog', *Bulletin of the Board of Celtic Studies*, 30.3–4 (Nov. 1983), 348–55.

ap Gruffudd Maelor, another of Emma's sons. On this issue, too, native Welsh law was ascertained: when anyone left their lands, for fear of war or for other reasons, and departed from Wales, the lord might seize the land as his escheat and do what he liked with it.[37] It seems that Emma may have fled the war-torn Maelor district.

Although Overton was soon restored to Emma, her claim to Eyton was complicated by the dower interests of her daughter-in-law Margaret, widow of Madog ap Gruffudd Maelor and, as it happens, also the sister of Llywelyn prince of Wales. After Madog's enfeoffment in Overton and Eyton by Llywelyn, he had granted the latter to his wife Margaret as (pseudo) dower, presumably under the same directives that had earlier permitted Emma's enfeoffment in Overton.[38] The need for further action was avoided when the two widows came to an agreement: the manor of Eyton was to be restored to Emma and Margaret was to hold it of her at farm at ten marks *per annum*. Margaret evidently had enough on her plate as it was, for the sources reveal that she too was picking up the pieces left by the depredations of her powerful brother.[39]

Emma d'Audley's situation also highlights the meeting of two principal legal cultures, English and Welsh, and the effects of a dynamic interplay between divergent legal norms and practices upon aristocratic widows of the northern March – and especially on those who had married beyond Offa's Dyke. In entering a union with a Welsh man, Emma perforce acquired Welsh status, at least in the eyes of the society she had joined.[40] In the classical Welsh law of women, she should have had no rights in any land governed by Welsh tenure, her property interests in widowhood taking the form of moveables instead.[41] Yet it is also clear, as J. Beverley Smith has demonstrated, that by the mid-thirteenth century, even before the Statute of Rhuddlan (1284) had ironed out the contrast between *cyfraith Hywel* and the common law of England, widows of Welsh rulers occasionally received landed dower, along English lines, in Welsh territories.[42] Emma d'Audley and her daughter-in-law, Margaret, Angharad widow of Owain ap Maredudd (d. 1275) of Ceredigion, and the unnamed wife of Owain's father were among such women.[43]

This spirit of compromise (if indeed that is what it was) or the adaptability of practice and procedure in the March and adjacent regions of *pura Wallia* is scarcely clearer than in the arrangements made by Gruffudd ap Gwenwynwyn for the distribution of his lands after his

[37] *Inq. Misc.*, no. 1095; Seebohm, *Tribal System*, App. D, 103.
[38] *Welsh Assize Roll*, ed. Davies, 245–6.
[39] *Ibid.*, 246–7.
[40] Davies, *Lordship and Society*, 307.
[41] Davies, 'The Status of Women', 98, 100–1.
[42] Smith, 'Dower in Thirteenth-Century Wales', generally.
[43] Above, p. 66; TNA, C146/9502; *CPR*, 1232–47, 487.

death. His English-born widow, Hawise Lestrange, was to have a dower third and his eldest son, Owain, lordship of the entire patrimony, as was the practice in England; those of Gruffudd's other sons who remained in the secular world (two became clerics) were to enter into a partible Welsh inheritance, each holding of the eldest brother.[44] The exact forces at work behind the creation of dower in land held by Welsh tenure is not clear; but it is highly possible that those 'dowering' Welshmen who entered into unions with English or Marcher lineages were guided by the demands of their in-laws. In more general terms, proximity or kinship to these lineages may have urged them to provide land for widows, like Angharad, who were not themselves of English or Marcher birth.[45]

If the issue of Emma d'Audley's dower was not already complicated enough, her recovery of the manor of Overton was ultimately conditional upon the will of Edward I, whose interference in, and exploitation of, the Maelor region in the late thirteenth century was nothing short of notorious.[46] Having been granted restoration to Overton, Emma was compelled to acknowledge before the bench that she would return the same land to the king if he chose to grant her property elsewhere in England for the term of her life.[47] And this is exactly what the king did. In October 1277, seemingly even before Emma had even re-entered Overton, Edward I had already notified Chancery that he intended to make an exchange with her. Thirteen months later the widow traded the land for an annual pension from the farm of the town of Derby, together with two manors in eastern Shropshire, free from any service obligations.[48] While Emma was clearly well rewarded for her compliance, it is impossible to ignore the fact that the king's uncompromising agenda in northern Powys at this interval had overridden both Emma's interests in her late husband's estates and the rights of the heirs to the reversion of those lands. Then again, Emma may actually have preferred the relative peace and security of dower in the lowland English territories.

[44] *Calendar of Chancery Rolls, Various, 1277–1326* (HMSO, 1912), 'Welsh Rolls', 171–3, 179, 328–32.

[45] Although Ceredigion was geographically remote from England and Angharad herself from the native princely dynasty of Cydewain, her father-in-law had associated with, and married into, a Marcher family of south-west Wales during the 1240s; and Angharad herself went on to marry into Shropshire society after her first husband's death: Smith, 'Dower in Thirteenth-Century Wales', 351, 353.

[46] In late 1277 Edward I, determined to extend his influence in northern Powys, had already begun extinguishing and buying out opposing interests in the whole of Maelor: Davies, *Lordship and Society*, 4, 340.

[47] *Welsh Assize Roll*, ed. Davies, 239.

[48] *Calendar of Chancery Warrants, 1244–1326* (HMSO, 1927), I, 4; *CCR*, 1272–9, 513; *CPR*, 1272–81, 282–3.

Estate management

On the death of the husband an extensive range of managerial and administrative concerns fell to the widow, who as an independent member of landed society was, if not necessarily more active, certainly far more conspicuous than the married woman. What becomes apparent at first glance is the extent to which the functions and duties carried out by the independent, adult male were transferable to the independent, widowed female in the context of estate management. Both were prominent members of landholding society and, with the notable exception of bearing arms, the widow carried out much the same tasks as the male lord. She would presumably already have had extensive experience of estate management gained during marriage and, where her dower was concerned, functioned as an agent of continuity between old lord and new.

The FitzAlan demesne manors of Cound, Wroxeter, Acton Round and Upton Magna brought with them a host of duties and perquisites, which few were inclined to neglect. By the end of the thirteenth century, the FitzAlan demesnes in both frontier and lowland England represented a growing enterprise involving vast acreages of arable, meadow and farmland, large numbers of livestock, the exploitation of the waste, forest and waters of the lordship (a key means of asserting control over Welsh communities),[49] and presumably also the hives, bird decoys and the like found on the neighbouring Corbet estates.[50] Although no estate records survive to reveal any direct evidence of widows' exploitation of demesne lordship, Alice d'Orreby's readiness to defend her game reserves, those jealously guarded features of the vast Marcher pasturelands, is evident in her complaints against park-breaking – complaints which, moreover, suggest that gender was not perceived as an impediment to demesne exploitation (or, indeed, to aristocratic recreational pursuits like hunting). Moreover, the widow who neglected the upkeep of the various instruments of demesne exploitation in her late husband's lands, or who allowed the destruction of forests, failed to keep land in cultivation, depleted animal-stocks or facilitated asset-stripping of any sort, was liable to prosecution. The responsibility of the widow as caretaker of the patrimonial third was critical and enforceable, as Maude de Verdun was to learn to her cost in March 1278, when she and her second husband, Richard de Amundville, were sued for waste in the woodlands which belonged to her dower.[51]

---

[49] Davies, *Lordship and Society*, 105, 120–7.

[50] *Two Estate Surveys*, ed. Clough, XXVIII–IX; Davies, *Lordship and Society*, 151 (see also Davies, *Conquest, Coexistence and Change*, ch. 5 and esp. 118–19); Staffordshire Record Office, Stafford Papers, 1/2/240–4.

[51] Eyton, *Antiquities*, IV, 122.

More than in lowland England, baronial estates of the Welsh frontier placed enormous emphasis on judicial rights and on the seigneurial court, the instrument of lordship *par excellence*. While the FitzAlan widows were excluded from control over the great central courts at Oswestry and Clun, the lowland manor of Wroxeter, held in dower by Hawise de Blancmister and Maude de Verdun respectively, certainly included pleas of bloodshed and hue-and-cry, as well as the maintenance of a gallows.[52] In the barony of Caus, Alice d'Orreby's grievances against her stepson Peter Corbet II highlight the importance placed by lords on judicial rights over tenants, including the hearing of pleas in the manorial courts and entitlement to amercement, distraint and attachment.[53] For widows like Alice d'Orreby, who had no inheritances of their own, their judicial rights within their dower estates were arguably not only lucrative money-earners, but also important symbols of their own power and authority within the parameters of their lordships, which they could not easily have relinquished without loss of prestige.[54]

Rees Davies has reminded us, too, that judicial lordship meant far more to medieval lords than law-keeping in the strictest sense. Judicial lordship lay at the very heart of the relationship between lord and tenant, and the court represented the intersection of their interests: here the lord 'defined the services of his tenants and compelled them to pay their dues, supervised their land sales, registered their land-deeds, collected their death duties and reliefs, and exacted fealty from them'.[55] Here, too, he ensured that his tenants' needs were met. Just as the lord expected to realise his or her rights over men, so his vassals anticipated the continuity of good lordship during a dowager's governance: the FitzAlan vassal Fulk FitzWarin of Whittington, whose services on a manor called 'Hilfrich' were assigned in dower to Isabel de Mortimer in 1272, could no more have made allowance for Isabel's failure to fulfil her responsibilities as lord than Isabel and her advisers would have tolerated any dereliction of duty by Fulk, the tenant.

Moreover, the gendered role of medieval women (particularly of queens) as intercessors, highlighted by Pauline Stafford and John Carmi Parsons,[56] may also have had particular resonance in the context of female lordship in medieval England, for a number of Shropshire widows directly

---

[52] *Inq. p.m.*, II, no. 356; Eyton, *Antiquities*, VII, 310.

[53] *CPR*, 1301–7, 355.

[54] In 1305 Alice even challenged her own son, John Corbet, then only a child, for further dower in Shropshire: TNA, CP40/154, m. 235d.

[55] Davies, *Lordship and Society*, 150.

[56] Pauline Stafford, *Queen Emma and Queen Edith: Queenship and Women's Power in Eleventh-Century England* (Oxford, 1997), 150, 181; John Carmi Parsons, 'The Intercessionary Patronage of Queens Margaret and Isabella of France', in *Thirteenth-Century England*, VI, ed. Michael Prestwich, R. H. Britnell and Robin Frame (Woodbridge, 1997), 145–56; *idem*, 'The Queen's

petitioned a higher authority on behalf of tenants and other dependants. Most notably, when William Milicent of Ludlow was dispossessed of his lands while at court on business, his lord, the dowager lady of Chelmarsh, wrote to the chancellor, Walter de Merton, on Milicent's behalf.[57] Soon after the death of her first husband, Ralph le Botiler, Maude Pantulf likewise petitioned the king seeking redress for her 'men of Wem'.[58] The intercessory function of the lordly widow may, in fact, have been rendered all the more critical in the March by the twin facts that judicial lordship was more comprehensive (through lack of conflicting or superior authority),[59] and that a woman could not take up arms on behalf of her tenants, a remedy that was not uncommon in a region where barons and knights could wage war at will.[60]

Figures like William Milicent of Ludlow also remind us of the existence of staff who served the lord in regulating the day-to-day business of lordship over men and land. In large measure, the operation of the lord's deputies, seneschals, constables, stewards and the like, especially at the local level, helps to explain the ease with which noble widows stepped into the breach on the death of their husbands and, by the early fourteenth century, could hold anything up to an entire barony in jointure. The role of the individual lord, or even of gender, in influencing the actions of men and women in medieval England is not in doubt; but it is also true that neither the baron of Clun and Oswestry nor his widow personally supervised the 'Monday-acres' of the cottars on their Wiltshire demesnes, collected rent from the lessees installed at Acton Round after 1300, presided in the local courts, or kept watch from the castle turrets (except, perhaps, in siege conditions).[61] Far more at issue was the skill with which the widow, like her late husband, was able to function as a manager of property and people, a delegator of responsibility and a figurehead of power and lordship in the locality. This was as important a question for male lords as female.

Where the widow's role as lord had the potential to become more awkward, however, and where the lord's gender did become a central issue, was in a region where militarism was still a feature of everyday life. On the Welsh frontier before the final conquest of Wales, military power was not merely the 'original foundation and ultimate sanction of lordship',[62] but also remained an immediate necessity long after the winds

Intercession in Thirteenth-Century England', in *Power of the Weak: Studies on Medieval Women*, ed. Jennifer Carpenter and Sally-Beth MacLean (Urbana, IL, 1995), 147–75

[57] TNA, SC1/7, no. 166.

[58] TNA, SC1/19, no. 185.

[59] Davies, *Lordship and Society*, 151.

[60] Davies, 'Kings, Lords and Liberties', 41.

[61] See *Two Estate Surveys*, ed. Clough, xxx and generally.

[62] Davies, *Lordship and Society*, 67.

of change had swept across lowland England. Seemingly most difficult to square with frontier life was the widow's automatic right to control an entire, fortified and strategic frontier lordship as her own inheritance. A number of high-ranking Marcher women inherited fortresses of varying size and importance. Indeed, it was hard to avoid doing so in a land that positively bristled with fortifications and where, more than anywhere else in England, the castle was truly the *caput* of the lordship.[63] In the most salient example from Shropshire, Isabel de Say, granddaughter of Earl Roger de Montgomery's henchman Robert 'Picot' de Say, became lady of Clun in her own right in the mid-twelfth century, and rightful lord of the single most important castlery on the Shropshire frontline.

Isabel de Say's almost constantly married state between *c.* 1155 and her death in 1199 (she married three times with little intermission) does not go unnoticed, and probably had as much to do with military expediency as with her exceptional value on the local marriage market. In 1160, at a time when Welsh attacks on the frontier were carried out with alarming regularity,[64] and when William FitzAlan II, Isabel's son from her first marriage and the heir to Clun and Oswestry, was little more than five years old, it was perhaps considered prudent to transfer the reins of military power at Clun to a male lord. That Magna Carta was still some years away makes it quite possible that the Crown intervened directly in Isabel's marital status. Henry II certainly demanded much of her second husband, who by marriage effectively became a 'ring-in' for FitzAlan lordship in Clun: Geoffrey de Vere was made sheriff of Shropshire in 1165. Moreover, the pipe roll evidence clearly reveals that, rather than remaining with Isabel in the period of her widowhood between the death of her first husband in *c.* 1160 and her marriage to de Vere in *c.* 1165, her own capital fortress at Clun was transferred to the control of the sheriff.[65] Assuming that Isabel was a legal adult in 1160 – and, admittedly, this is not certain – then the Crown's action was remarkable.

Yet the relationship between widow and fortress on a militarised frontier is not as cut-and-dry as this example might suggest, for there were also individuals for whom widowhood in a turbulent frontier zone enabled them to carve out an alternative means of participation. This was an essential paradox of Marcher life. While Isabel de Say was afforded few openings for independent castle administration on her own inherited estates, other dowagers assumed roles directly associated with the management of fortresses on their late husbands' properties. Not only did Isabel de Mortimer have dower in Shrawardine Castle – a stronghold

---

[63] *Ibid.*, 71, 76.
[64] Frederick C. Suppe, *Military Institutions on the Welsh Marches: Shropshire, AD 1066–1300* (Woodbridge, 1994), 56, 156–7.
[65] *Pipe Rolls*, 6 Henry II, 26, 7 Henry II, 40,8 Henry II, 6, 9 Henry II, 4.

of lessening but not inconsiderable importance in 1272[66] – but in 1280 she was also appointed to the custody of her late husband's castle of Oswestry on the Shropshire frontline. Precisely what Isabel de Mortimer's role at Oswestry entailed is difficult to determine. The wording of her appointment on the patent rolls is singularly vague; but among her final duties was the arming and victualing of the fortress for the incoming garrison at the commencement of the second Welsh war in 1282, suggesting that even if she were not the resident castellan, her custody gave her oversight of the martial aspects of the castle's administration. As I shall presently discuss, Isabel's command of Oswestry Castle also belonged both to her own broader enterprise in her late husband's lands and to Mortimer ambition in middle and northern Marches at this time.

The appointment of women to the custody of castles was neither entirely novel nor purely honorary, particularly under politically sensitive or highly irregular circumstances. The redoubtable Nicholaa de la Haye was made castellan of Lincoln Castle in 1215, an appointment which Louise Wilkinson has revealed rested on a combination of hereditary claim to the post and prodigious personal ability, and belonged squarely to the context of King John's deteriorating fortunes.[67] Over a century later, Aline, widow of the Shropshire lord and royal administrator, Edward Burnel of Acton Burnell, was granted custody of the great royal citadel of Conway in Caernarvonshire from January to October 1326.[68] Aline was a Despenser and the Despensers were in grave danger: they had not troubled to cultivate a party of supporters in England and, with resentment against them building, turned to family members to hold key positions.[69] As an autonomous and clearly robust member of landed society – she lived until 1363 – Aline was perhaps not such an extraordinary choice for the office. The notice of her appointment entered on the original patent roll states that she was to receive 'the keepership of our castle of Conway (*custodiam castri nostri de Coneweye*)' during pleasure; she took office at her own risk, being responsible for the safe keeping of the castle and receiving an allowance.[70] The castle came fully stocked

[66] D. J. C. King, *Castellarium Anglicanum: An Index and Bibliography of the Castles in England, Wales and the Islands* (2 vols., Millwood, NY, 1983), 45–6. At the end of the thirteenth century Shrawardine still had one of its two earlier 'muntatores' (mounted soldiers). Suppe, *Military Institutions*, 69.

[67] Louise J. Wilkinson, *Women in Thirteenth-Century Lincolnshire* (Royal Historical Society Studies in History, new series, 2007), 13–26.

[68] *CPR*, 1324–7, 215; *Calendar of Fine Rolls* (22 vols., HMSO, 1911–62) [hereafter *CFR*], 1319–27, 421.

[69] See Nigel Saul, 'The Despensers and the Downfall of Edward II', *English Historical Review*, 99 (1984), 1–33.

[70] TNA, Chancery and Supreme Court of Judicature: Patent Rolls [hereafter C 66] / 169, m. 5.

with armour and victuals, and Aline presumably had to answer at the Exchequer for the issues of the castle, as her successor was required to do.[71] As a linchpin of her family's ambition she may have been expected to reside there during her tenure.[72]

Similarly, the dowager countess of Arundel, Isabel widow of Earl Hugh d'Aubigny (d. 1241), was made constable of the royal castle of Portchester, with an annual stipend of 16 marks, for the period of March 1268 to May 1272. She, too, assumed the usual duties of building maintenance and rendering account at the Exchequer.[73] In two separate notices on the original liberate rolls Isabel d'Aubigny is referred to both as *constable* of Portchester Castle and as *custos* or keeper, terms which, at least as far as male post-holders were concerned, appear to have been largely interchangeable.[74] In this particular case, any attempt to establish whether the Latin nouns *constabularius* or *custos* were rendered as masculine or feminine when applied to women, and thus whether (in theory at least) contemporaries might have viewed the post as inherently gendered, is foiled by scribal abbreviation and Latin grammar: in the first instance the scribe has simply written *constabul'*, and in the second the word *custos*, of Greek derivation, is both masculine and feminine in form.

Nevertheless, the existence, recorded elsewhere,[75] of terms like *cunestabularia* and *châtelaine* (the latter also denoting lady's girdle from which hung personal and household keys) suggest that not only did there exist scope for female appointment, but that contemporaries had a theoretical place for female post-holders that found its way into the vocabulary of government. It was not especially common to find female keepership, constableship or custodianship – terms that were vague, overlapping and sometimes interchangeable[76] – but it was far from unheard of. Legal status and managerial acumen where what really mattered in the first instance.

When it came to the militarised and often turbulent March of Wales, however, the normative relationship between the noblewoman and the castle became rather more problematic. On the one hand the fluidity and adaptability of aristocratic life on the March meant that independent

---

[71] *CPR*, 1324–7, 215; *CFR*, 1319–27, 421.

[72] *CFR*, 1319–27, 418.

[73] *Calendar of Liberate Rolls, 1226–1272* (6 vols., HMSO, 1917–64), V, 290, VI, 214; *CPR*, 1266–72, 204.

[74] TNA, Chancery: Liberate Rolls [hereafter C62]/43, m. 3; C62/48, m. 8.

[75] *A Dictionary of Medieval Latin from British Sources*, prepared by R. E. Latham, D. R. Howlett *et al.* (1975–present), I, 456; R. E. Latham, *The Revised Medieval Latin Wordlist from British and Irish Sources* (Oxford, 1965; repr. 1999), 109.

[76] The overlap between wardship and the duties inherent in royal constableships is discussed in John Rickard, *The Castle Community: The Personnel of English and Welsh Castles, 1272–1422* (Woodbridge, 2002), 45.

landed women like Isabel de Mortimer might, with tenacity and ability, carve out a leading role in the management of strategic fortresses and the holding of the frontline. Indeed, it was sometimes the only suitable course of action. On the other hand, the very warlike nature of the frontier region also dramatically increased the likelihood that the female lord might be denied, or stood down from, castle governance: combat offered little room for women in thirteenth-century England and Wales, except under extraordinary circumstances.[77] The ambitious and fully able Isabel de Mortimer was removed from control of her late husband's castles when full-scale war with the Welsh broke out in 1282.

The widowhood of Isabel de Mortimer

Isabel de Mortimer, daughter of Roger de Mortimer of Wigmore and Maude de Braose, was not an heiress. Her brother Edmund was destined to inherit her family's burgeoning estates, and her own value lay principally in the marriage market and the connections her marriage would forge between her natal family and kin and those of the man she married. Still in her teens, Isabel was married to the heir apparent to the neighbouring frontier baronies of Clun and Oswestry and the earldom of Arundel, and much of her young life was spent under the guidance and protection of her husband and his family. Despite (perhaps even because of) Isabel's limited access to land through birth, her widowhood saw her determinedly carve out an administrative portfolio within her late husband's estates, which she continued to manage on behalf of the Crown until shortly before her second marriage in 1285.

We have seen above that Isabel de Mortimer's extensive dower assignment differed from that of her two immediate predecessors to FitzAlan widowhood in its inclusion of the manor and castle of Shrawardine, traditionally an important staging post along the lower northern March. Although they were soon to become more settled, the conditions of the March in the 1270s were nevertheless still such that they directly interfered with the straightforward allocation of Isabel's dower, which, for a variety of reasons, had to be assigned to her piecemeal over a number of years.[78] The requisite pre-dower surveys of the FitzAlan estates had been carried by the August of 1272, when a strikingly detailed snapshot of the FitzAlan territories in the March and the d'Aubigny inheritance in lowland England, and of their division between Isabel as John III's widow and the king as default guardian of the young heir and his estates, was entered on the close rolls.[79] Isabel's interests were

---

[77] Examples do exist of English noblewomen in warfare, typically under urgent, defensive conditions. The issue is raised by Wilkinson, *Women in Thirteenth-Century Lincolnshire*, pp. 22–3.

[78] *Rot. Fin.*, ii, 574–51; *CPR*, 1266–72, 653; *CR Hen. III*, 1268–72, 499.

[79] *CR Hen. III*, 1268–72, 505–15.

extensive and valuable. In Shropshire she received not only Shrawardine manor and castle, but also a third of the issues of the markets, fairs, ale tax (*prisa cervisie*), the Oswestry borough courts and watermills, as well as extensive arable, meadow, moorland and woodland rights.[80] In Welshry she was to have an array of interests attached to the barony of Oswestry.[81] A series of knights' fees were also assigned to the young widow, the most notable of which were held by John Lestrange and Fulk FitzWarin.[82] Nor did Mortimer control over the FitzAlan inheritance in the March stop at Isabel, for her father Roger was soon granted custody of the manor and castle of Clun, £100 of adjacent land and the Shrawardine satellite of Ensdon, to hold until Richard FitzAlan came of age.[83]

As the royal letters close reveal, the assignment of Isabel de Mortimer's dower was a far simpler task in lowland England than on the troubled border. Even after the substantial and carefully thought-out allocations outlined above, there remained sizeable omissions in Isabel's dower, largely consequent upon the activities of Llywelyn ap Gruffudd on the frontier at Clun during the 1260s. In the months and years that followed Isabel's initial dowering, several additional allocations were made to her, including a stop-gap measure implemented by her father, Roger de Mortimer;[84] but, although Isabel's dower claims in the honour of Arundel appear to have been settled by mid-1274, it was nearly twelve years before she finally received the full third that she was entitled to in her late husband's border territories. It was not until the end of 1284 that the final settlements were carried out: Isabel received seven towns in the Welshry of Portlock, together with extensive interests in the borough and forest of Clun and in the Tempseter Welshry of Clun.[85]

The hill district of Tempseter, west of Offa's Dyke and largely Welsh in character,[86] had been occupied by Llywelyn ap Gruffudd from the late 1260s until he was ejected by Isabel's father, Roger de Mortimer, in 1277.[87] Although Mortimer, as custodian of Clun, had thus reclaimed the barony's western-most lands, no action was taken toward dowering Isabel in the region until both her father and the prince of Wales were dead. Nor does Isabel appear to have made any attempt to sue for dower here, and it is possible that Mortimer's substitute gift of Ensdon in Shrawardine,

---

[80] *Ibid.*, 506–7, 508–9.

[81] *Ibid.*, 510–11.

[82] *Ibid.*, 514–15.

[83] *Ibid.*, 512.

[84] *CPR*, 1266–72, 716; *CCR*, 1279–88, 227, 260–2.

[85] The total annual value of this assignment was £10 17s 7d, in addition to biennial rents of 53s 4d: *CCR*,1279–88, 262.

[86] Sylvester, *Welsh Borderland*, 328–32.

[87] *CCR*, 1279–88, 227. See also the inquisition of 1267 quoted in Eyton, *Antiquities*, X, 231 n. 3.

and of additional issues of Oswestry mill, both of which derived from the heir's portion of the FitzAlan estates held in trust by Mortimer, was a private agreement between father and daughter intended to supplement her existing dower and forestall any need for litigation. Once Isabel had been granted custody of her Welshry interests at Clun, she was required to return Ensdon and the issues of Oswestry mill to the executors of her late father's will.[88]

The requirements of administration and management attached to her dower estates alone must have presented Isabel with a formidable challenge. Not only was she faced with the day-to-day running and longer-term maintenance of these holdings, but restiveness of the March on the eve of the final Edwardian campaigns in Wales probably heightened the need for security and vigilance in her Shropshire territories. Isabel's lands in the March were flanked by the custodial interests of her father, who held both the Clun castlery and his grandson (Isabel's son) in wardship, thereby presumably providing military support in the region and, perhaps too, paternal guidance; but Isabel herself may well have taken something from the lessons of her past. During the early days of Isabel's marriage, Llywelyn ap Gruffudd had seized control of the western fringes of Clun from her father-in-law, John FitzAlan II. Neither Isabel nor her ambitious and war-hardened father, who had lost extensive possessions in the March to Llywelyn between 1258 and 1263,[89] were likely to have forgotten those times in a hurry. Isabel had presumably also witnessed much of the civil strife of the mid-60s, which was largely played out in the March and contiguous counties, and in which her father and father-in-law had ultimately become prominent royalist partisans.[90] Indeed, it was to Isabel's own mother, Maude de Braose, that Simon de Montfort's severed head and genitals were said to have been sent as a trophy in 1265.

By 1276, only four years after her husband's death, Isabel de Mortimer had also begun to carve out a business enterprise for herself over and above her dower territories. In January 1277, in what appears to have been the first in a series of steps toward the deliberate augmentation of her footholds in the FitzAlan lands, Isabel obtained custody from the Crown of properties directly abutting her dower in the county of Sussex. Comprising lands and rents in Westdon and Charlton and a moiety of the hundred of Stockbridge, valued at around £35 a year, these interests

---

[88] *CCR*, 1279–88, 227, 260–2.

[89] *Brut y Tywysogion or The Chronicle of the Princes. Peniarth MS. 20 Version*, ed. T. Jones (Cardiff, 1952), 110, 112; R. Pauli, 'Annales monasterii de Waverleia, A.D. 1–1291', in *Monumenta Germaniae Historica, Scriptores* 27, ed. F. Liebermann and R. Pauli (Hanover, 1885), 458–64, at 370; Tout, 'Wales and the March', 71, 86.

[90] See Tout, 'Wales and the March', generally.

were to be held in trust until her son came of age.[91] By 1280 Isabel had also taken control of the castle and the entire honour of Arundel[92] as well as the farm of the hundred and township of Oswestry in the Shropshire March.[93] As long as she kept abreast of the requisite yearly payments – and there is every indication that she did so[94] – Isabel de Mortimer could expect more or less free rein in the managements of land, and the administration of the courts and other perks of lordship. But more was to still come. In November 1280, in response to her own petition to the king the year before, Isabel was awarded full custody of the castle of Oswestry hard on the Welsh frontier.[95]

Isabel's custodial tenures came with several attendant obligations, including providing the abbot of Vale Royal in Cheshire with a total of £300 a year for his building works, and ensuring that the archbishop of Canterbury received twenty-six deer a year from the forest of Arundel, in accordance with a grant made by an ancestor of her late husband. She was also ordered to allow the archbishop to hunt in the forest every year on his way to and from his manor of Slindon in central Sussex.[96] Isabel's management skills were clearly sound, and perhaps even above average, and I have suggested elsewhere that she may have been involved in the extensive survey of the FitzAlan estates undertaken at the end of the thirteenth century and known today as 'Book A' of the *Two Estate Surveys of the FitzAlan Earls of Arundel*.[97] Most tellingly, Isabel's view of her own ability as equal to that of any male lord was expressed in another petition to the king around 1279, in which she requested grace of scutage on the grounds that she had defended the March as well as her neighbours during the Welsh war of 1277; if granted the waiver, moreover, she pledged to redirect the same funds toward the castle of Oswestry which was dilapidated (*decheu*).[98] Isabel was clearly willing to bargain with the Crown for the augmentation of her interests, and it is interesting that she did so around the time that her father was rewarded for his role in the same Welsh war.[99]

The prominence of Isabel's natal family during her adult career, and her own part in the fulfilment of Mortimer ambition in the March, are

[91] *CFR*, 1272–1307, 74, 7, 127; *CPR*, 1272–81, 372.

[92] *CPR*, 1272–81, 372; *CFR*, 1272–1307, 127.

[93] *CPR*, 1272–81, 311, 404

[94] *CCR*, 1279–88, 373.

[95] TNA, Special Collections: Ancient Petitions [hereafter SC8]/62, no. 3077; CPR, 1272–1281, 404.

[96] *CPR*, 1272–1281, 311, 404, 416; *CCR*, 1279–88, 93, 171.

[97] Emma Cavell, 'Noblewomen in Shropshire and the Adjacent March of Wales' (D.Phil. thesis, University of Oxford, 2007), 265.

[98] TNA, SC8/62, no. 3077.

[99] C. Hopkinson and M. Speight, *The Mortimers, Lords of the March* (Almeley, 2002), 67.

not acknowledged by historians, but are without doubt critical to the history of the region on the eve of the Edwardian conquest of Wales. From the very commencement of Isabel's thirteen-year widowhood, her father was the guardian of her infant son, the future earl of Arundel, Richard FitzAlan, and of the larger part of the FitzAlan barony and castlery of Clun, creating a circumstance in which Isabel's own sphere of influence lay check-by-jowl with that of her father in the northern and middle Marches. These factors alone must have encouraged regular communication between father and daughter, but the evidence that Roger de Mortimer supplemented his daughter's dower holdings in the barony of Clun during Llywelyn ap Gruffudd's occupation of Tempseter suggests that theirs was a cooperative relationship. Roger de Mortimer had been assigned responsibility for the security of the middle March during the Welsh campaign of 1277, and may actively have enlisted his daughter's assistance in extending his influence along the frontier, and particularly to secure the region around Clun. Between the two Welsh wars Roger and Isabel de Mortimer (with the assistance of Maude de Braose) together controlled most of the western front from the lower edge of Cheshire to southern Herefordshire.

If this period was 'the high summer of Roger de Mortimer's career', as historians have stated,[100] it was also his daughter's finest hour. By creating and running a business enterprise in her late husband's properties that bolstered her dower territories, Isabel not only supplemented her own power and wealth in widowhood, but dramatically increased Mortimer influence in the March (and elsewhere). She was a mainstay of Mortimer power in the FitzAlan territories at the end of the thirteenth century and, as she herself acknowledged, an important contributor to the security of the March on the eve of Edward I's final conquest of Wales. It is impossible now to determine where the ambition of Isabel's natal family ended and her own personal drive began – nor should they necessarily be separated out – but it seems certain not only that she and her father, and perhaps also her mother, reinforced each other's career successes in the decade between 1272 and 1282, but also that she was herself, like the far better known Maude de Braose, an ambitious, determined and fully capable woman. Given that she petitioned for grace of scutage and custody of Oswestry Castle around the same time that her father received reward for his services in the first Welsh war, and that she deliberately emphasised her own role in frontier security, Isabel was probably as eager for recognition and reward as the indefatigable Roger de Mortimer of Wigmore.

[100] *Ibid.*, 69.

In June 1282, a new war against Wales underway, Edward I took the decision to relieve Isabel of her custodies in Oswestry and Arundel, and from Rhuddlan in August that year he ordered that these same interests be made over to Isabel's thirty-year-old brother, Edmund de Mortimer.[101] Still at Rhuddlan in November, the king ordered that Isabel's accounts for Oswestry Castle be audited and that she be reimbursed for all expenses incurred in fitting out the castle after the commencement of the war.[102] With a full-scale Crown enterprise underway in Wales and Isabel herself in no position to wield a sword, Edward I presumably wished to place the greater Mortimer and FitzAlan castles under the command of a single, strenuous leader, who could be relied upon to hold the middle and lower northern Marches and to fight when necessary. By August 1282, moreover, Isabel's notably supportive father, Roger de Mortimer, had only eight or ten weeks left to live, and Edmund was emerging as head of the Mortimer family. Perhaps Isabel's influence was deliberately stymied by her younger brother, irritated by their father's reliance upon his sister rather than him, or perhaps she was a casualty of the will of Edward I, whose policy toward the governance of the March may have undergone re-appraisal on the eve of the conquest of Wales (or, indeed, the demise of the once powerful Roger de Mortimer). We do not know what Isabel thought of her total dispossession of her Marcher *and* lowland custodies, but given the self-belief she expressed in 1279, she may not have been entirely pleased. Deprived of her custodial enterprises at the end of 1282, Isabel had re-married by 1285 and was once again shrouded by that greater obscurity that had surrounded her marriage to John FitzAlan III.

Conclusions

The main purpose of this essay has been to consider some of the implications for the English noble widows of life on a military frontier. The widow's dowering in a frontier region certainly seems to have brought its own unique considerations to the bargaining table. The importance of the lordship's military integrity and the centrality of the fortified *caput* and castlery underscored the generally held principle that a widow's dower should not be allocated in the most important of her late husband's estates. Few Shropshire widows in the period under discussion received dower either in property that had been central to their late husband's lordship, or in the traditional hotspots of the border. To the threat of border skirmishing or larger-scale land seizures, such as were perpetuated by Llywelyn ap Gruffudd in the 1260s, might also be added the scope for the

---

[101] *CFR*, 1272–92, 163; *CPR*, 1281–92, 32.
[102] *CCR*, 1279–88, 170.

circumvention of royal authority and resistance of legal process offered by Marcher immunities – to say nothing of the character of some of those war-hardened *marchiones* who inhabited the region. Family relations, complex at the best of times (especially where step and in-law relationships were involved), might be further problematised by the introduction of inter-cultural marital alliances into the mix. Yet these factors, doubtless highly variable, not only reveal the unique conditions of the frontier and their effect on widows' dowering, but also throw into relief the agency of the widow herself in the working-out of her dower, and in its defence and maintenance.

Despite the potential for trouble between widow and heir, there is also evidence to suggest that, far from being automatically resented as a burden on the heir's lordship, the widow was often seen as an agent of continuity, especially during a protracted minority: she was already familiar with the estates she held and integral to the web of connection and kinship embracing the aristocratic family. Her managerial expertise, and that of the men and women responsible to her, was perhaps particularly useful with regard to regions where Welsh or hybrid customs obtained – customs which might have confounded the outside lord but with which she and her staff were presumably familiar. I have also suggested, moreover, that the noble widow might have had an intercessory role between her tenants and her own lord (usually the Crown), that was especially important in a region where judicial lordship was all but comprehensive, and where the female lord could not fight on behalf of her tenants.

Indeed, the bearing of arms was the main sticking point for female lordship, and it has been necessary therefore to examine the implications of militarism on the widow's tenure of castles, and the nature of her control over fortresses in a region where the waging of war was a relatively immediate concern. I have suggested above (and am not alone in doing so) that the actual bearing of arms was the only area of castle governance from which women were barred. It was only when warfare loomed that that the female lord might find herself sidelined. Isabel de Mortimer was relieved of her custody of Oswestry and Arundel Castles when war with the Welsh broke out for a second time in 1282; Isabel de Say of Clun either eschewed, or was debarred from, the administration of her own inherited castlery on the doorstep of native Wales during the second half of the twelfth century.

Life on the March could certainly be difficult for women; but it also brought them opportunities for action, underscoring the critical importance of their functions as managers of land and family, and enabling certain dowagers to carve out prominent roles in the maintenance of frontier security. The close study of noblewomen of Shropshire and the adjacent March of Wales not only sheds light on the lives, roles and personalities of women who lived in the region, thereby also adding to what we know about the English medieval noblewoman generally, but also clearly demonstrates that this ostensibly male, militarised zone cannot, in fact, be fully understood without the inclusion of the female members of aristocratic society. Nothing is more telling than the (hitherto unacknowledged) fact that Isabel de Mortimer, daughter of far more famous parents, Roger de Mortimer and Maude de Braose, actively helped her father to hold the frontier at Shropshire on the eve of the Edwardian Conquest of Wales.

Transactions of the RHS 17 (2007), pp. 83–99 © 2007 Royal Historical Society
doi:10.1017/S0080440107000540   Printed in the United Kingdom

THE BURDEN AND CONSCIENCE OF
GOVERNMENT IN THE FIFTEENTH CENTURY

The Prothero Lecture

By Jeremy Catto

READ 5 JULY 2006

ABSTRACT. This study argues that the experience of government, though more
clearly articulated after 1400, did not engender *realpolitik* and made princes and
ministers, both the old nobility of service and the newer graduate careerists, more
acutely aware of issues of conscience. It traces the anxieties provoked by political
experience, their relation to the new spiritual literature addressed to persons with
active responsibility, and their resolution after 1410 in a new, tough, realistic but
morally sensitive approach to government, associated above all with Henry V of
England.

'A reputation for meanness disgraces the King and detracts from the
royal dignity.' This banal sentiment can be taken as characteristic of
the jumbled sentiments and moralisations to be found in profusion in
the extensive literature of political advice produced between the middle
of the twelfth century and the middle of the fifteenth: the genre of 'Mirrors
for Princes'. It is found in perhaps the last example of the genre to
come to the eyes of an unimpeachably legitimate English king, the *De
quadripartita regis specie* written for Richard II in the 1390s and found in his
Book of Geomancy, and is distilled from the *Secreta secretorum*, the pseudo-
Aristotelian tract served up in various dishes to any number of princes
of the fourteenth century.[1] Richard II's form of it lies near though not
quite at the end of a succession of moral political tracts for the use of
princes in which the political thought of the University of Paris from John
of Salisbury through Giles of Rome to Marsilius of Padua is distantly
reflected. At the turn of the fifteenth century it was being superseded by
a new form of political literature, more realistic and more specific, which
is found in the memoranda of ministers and officials, also for the use of

---

[1] *De quadripartita regis specie*, ed. J.-P. Genet in *Four English Political Tracts of the Later Middle
Ages* (Royal Historical Society, Camden, fourth series, XVIII, 1977), 22–39. On the genre see
Wilhelm Berges, *Die Fürstenspiegel des hohen und späten Mittelalter* (Leipzig, 1938).

princes, a literature which reached its most general form in the sixteenth century in the works of Machiavelli and Giovanni Botero. The essence of this kind of literature is its distillation of the *experience* of government into political advice primarily on particular issues, though in Machiavelli's case of a more general nature. My purpose today is to identify some strands and themes in the experience of government by princes and their ministers in the fifteenth century. I will concentrate primarily though not exclusively on the English experience of government, and especially though again not exclusively on the early part of the century. I will argue that the supersession of general moral precepts by particular prudential advice after 1400 was not an expression of political cynicism or *realpolitik*: that it was offered by councillors careful of their conscience; that the conscience of the prince was at the centre of fifteenth-century political decision-making; and that in an era when government was exercised by an educated military nobility and a cadre of graduate careerists, both of whom were demonstrably sensitive to inward moral pressure, specific political decisions were discussed as particular *casus conscientiae* on which confessors might advise, but for which in the court of heaven princes and their servants would have to account.

The psychology of government in the fifteenth as in any other century has perhaps never been dissected so ruthlessly as Augustine of Hippo had done in the *City of God*. In spite of his acute sense of evil, he knew that it could not simply be summed up as *libido dominandi*, the mindless ambition for power. Rather, he had described it in terms of irresoluble tension, for instance in the work of a judge whose irremediable ignorance of the circumstances of his case, as he peers through 'the mists of mortal society', condemns the innocent to death: but 'he has to sit; he is bound to it by his place, which he holds it wickedness not to discharge, and by the state's command, which he must obey'.[2] This is of course the universal curse of responsibility, in the fifth, fifteenth and twenty-first centuries. Historians are perhaps rather inclined to take the lust for power for granted in describing the political conflicts of the past, attributing to their subjects the simple appetite of Madame Nhu, the redoubtable South Vietnamese lady of the 1960s, who reportedly misquoted Acton: 'power is delightful: absolute power is absolutely delightful'. The contemplative writer Walter Hilton was more realistic, focusing on the responsibilities of power in the febrile 1390s: temporal men, as he wrote, 'which have sovereignty with much possession of worldly goods, and have also as it were lordship over other men for to govern and sustain them, as a father has over his children, a master over his servants, and a lord over his tenants' could receive 'of our Lord's gift grace of devotion' and participate

---

[2] Augustine, *De civitate dei*, XIX. 6.

in some way in the contemplative life.[3] For Hilton, unlike his monastic predecessors, worldly responsibility was natural, and open to grace, and he addressed those who held it. He could have had in mind not just sober and respectable statesmen like Thomas Arundel, archbishop of York and later of Canterbury whose circle promoted contemplative literature, but young active and ambitious laymen such as Thomas Mowbray earl of Nottingham, founder, about the age of thirty, of Axholme Charterhouse (1395–7), or the even younger and more dizzyingly ambitious Thomas Holand, duke of Surrey, founder of the Mountgrace Charterhouse at the age of twenty-six in 1397.[4] These Carthusian houses would play an active part in bringing Hilton's practice of the 'mixed life' of contemplation and action to the notice of the Lancastrian political world. Their young founders, manoeuvring precariously in a capricious court, are unlikely to have enjoyed so robust a luxury as *libido dominandi*. They must, however, have at least understood the Carthusian call to inward reflection in the exercise of public office.[5]

In England in 1400, as in most other parts of Europe, public office was the monopoly of two groups of contrasting experience. One, the more traditional, was a nobility of service – a *noblesse*, in the wider French sense – whose apprenticeship had been served in war, in diplomatic missions, on local commissions such as the justices of the peace and in the government of their own estates.[6] The other was a cadre of graduate careerists, with degrees in civil or canon law or in theology, and nearly always in at least minor orders. Akin to the latter category but with some characteristics of the first group were common-law judges trained in the Inns of Court by methods parallel to those of the universities (but by 1400 almost all laymen), and clerks of Chancery or the Privy Seal apprenticed in their departments, like the poet Thomas Hoccleve (most of whom, at that date, were in minor orders).[7] The experience of the graduate cadre lay in the legal or administrative service of princes, focusing above all on the art of persuasion, exercised indifferently in secular and ecclesiastical business. The general sophistication and ability of the first group has long been

---

[3] *Walter Hilton's 'Mixed Life' edited from Lambeth Palace Ms 472*, ed. S. J. Ogilvie-Thomson (Salzburg, Salzburg Studies in English Literature, 1986), 15 (spelling modernised).

[4] E. Margaret Thompson, *The Carthusian Order in England* (1930), 218–38; Alastair Dunn, *The Politics of Magnate Power* (Oxford, 2003), 63–6, 69–72.

[5] On the attraction of Carthusian foundations to European princes and their nobility, see the contributors to *Princeps i reis: promotors de l'Orde Cartoixà*, ed. Concepció Bauçà de Mirabó Gralla (Palma de Mallorca, 2003).

[6] For the wider definition of the nobility – equivalent to the French *noblesse* – implied here see K. B. McFarlane, *The Nobility of Later Medieval England* (Oxford, 1973), 6–7, 122–5.

[7] These emerging professions are discussed by the contributors to *Profession, Vocation and Culture in Later Medieval England: Essays in Memory of A. R. Myers*, ed. Cecil H. Clough (Liverpool, 1982), and those to *Concepts and Patterns of Service in the Later Middle Ages*, ed. Anne Curry and Elizabeth Matthew (Woodbridge, 2000).

established; there is some evidence for the primary education of noble children in the 1390s and the 1410s, showing that their literacy in Latin was taken for granted.[8] Where their inventories survive, they indicate that the lay nobility possessed substantial numbers of books. For all we know, cultivated learning may have characterised them for several previous generations: what was perhaps new is evidence that the generations born after 1350 had independent and individual religious views and tastes. We know that Thomas of Woodstock duke of Gloucester caused a debate between a rather Lollard-minded secular clerk and a friar to be held in his presence, and that he possessed a copy of the Wycliffite scriptures; we know that Sir William Beauchamp Lord Abergavenny patronised Lollard preachers, while nursing a devotion to the Holy Name of Jesus; we know of Henry Lord Fitzhugh's devotion to St Brigit and his cousin Lord Scrope's collection of contemplative texts. We can reconstruct the confessional practice of Humphrey de Bohun earl of Hereford and the prayers of his two daughters, and we may be able to identify the devotional reading of his countess, whose influence on her grandson Henry V was considerable.[9] This is a cross-section of the nobility selected only by the chance of surviving evidence; it would seem to imply that a private religious life, perhaps sharpened by confession, was becoming the norm. This does appear to be a novelty of the years about 1400. The religion of the men in this group, active in government and warfare as they were, gave them no respite from the violence, the moral compromises and the inevitable betrayals inseparable from public life under Richard II and Henry IV. It may, at least, have stirred the consciences which their personal devotion must have sharpened.

The mentality of the graduate cadre, whose part in the counsels of princes was growing rapidly in the years around 1400, is more difficult to pin down. Careerists with their way to make in the world like their lay contemporaries, the bare record of their offices and preferments gives

---

[8] See McFarlane, *Nobility of Later Medieval England*, 243–5, and J. I. Catto, 'Religion and the English Nobility in the Later Fourteenth Century', in *History and Imagination, Essays in Honour of H. R. Trevor-Roper*, ed. Hugh Lloyd-Jones, Valerie Pearl and Blair Worden (1981), 43–55.

[9] The duke of Gloucester's debate in Dublin, Trinity College MS C.iii. 12, fos. 212v–219; for his Bible, London, British Library MSS Egerton 617 and 618, see Viscount Dillon and W. St John Hope, 'Inventory of the Goods and Chattels Belonging to Thomas Duke of Gloucester', *Archaeological Journal*, 54 (1897), 275–308, see 300; on Sir William Beauchamp see J. I. Catto, 'Sir William Beauchamp between Lollardy and Chivalry', in *The Ideals and Practice of Medieval Knighthood*, III, ed. C. Harper-Bill and R. Harvey (Woodbridge 1990), 39–48; on Fitzhugh and Scrope, C. L. Kingsford, 'Two Forfeitures in the Year of Agincourt', *Archaeologia*, 70 (1918–20), 71–100, see 93–4 (inventory of his books); and Jonathan Hughes, *Pastors and Visionaries* (Woodbridge, 1988), 74–5. On the devotions and reading of the Bohun family see M. R. James, *The Bohun Manuscripts* (Oxford, 1936); and Catto, 'Religion and the English Nobility', 49.

the impression of coldly ambitious pluralists whose university degrees were just a step to the rewards of practice in the ecclesiastical law courts, government sinecures and the episcopal bench. But the case of the most powerful and most richly rewarded of them all, Thomas Arundel, the archbishop of Canterbury restored by Henry IV and perhaps his closest confidant throughout the reign, indicates otherwise. The few intimate glimpses we have of him, personally interviewing heresy suspects and listening patiently to the holy woman Margery Kempe, while she expounded her revelations and her practice of weeping aloud in church 'til sterrys apperyd in the fyrmament', confirm the indirect evidence of his promotion of contemplative practice among the laity.[10] If as archbishop he consistently sought to strengthen a common, uniform faith and a common form of worship among his flock, he and his circle of Cambridge church lawyers persevered with equal tenacity in making the English works of Richard Rolle, Walter Hilton and Nicholas Love easily available – the classics, to modern eyes, of late medieval contemplative literature.[11] These books did much to make familiar the practice of expressing complex ideas in English. They also had almost official status, being at the elbow of princes and ministers. Among contemporary intellectuals with university degrees Arundel was undoubtedly one of the more strong-minded. The experience of public affairs upon his generation of graduates as they progressively found places in the service of government seems to have been, on the evidence of surviving comments of a personal kind, rather more stressful. The university-educated clergy, sometimes theologians but more often canon or civil lawyers, filled the councils of every prince and were the backbone of secular diplomacy. They had a pivotal role both in directing the conscience of princes and ministers, and in filling the office of minister themselves. Their gradual infiltration of the higher dignities of the church, and thereby the councils of princes, seems to have modified significantly the political culture of the age: by making available intelligent and rational advice, they encouraged secular princes to cooperate, to be less quick to take offence and to develop lines of action closer to what in modern language would be called policy. In return, they earned the rewards of what French scholars have termed the *régime bénéficial*, the system of ecclesiastical patronage through which princes, popes and the higher clergy sustained persons in their service. The system might seem to offer graduate careerists both self-respect and material comfort, gently guiding the caravan of state while grazing in the pastures of the church.

[10] See *The Testimony of William Thorpe*, in *Two Wycliffite Texts*, ed. Anne Hudson (Oxford, Early English Text Society o.s. CCCI, 1993); *The Book of Margery Kempe*, ed. S. B. Meech and H. E. Allen (Early English Text Society o.s. CCXII, 1940), 37.

[11] Hughes, *Pastors and Visionaries*, 193–205.

Where, however, the private and authentic voice of the graduate cadre can be detected, among their highly articulate but overwhelmingly formalised utterances, a more jarring note than the sound of the contented ruminant is repeatedly struck. That the evidence of personal responses to the *régime bénéficiale*, where responses have survived, indicates an underlying anxiety is not perhaps so surprising to those who have witnessed, or experienced, the crises of conscience of intellectuals, deraciné or otherwise, in the twentieth century. Even in the fourteenth century they were recruited and consulted not to be routine pen-pushers, but to provide ideas and arguments as discomfiting to some as they were convenient to others. These voices were only occasional, and as they were barely raised at all among the reticent English, the cases I shall cite are primarily though not entirely continental. The first two are those of graduates who became spiritual leaders. Gerard Groote was a not particularly distinguished product of the canon law faculty of the University of Paris, who took no degree, but about 1370 represented his native town of Deventer in a case before the Roman curia. His private fortune and his canonries at Aachen and perhaps Utrecht kept him in comfort, but an illness in 1372 provided the catalyst for Groote to formulate to himself his dissatisfaction with an undemanding way of life, which provoked a conversion experience. His rather incoherent notes, his *Conclusa et proposita*, record the process of his renunciation of its various elements: of ambition, of everything he had learnt in the arts course in Paris; of his legal expertise, unless called on for charity; of his acquired perquisites, the canonries, and of his inherited property.[12] This was no simple religious conversion. Groote had no idea how to lead a life in accord with his uneasy conscience; he tried a spell of residence at Aachen, the life of a recluse in a corner of his former property in Deventer, and a vocation at the local Carthusian house at Monnikhuizen, before realising that his destiny was to preach among the rural population of the Low Countries. His missionary base was a community of like minded graduates which formed around him at Deventer, bound by no kind of vow and therefore known (though not in Groote's time) as the Brethren of the Common Life. Their simple form of the contemplative life, akin to the 'mixed life' advocated by Walter Hilton, would have a profound influence as the Devotio Moderna. But its roots in Groote's anxiety about the easy life open to church lawyers comes out in a letter to a Parisian student contemporary: Paris, and above all its law faculty, were the source of the evil in the world, the place where pharisees taught 'ancient human codes of law, out of accord with the law

---

[12] Groote, *Conclusa et proposita*, in *Thomas a Kempis opera omnia*, ed. M. J. Pohl (7 vols., Freiburg, 1910–22), VII, 87–107, and translated summarily in *Devotio moderna: Basic Writings*, ed. John van Engen and Heiko A. Oberman (New York, Classics of Western Spirituality, 1988), 65–75.

of God'.[13] This did not prevent him citing canon law texts read at Paris in his many moral tracts. His letter affords a glimpse, the more convincing for being indirect, of the burden of guilt he carried on account of his education and career; that his training had been conventional and his use of it straightforward awakens the suspicion that his personal experience may just have articulated the anxieties of a generation.

If Gerard Groote might well have served one of the princes of the empire, the duke of Guelders or the bishop of Utrecht, the chances of Walter Hilton's advancement were better still. One of the circle of lawyers in the Ely consistory court in the 1370s, he was well placed to rise, like Richard Scrope and others, with the fortunes of his bishop, Thomas Arundel, to a place of authority under the English crown. But he too threw up his career for an uncertain future, trying to live the life of a recluse and perhaps other spiritual avocations before finding peace in the small priory of Thurgarton. Hilton's anxiety comes out in a letter to an unnamed correspondent who like him had given up benefices, honours, the favour of the great and the praise of his family – probably a lawyer therefore – and was now a solitary. The anonymous master's renunciation had not stilled his interior turmoil, which had moved him to lament to Hilton. But Hilton dealt savagely with his complaints: he had not rid himself of his worldly desires, but had translated them into spiritual pride. It soon becomes clear that Hilton's unmerciful response and brusque dismissal of the hermit's lifestyle was really directed at himself: 'What are we doing, the two of us and our like, lazy and useless men standing idle all the day long?'[14] He was articulating the burden of guilt accumulated in his professional career, which had not been eased by his new life of pious solitude. At a later and more serene stage of his life he was able to set out a programme of spiritual exercises for graduate careerists active in the world, but in this agonised letter, written perhaps in the early 1380s, we can, I think, hear the interior voice of a whole new cadre of government: the highly educated, professional holders of higher degrees from universities, fortunate in the value newly placed on their expertise by princes and ministers, and accordingly rewarded with comfortable benefices, whose tender consciences nevertheless were disturbed by their involvement in the brutal world of politics and worldly ambition.

[13] *Gerardi magni epistolae*, ed. W. Mulder (Antwerp, Tekstuitgaven van Om Geestlijk Erf III, 1933), ep. IX, 27–30.
[14] *Tractatus de imagine peccati*, in *Walter Hilton's Latin Writings*, ed. J. P. H. Clark and Cheryl Taylor (2 vols., Analecta Carthusiana CXXIV, Salzburg, 1987), I, 73–102, see 90. On Hilton's career see A. B. Emden, *Biographical Register of the University of Cambridge to 1500* (Cambridge, 1963), 305–6.

The voices of Gerard Groote and Walter Hilton may express the moral perplexities of the graduate careerist, but when we hear them they were not close to any centre of power. The circle of intellectuals in 1390s Paris among whom Jean Gerson was a leading member was, however, close to the French court and to that of the pope of the Avignon obedience, Benedict XIII, and eloquently expressed in their correspondence and pamphlets their acute discomfort at the moral dilemmas in which proximity to power placed them. One focus of discomfort was, of course, the Great Schism itself, but the Schism was only a particularly scandalous example of the personal ambition which the *régime bénéficial* promoted. One of the more fastidious of Gerson's circle, Nicholas de Clamanges, who had become secretary in the chancery of Pope Benedict, wrote about 1400 one of the best-known denunciations of the corruption of the papal court, his *De ruina ecclesiae*: 'the frauds, the strategems, the backbiting, the bribery, the assaults on the rights of innocent people, the corrupt judgements', the pride and greed of cardinals with their pluralism and simony – these vices, far from being selected at random, were the precise indictments of a well-informed insider.[15] Nicholas went on to describe accurately the process of application for papal provisions by the recommendation of princes, indignantly pointing out how popes consolidated their position by seeking the good will of temporal powers. He was no more indulgent to bishops, whose way of life made it just as well that they were absent from their sees, and ended by hoping for the thorough humbling of the church. These puritanical sentiments, much employed in reformation controversy, could not have been made with such force had Nicholas not had first-hand experience of the curia at Avignon. Equally, their author's circumstances give them further significance. At the moment of writing them, he was enjoying the emoluments of the office of treasurer of Langres, a benefice bestowed on him directly for his services in the curia. Though he could have claimed that without the support of his benefices he would have been unable to fulfil his duty as papal secretary, so could the other beneficiaries of papal provisions, and a similar claim could be made for the whole body of graduate careerists on whose behalf the *régime bénéficial* had grown up. As a privileged alumnus of the Collège de Navarre with a passion for classical literature, Nicholas may have avoided the vulgar clamour for ecclesiastical places, but his studies could no more than his secretarial duties have been sustained without them. We can be sure that, as an acute and reflective observer, he was aware of the paradox. *De ruina ecclesiae* is a lament on the inexorable progress of patronage which evokes an ideal concept of clerical life; it hardly sets out a

---

[15] Nicholas de Clamanges, *De corrupto statu ecclesiae* (more properly titled *De ruina ecclesiae*), in *Nicholai de Clemangiis Opera Omnia*, ed. J. M. Lydius (Leiden, 1613), 10; and *La traité de la ruine de l'église*, ed. A. Coville (Paris 1936), p. 121.

practical programme for reform. It is also a witness to the uncomfortable moral position of the graduate careerist as he surveyed his natural habitat, the superstructure of the church.[16]

Such protests arising from the Schism were personal *cris-de-coeur* rather than coherent plans of reform. We find another at much the same time and not directly provoked by the Schism in Gerson himself, who gave voice to his own disgust with the business of government at the French court. Brilliant, successful and discontented, he was chancellor of the University of Paris and an admired court preacher. In such a milieu he was naturally compelled to be sociable, and it irked him. As he wrote to an unknown correspondent (possibly Pierre d'Ailly) from Bruges in February 1400, he had to let himself be carried this way and that in the court, being polite to grandees who disliked him; above all, he had to listen to friends, *importunissimi amici*, urging him to promote the ignorant and the corrupt. In order to live, he had to be an absentee pastor when he should be edifying his flock by precept and example. So he had resolved, or almost resolved, to resign the chancellorship and retreat into a life of contemplation in his church at Bruges, leaving it to others to cope with the discontents of office.[17] But Gerson was made of sterner stuff than his sensitive friend Nicholas de Clamanges. He gradually realised that his students, budding careerists that they were, could at least be improved if they were aware of the contemplative life, and like Walter Hilton's readers partake of it in the interstices of their activities. His lectures on mystical theology, a new departure in the Paris theology faculty, were delivered in 1402 and 1403. We hear no more of his painful conscience. This more resolute Gerson, sustained by his new sense of purpose, is the familiar figure who would contribute powerfully to the reform of the church at Constance.[18]

These Parisian intellectuals could be dismissed as untypical, with their Proustian sensibilities, of the ambitious careerists of their time. But it would be difficult to dismiss in this way a man of business such as Matthew of Cracow, who was effectively the prime minister of Rupert III of the Palatinate, king of the Romans from 1400 to 1410, and whose vision of evil at the curia of Boniface IX, Pope Benedict's rival, is one of the most impressive witnesses to the disturbed conscience of an intellectual in politics. Born in Cracow in 1345, he read arts and

---

[16] On Nicholas see Christopher Bellitto, *Nicolas de Clamanges: Spirituality, Personal Reform and Pastoral Renewal on the Eve of the Reformations* (Washington, 2001); and Ezio Ornato, *Jean Muret et ses amis Nicolas de Clamanges et Jean de Montreuil* (Paris and Geneva, 1969).

[17] The letter is in *Jean Gerson: oeuvres complètes*, ed. P. Glorieux (10 vols., Paris, 1960–73), II, 17–23.

[18] On Gerson's productive interval at Bruges, see J. L. Connolly, *John Gerson, Reformer and Mystic* (Louvain, 1928), 75–6; and D. C. Brown, *Pastor and Laity in the Theology of Jean Gerson* (Cambridge, 1987), 6–7.

theology in Prague and incepted in 1384. He was at once involved in the pastoral work of the great reforming archbishop of Prague, John of Jenstein, as a preacher and confessor; a sermon-cycle survives, and a work on confession and a dialogue between reason and conscience show him addressing individuals as well. Clearly sympathetic to the contemplative life, he was one of the proposers in the process of canonisation of Bridget of Sweden. However his vocation was the proper government of the institutions of the church. He was called to Cracow in 1390 to assist in the reorganisation of the university, and in 1394 to perform the same service in Heidelberg. Effectively the head of the university until 1406, he was one of the counsellors of the Elector Palatine Rupert from 1400 king of the Romans and emperor-elect), and was made bishop of Worms from 1406 to his death in 1410. Matthew, as one of the most active figures in the German church, was well placed to represent the emperor-elect at the Roman curia in 1403 and 1404; unlike Nicholas of Clamanges, he appeared as a mature, confident and independent churchman, ready to deal with the curia as an equal.[19] His *De praxi Romanae curiae* is a brisker and more practical work than *De ruina ecclesiae*, written more in a spirit of exasperation than rhetorical lamentation, but its author's shocked reaction to the 'negligent' disposition of ecclesiastical benefices by the curia is unmistakable. His enumeration of the church's evils was more or less identical to that of Nicholas, though characteristically he offered a feasible remedy, the abolition of expectatives, or promises of future promotion to benefices. His deep respect for the papal office did not alter the plain truth, in his eyes, that 'if the pope lacked the cooperation and loyalty of the church, then what was he, and who would take any notice of him? Just as a prince without the allegiance of his subjects and the help of the public could do nothing further.' Matthew's no-nonsense style does not however disguise the clear implication, that his vision of evil in the church was framed in the eye of interior conscience. He compared it to the burning bush which appeared to Moses, 'the friend of solitude', in contemplation in the desert; Matthew, a sinner, and 'the companion of many a curious notion (*curiosae considerationis*)' also looked out upon the exterior world, and saw the ecclesiastical estate, the clergy, burning in as terrible a fire. 'If this is a real vision, crystal clear to anyone who wants to see it – let it open their eyes ... and talking, writing, counselling,

---

[19] On Matthew of Cracow's career see *Die Deutsche Literatur des Mittelalter: Verfasserlexikon*, ed. G. Stammler *et al.* (10 vols., Berlin 1977–99), VI, 172–82 (article by F. J. Worstbrock). On his circle of graduate careerists at the court of Rupert III see Peter Moraw, 'Beamtentum und Rat König Ruprechts', *Zeitschrift für die Geschichte des Oberrheins*, 66 (1968), 59–126; Peter Moraw, 'Kanzlei und Kanzleipersonal König Ruprechts', *Archiv für Diplomatik*, 15 (1969), 428–531; and Hartmut Boockman, 'Zur mentalität spätmittelalterlicher gelehrter Räte', *Historische Zeitschrift*, 233 (1981), 295–316.

preaching, let them speak out with me'.[20] The busy German churchman lacked the highly strung sensitivity and the literary culture of Nicholas de Clamanges, and the inner vision of Gerson. This makes all the more telling his clear appreciation of the self-destruction of the *clerus*, his own estate as a successful graduate careerist.

These voices, provoked largely but not entirely by the general crisis of the Schism, provide broad evidence of the anxiety which involvement in the public sphere produced among the graduate cadre around the year 1400. It was a protean anxiety, experienced in many different ways of which I have given only a few examples: one could add, in Bohemia, the apocalyptic preaching of graduates of the University of Prague, among whom Jan Hus was the latest, or in Italy the wide-ranging debate on the contemplative and the active life, in Italian terms the life of ideas and that of the responsible citizen, conducted notably by Coluccio Salutati, the enlightened but conscientious chancellor of Florence. His approach to this standard monastic topos fluctuated, though it hardly amounted to an attempt to find a moral basis for the pursuit of politics and public affairs, either in the form of Walter Hilton's defence of the mixed life or that of his disciple Leonardo Bruni's Ciceronian justification of active politics.[21] But however widespread and multiform the anxieties of intellectuals, the imperatives of government required decisive action, and in the minds of princes in the first decade of the new century above all in bringing to an end a papal schism which threatened the legitimacy of every secular power. Decisive action, involving numerous European princes and more to the point the graduate careerists who advised them, was indeed forthcoming. It is tempting, though probably not quite accurate, to place the watershed between this common mood of fastidious detachment on the part of intellectuals, and the more committed and businesslike attitude of the next generation, at this juncture, the high summer of 1408, when a common decision to depose both the schismatic popes, a decision which graduate councillors in high ecclesiastical and temporal office had to take for themselves, was finally taken in the councils of the kings of France, England and a number of other princes, and in the two colleges of cardinals. What it cost some of them to accept this personal breach of faith and departure from the letter of ecclesiastical law can be detected in the correspondence of the strong-minded Pierre d'Ailly, the bishop of Cambrai, who had, until now, consistently and conscientiously

---

[20] *De praxi romanae ecclesiae*, in *Monimenta Medii Aevi*, ed. C. W. F. Walch (2 vols., Gottingen, 1757–60), I, 24–6, 95, 99; a better but less easily available text is *Mateusza z Krakowa De praxi romanae ecclesiae*, ed. W. Senko (Wroclaw, 1969), 86–7, 120–1, 122.

[21] Coluccio Salutati, *De seculo et religione*, ed. B. L. Ullman (Florence, 1957). See Ronald G. Witt, *Hercules at the Crossroads* (Durham, NC, 1983), 195–208. His earlier, unfinished and now lost *De vita associabili et operativa* was evidently a defence of the *vita activa* which his career, of course, exemplified.

maintained his allegiance to Benedict XIII.[22] How it affected the more reticent Archbishop Arundel is not known.[23] But the decision was taken, with careful consultation among canon lawyers and with reference to the Aristotelian principle of *epieikeia*, the idea that necessity knows no law. Its broad acceptance was not the result of theoretical arguments by canonists or theologians, but arose in the course of diplomatic deliberations, and led to an international congress, the Council of Pisa. Once the decision had been made, it released, in a spirit of palpable optimism, extraordinary energies on the part of the leading theologians and canonists of Europe. Their constructive joint action to end the papal schism was followed by a serious attempt to correct the abuses which they detected in the government of the church, in two general councils of an entirely new character: in effect, a genuine and even enthusiastic gathering of those graduate careerists whose malaise in previous years had been so paralysing. Its modest beginning with perhaps a hundred theologians gathered for about eight weeks at Pisa in 1409 allowed only for minimal common work; the more definitive reunion at Constance in 1414, with an elaborate committee organisation and several years of discussion, was as the work of Phillip Stump has now shown highly constructive in modifying several aspects of the *régime bénéficial*, the system of preferment which supported the graduate careerist but which troubled his fastidious conscience.[24] Many, perhaps most, of the delegates represented absent ruling princes or prelates; but it is clear that in most of the details of the reform programme they acted on their own judgement as professional canon lawyers and theologians, and the effect of their representative status was really to involve the lay powers in backing their decisions. The novelty of the international congress and the significance of its precedent in the gestation of the modern state can hardly be overstressed. Constance would be the paradigm of similar gatherings of princely councillors and diplomatists, whose effective role was often to educate their masters in a more enlightened self-interest, at the Council of Trent, at Münster in Westphalia, at the Treaty of Utrecht and at the Congress of Vienna. Such gatherings of educated and internationally minded public servants, infrequent as they were, would prove to be indispensable lubricants

[22] A. Combes, 'Sur les "Lettres de consolation" de Nicolas de Clamanges à Pierre d'Ailly', *Archives d'histoire doctrinale et littéraire du Moyen Age*, 13 (1940–2), 359–89; *Jean Gerson: oeuvres complètes*, ed. Glorieux, II, 105–7. See B. Guenée, *Between Church and State* (1991), 216–21.

[23] The only indication is his supposed critical phrase about the papal prerogative of granting benefices *ad votum suum*, referring to the pope as an 'overseas bishop' as alleged by the dean of Oriel College, Oxford. This imputation on the archbishop's orthodoxy was however implicitly denied in his inquiry into the conduct of the Oriel fellows. See *Snappe's Formulary and Other Records*, ed. H. E. Salter (Oxford, Oxford Historical Society LXXX, 1924), 201.

[24] Phillip H. Stump, *The Reforms of the Council of Constance, 1414–1418* (Leiden, 1994).

in the European state system, in the nineteenth as in the fifteenth century.

The change of mood seems to have allowed ministers and councillors to articulate their advice in a new and more practical language. The second decade of the fifteenth century was the first age of the political memorandum, one of the earliest examples of which is the document drawn up for Henry V about November 1418 to set out the possible case for an alliance with the Dauphin Charles, perhaps by Dr Philip Morgan or Dr John Kemp. This is a notably realistic briefing, which makes no bones about the cost of the king's wars and the refusal of the enemy to treat with him; logically argued, and acute in working out the possible outcome of various courses of action, it is devoid of moralistic sentiments. On the other hand it is not in any crude sense Machiavellian or amoral: the author took due account of the royal conscience, posing the question 'whether the King may with his worshippe and in conscience and also savyng of his title to the coroune of France werreie with (that is, make war as an ally of) the Douphin'.[25] In the following October Philip, the new duke of Burgundy, sought the advice of his council as to whether he should accept the terms of peace offered by Henry V, in the new situation created by the murder of the duke's father by partisans of the dauphin, which might involve his renouncing his pledged allegiance to King Charles VI. The advice was proffered in scholastic form, with arguments listed for and against. Like Henry V's councillors, the duke's advisers took careful note of the point of conscience respecting his allegiance, and also of his honour were his father's murderers to be left unpunished, 'if [the duke] does not agree soon to the terms, he might not recover what he requires in respect of his honour and his profit'.[26] The memorandum seems to be the first of a genre which would soon be common in the records of Philip the Good's government, notably from the pen of Hue de Lannoy, the governor of Holland.[27] They are cognate with the opinions recorded more or less verbatim in the Florentine *Consulte e pratiche*, among which Professor Brucker has noted, about 1410, a distinct change from sentiments expressed by the spokesmen of particular families, guilds or neighbourhoods to the remarks of 'discrete individuals formulating independent opinions ... whose views carried weight by virtue of their particular expertise or status in the regime'.[28] Acting as the Florentine

---

[25] *Proceedings and Ordinances of the Privy Council of England (1386–1542)*, ed. N. H. Nicholas (Record Commission, 1834–7), I, 350–8, see 353–4.

[26] Paul Bonenfant, *Du meutre de Montereau au traité de Troyes* (Brussels, Académie Royale de Belgique, Mémoires de la Classe des Lettres, Collection in-8o, 2nd series, LII, fasc. 4, 1958), 216–21, see 219.

[27] See for instance the two translated by Philip Vaughan, *Philip the Good* (1970), 22–4, 103–7.

[28] Gene Brucker, *The Civic World of Early Renaissance Florence* (Princeton, 1977), 289.

equivalent of an English or Burgundian councillor, one such prominent individual, Agnolo Pandolfini, explicitly put experience above theoretical knowledge (*scientia*) in coming to decisions.[29] The quality of official advice given in such documents indicates that their authors, whether clerical or lay, were both experienced and educated, and its unsentimental tone is not a sign that the conscience of the Prince is to be ignored. Rather, it is an indication that a disciplined conscience, guided more by the accumulated wisdom of the experienced confessor than by abstract moral principles, was the right attribute of a prudent prince or for that matter of a wise minister or councillor. We can see why so many of them in this generation, both princes and ministers, laity and clergy, soldiers and statesmen, having, in Walter Hilton's words 'sovereignty with much possession of worldly goods', should have left evidence of an active conscience in their devotional books and charitable support of Carthusian houses dedicated to circulating such books, or, to quote Hilton again, to have 'receyued of our Lord's gift grace of devocioun, and in partie savoure of spiritual occupacioun'.[30]

In this same second decade of the fifteenth century the Carthusian Order acted, with startling rapidity, to supply the political world with practical spiritual guidance, in the form of suitable texts culled from recent contemplative literature. Many of these texts, originally in various vernaculars like the *Dialogo* of Catherine of Siena or Jan Ruysbroeck's *Van de blinkenden steen*, were translated into Latin and some of them then retranslated into other vernaculars: Catherine's *Dialogo* was available in English as *The Orcherd of Syon* before 1420. Other texts were collected in carefully edited anthologies such as the *Donatus devocionis*, excerpts of which were written out by John count of Angoulême, in his own hand as a spiritual exercise, probably when he was a prisoner in England in the 1420s.[31] The original impetus of this complex and apparently coordinated work may have come from Stefano Maconi, the Carthusian translator of Catherine's *Dialogo* into Latin, who was prior general of

---

[29] *Ibid.*, 290 and note. A German example which deserves to be better known is the 'political testament' or advice to his successor composed in 1438 by Raban of Helmstatt, bishop of Speyer, in Karlsruhe, Generallandesarchiv 67/302, fo. 173, ed. F. J. Mone, 'Politische Testament des Bischofs Raban von Speier', *Zeitschrift für die Geschichte des Oberrheins*, 9 (1860), 193–201.

[30] Walter Hilton's 'Mixed Life', ed. Ogilvie-Thomson, 15–16.

[31] On the copying of texts as a religious exercise see A. I. Doyle, 'Publication by Members of the Religious Orders', in *Book Production and Publishing in Britain, 1375–1475*, ed. Jeremy Griffiths and Derek Pearsall (Cambridge, 1989), 109–23, esp. 114–16. Further devotional exercises in John of Angoulême's hand are in Paris, Bibliothèque Nationale MS lat. 3638; see Gilbert Ouy, 'Charles d'Orléans and his Brother Jean d'Angoulême: What their Manuscripts Have to Tell', in *Charles of Orléans in England, 1415–1440*, ed. Mary-Jo Arn (Woodbridge, 2000), 47–60, see 54–5.

the Order's Urbanist half from 1398 to 1410.[32] By 1417, the practice of preparing texts for a lay readership was widespread enough for compilers to need guidance on preserving or restoring a correct version, guidance supplied in the handbook of textual criticism written by a Carthusian of the Grande Chartreuse, Oswald de Corda, in his *Opus pacis*.[33] The surviving fragments of these texts written out in the hands of occasional lay noblemen or women are evidence that their efforts were not wholly in vain.

This body of literature gave firm and orthodox guidance to the political world. But it was left to Henry V to make the disciplined conscience the linchpin of an aggressive and highly controlled style of government, in which both the lay nobility and the graduate careerists would equally put their independent intelligence and their several professional skills to his demanding, exhausting but satisfying and in the end life-transforming service. For his deeply personal religion, we have the evidence of his chaplain:

> For this prince, after he had first taken his seat upon the throne of the kingdom, wrote out for himself the law of Deuteronomy in the volume of his breast, and may God of his immeasurable mercy grant that, as he began, he may read it all the days of his life, in order that he may learn so to fear the Lord his God ... For from the very beginning of his assumption of government, so fervently had he been devoted to the hearing of divine praises and to his own private prayers that once he had begun them there was not anyone, even from amongst his nobles and magnates, who was able by conversation, however brief, at any time to interrupt them.[34]

This is a description of Henry V in the privacy of his chamber, but the author treats it as the starting point of a style of government. It is a style of ruling the essence of which is in the phrase 'learning to fear'; to fear God in the person of the king, the avatar of Moses, who in Deuteronomy lays down in detail the canons of an orthodox way of life for a disobedient people. Its public consequences were a programme of religious reform which had its heart in a projected monastic palace complex at Sheen, of which the Sheen Charterhouse and the Brigittine convent over the river at Syon were realised. These foundations became, as was clearly intended, powerhouses of intercessory prayer for the realm of England and the focus of orthodox guidance for the personal religion of the laity.

---

[32] See *Epistolario di Santa Caterina da Siena*, ed. E. Dupré Theseider (Rome, Fonti per la Storia d'Italia, 1940), xxiii–xli, and on Maconi, Giovanni Leoncini, 'Un certosino del tardo medioevo: Don Stefano Maconi', in *Die Ausbreitung kartäusischen Geistes im Mittelalter*, ed. James Hogg (Salzburg, Analecta Cartusiana LXIII, 1987–91), II, pp. 54–207. See M. C. Sargent, 'Transmission by the English Carthusians of Some Late Medieval Spiritual Writings', *Journal of Ecclesiastical History*, 27 (1976), 225–40.

[33] *Oswaldi de Corda opus pacis*, ed. Belinda A. Egan (Turnhout, Corpus Christianorum Continuatio Medievalis CLXXIX, 2001).

[34] *Gesta Henrici Quinti*, ed. Frank Taylor and John S. Roskell (Oxford, Oxford Medieval Texts, 1975), 155.

Another consequence, of course, was his project for founding an English empire in France which sometimes seemed to assume the moral force of a crusade. If these ambitious plans naturally put his graduate servants under great strain, they seem to have faced his service with professional stoicism and looked back on it, when Henry's short life was over, as the gold standard of good government; Henry Chichele, his diplomat and archbishop, would evoke the king's memory years later in his foundation statutes for All Souls College in Oxford, dedicating his foundation to the arduous service of the state.[35] The discipline and professionalism of Chichele seems a world away from the agonised consciences of Gerson and Nicholas de Clamanges.

The recovery of discipline over the conscience was a lasting feature of fifteenth-century government. It was achieved by hard, or hardened, men like Arundel, Henry V or Pierre d'Ailly, capable of intelligent cooperation as the Council of Constance showed, but prepared too to impose sanctions, including the extreme penalty, on those of their number, like Jan Hus, who put the demands of their private conscience before the discipline of unity. In the record of fifteenth-century government, references to the conscience of the prince abound; indeed the greater his prerogative, the sharper his sense of personal sin. It was a duty of ministers to reconcile princely misgivings with the dictates of prudence: in the words of the secretary of Ludovico il Moro duke of Milan, a ruler whose political career had been far from saintly, 'we must always be alert to the safekeeping of your conscience'.[36] The political classes of the fifteenth century had certainly been made aware of individual conscience, which at many points might be in conflict with their duty of service and cooperation in government. As a result one of the strongest features of the early modern state was its demand for commitment not only of service but of opinion; the principled cruelty of its discipline seems to have arisen from the fear of untrammelled conscience and the destruction it could bring. In that perspective, the concept of *raison d'état* was a doctrine of comfort for unquiet souls: as Machiavelli remarked, a prince should not worry if he incurs reproach, *non si curi di incorrere nella fama*, for his cruelty so long as he keeps his subjects united and loyal.[37] United and loyal – but in defiance of the variable dictates of their consciences, and under the tensile force and the artifice of the modern state. It was not surprising that princes should worry, living under constant moral pressure. For many of

---

[35] *Statutes of the Colleges of Oxford* (1853), I, Statutes of All Souls College, 4. See Jeremy Catto, 'The World of Henry Chichele and the Foundation of All Souls', in *Unarmed Soldiery*, ed. J. K. McConica (Oxford, 1996), 1–13, see 6–7.

[36] D. Bueno de Mesquita, 'The Conscience of the Prince', in *Art and Politics in Renaissance Italy*, ed. George Holmes (Oxford, 1993), 159–83, see 176–7.

[37] N. Machiavelli, *Il Principe*, chapter XV.

them, power was not delightful – that was a fantasy of the impotent – but a burden fit to crush all but the hardest men. Forced into judicial severity and bound by political imperative, princes and ministers must take what comfort they could in the doctrine of necessity, in the Aristotelian notion of *epieikeia*, as they had in 1408, or in the modern defence of *raison d'état*, as their confessors might allow, from the unsleeping accusations of their conscience.

Transactions of the RHS 17 (2007), pp. 101–28 © 2007 Royal Historical Society
doi:10.1017/S0080440107000552 Printed in the United Kingdom

'REPRESENTING' AFRICA: AMBASSADORS AND PRINCES FROM CHRISTIAN AFRICA TO RENAISSANCE ITALY AND PORTUGAL, 1402–1608*

By Kate Lowe

READ 10 MARCH 2006

ABSTRACT. During the fifteenth and sixteenth centuries, a number of sub-Saharan envoys and ambassadors from Christian countries, predominantly Ethiopia and the Congo, were sent to Portugal and Italy. This essay shows how cultural assumptions on both sides complicated their task of 'representing' Africa. These African ambassadors and princes represented the interests of their rulers or their countries in a variety of ways, from forging personal relationships with the king or pope, to providing knowledge of the African continent and African societies, to acquiring knowledge of European languages and behaviours, to negotiating about war, to petitioning for religious or technological help, to carrying out fact-finding missions. But Renaissance preconceptions of Africa and Africans, reinforced by the slave trade, and Renaissance and papal assumptions about diplomatic interaction, ensured that the encounters remained unsatisfactory, as this cultural history of diplomacy makes clear. The focus of the essay is on religious and cultural exchange and the ceremonial culture of embassies.

The great majority of black Africans in Renaissance Europe[1] were slaves, and the impetus for this essay came from a desire to investigate some who were not. High-ranking and important African ambassadors – and even their lowlier cousins, envoys – were at the other end of the spectrum to slaves, and offer an opportunity to analyse a variety of European representations of Africa and Africans generated by their presence and office.

As introduction, here are two stories concerning embassies from Ethiopia to fifteenth-century Italy[2] where the difficulties of

---

* Versions or portions of this essay have been presented at the University of North Carolina at Chapel Hill, North Carolina State University, Oxford University and Stanford University. I am grateful to these audiences for their helpful comments.

[1] For information on Africans in Europe between 1400 and 1600, see *Black Africans in Renaissance Europe*, ed. T. F. Earle and K. J. P. Lowe (Cambridge, 2005).

[2] This is not the place to address how African ambassadors fitted into the diplomatic scene in fifteenth- and sixteenth-century Italy in terms of the change from temporary ambassadors to ambassadors with a particular remit to resident ambassadors. On this change, see Garrett Mattingly, *Renaissance Diplomacy* (1955), 64–90, and Michael Mallett,

'representing'[3] one country to another, and the consequent perplexities of cultural difference, can be seen very clearly. Both have laughter, that most subtly nuanced and complex of cultural responses, at their centre. In the first, an Ethiopian embassy to Venice in 1402 brought as gifts for the doge and signoria '4 leopards, spices and various other pleasing items',[4] among which were a skin described as that 'of a wild man' and the skin of 'an ass of diverse colours'.[5] Francesco Novello da Carrara, the lord of Padua, was contacted by the Venetian government for help in transporting two of the leopards to Germany, and in return he asked that the skins be taken to Padua for him to see. His response to them was memorable – he laughed – and he later wrote to the doge, Michele Steno: 'I saw the skins with hilarity and pleasure.'[6] The second story comes from a letter written by Candido di Gagliano of the collegiata of S. Maria di Cividale in Friuli to his friend, Corrado Bojani, on 5 August 1404. Candido was in Rome. He described in vivid detail the visit to Rome of three Ethiopian ambassadors sent to obtain indulgences and absolution from sins for fellow countrymen, and to acquire saints' relics. Candido wrote that their reports of Ethiopia tallied completely with what was written in the 'Book of the Three Magi', owned by the law professor Angelo degli Ubaldi,[7] and that the Ethiopians willingly listened to the contents of this manuscript (some of which was concerned with Ethiopian Christianity), and while the interpreter was explaining it, 'they moved closer together, laughing and greatly enjoying [hearing] what we knew and appreciated about them, and about the names of their dukes, princes and popes'.[8]

Laughter is a rather complicated cultural signifier and decoding these scenes from Renaissance Italy is not altogether easy, but some of the more pressing contextual references and concerns can at least be mentioned. In

'Ambassadors and their Audiences in Renaissance Italy', *Renaissance Studies*, 8 (1994), 229–43 at 229–30.

[3] I am using this word in inverted commas to signal the multiple levels at which representation took place. In this period, the primary aim of embassies was not, in a formal way, to represent their countries, but to act as message-bearers, request-seekers and news-gatherers.

[4] N. Jorga, 'Notes et extraits pour servir à l'histoire des croisades au XVe siècle', *Revue de l'Orient latin*, 4 (1896), 25–118, 226–320, 503–622 at 252, and N. Jorga, 'Cenni sulle relazioni tra l'Abissinia e l'Europa cattolica nei secoli XIV–XV, con un itinerario inedito del secolo XV', in *Centenario della nascita di Michele Amari* (2 vols., Palermo, 1910), I, 139–50 at 142.

[5] Venice, Biblioteca Nazionale Marciana [hereafter BNM], MSS lat., cl. XIV, 93 (=4530), fo. 64r: 'una pelle de uno homo salvego e una pelle de uno aseno de diversi colore'; cited in C. Cipolla, 'Prete Jane e Francesco Novello da Carrara', *Archivio veneto*, 6 (1873), 323–4.

[6] Venice, BNM, MSS. lat., cl. XIV, 93 (=4530), fo. 67r: 'Vidi hilariter et iocunde pelles'; cited in Cipolla, 'Prete Jane', 324.

[7] Paul H. D. Kaplan, *The Rise of the Black Magus in Western Art* (Ann Arbor, 1985), 226n.

[8] Vittorio Lazzarini, 'Un'ambasciata etiopica in Italia nel 1404', *Atti del Reale Istituto veneto di scienze, lettere ed arti*, 83, 2 (1923–4), 839–47 at 842 (Italian translation) and 846 (Latin).

the 1402 story, the first skin must have been of an ape,[9] possibly a gorilla[10] or a chimpanzee, and the second most probably of a zebra. Renaissance Italians (with their interest in origins of all types) were fascinated by the notion of a wild man, and the ape skin must have fuelled these fantasies. Whether Francesco Novello thought he was seeing the skin of a wild man or of an ape is not recorded, but his hilarity may have signalled surprise or incongruity, occasioned both by the skin of the extraordinary hairy human/ape and by the striped zebra skin, as stripes in themselves could be considered funny. It is possible that Novello had an interest in Africa because at an early date he possessed at least two sub-Saharan African slaves; in October and November 1405, he gave two black female slaves to his doctor as payment for services rendered.[11]

In fifteenth-century Italy, the craze for menageries of wild and exotic non-European animals led initially to a steady stream of big cats, and later to the import of giraffes, elephants and rhinoceroses, all of which were passed around between princes and lords as welcome gifts. In addition to their connection to live, unfamiliar animals, the skins were also funny because as dead, unknown ex-animals they had no place in the European hierarchy of pelts. Animal skins in Europe were employed as status indicators, and were frequently chosen as ambassadorial gifts, but what status was represented (or indeed could be represented) by a zebra or an ape skin? The animal skins presented as gifts by the Ethiopians could have been chosen on account of their known novelty in Italy, for they would probably not have been exceptional or exceptionally costly in Ethiopia (now there are two types of zebra in Ethiopia and no gorillas, but it is difficult to be certain what the situation was in the fifteenth century). But it is also possible that the Ethiopians brought animal skins as gifts because they were the gifts usually given in Africa, and because in Africa as in Europe, animal skins were used as status indicators. According to the chaplain to the Portuguese embassy to Ethiopia in the 1520s, Francisco Álvarez, Ethiopian courtiers wore various animal skins (sheep, lion, tiger,

---

[9] On the association of sub-Saharan Africans with apes, see H. Janson, *Apes and Ape Lore in the Middle Ages and the Renaissance* (1952), 65 n. 97 and 67–9 n. 105. In a second note with exactly the same title as his one of the year before (see n. 5), C. Cipolla, 'Piete Jane e Francesco Novello da Carrrara', *Archivio veneto*, 7 (1874), 111, writes that the skin must have been of an orang utan.

[10] Cf. OED etymology: 'perh. Afr. for "wild man", in Greek account of Hanno's voyage 5th or 6th century B.C., adopted as specific name 1847'. According to Pliny the Elder, *Natural History*, with an English translation by H. Rackham (10 vols., Cambridge, MA, 1956–63), vol. II, Book VI, XXXVI, 200–1 (487 in English translation), Hanno sent the skins of two wild, hairy women/female apes he found in the Ethiopian islands back to the temple of Juno in Carthage, where they were displayed as curiosities.

[11] Giuseppe Gennari, *Annali della città di Padova* (3 vols., Bassano, 1804), II, 211, and Filippo Zamboni, *Gli Ezzelini, Dante e gli schiavi: Roma e la schiavitù personale domestica* (Rome and Turin, 1906), 249.

leopard) according to their rank.[12] Whatever the case, the Ethiopians would have been very surprised that their gifts engendered hilarity. A passage from the humanist Lapo da Castiglionchio the Younger's Dialogue *On the Benefits of the Curia*, written during the summer of 1438 in response to the start of the Council of Ferrara–Florence (1438–42), backs up the view that things or people perceived as 'strange' by Italians (which included nearly all foreigners) produced laughter:

> Lapo: Indeed the Byzantine emperor has come...followed by priests, high priests, legates and many translators from all the Eastern peoples and nations among whom the name of Christ is worshipped. The variety of their language, their character, their adornment, their dress, their bearing, and finally, their bodies themselves leads not only to delight but also to laughter and wonderment.
>
> Angelo: 'It is so. I mean, I never look at men of that sort without laughing.'[13]

The second story from 1404 reveals the other side of the coin – Ethiopian ambassadors laughing on account of Italian knowledge of Ethiopia. Why did the Ethiopians react in this way? What did laughter signify in this context? Were they laughing because it was so unusual to encounter accurate information in Italy about Ethiopia and Ethiopian Christianity? Or were they in reality laughing out of a sense of cultural superiority because they were enjoying hearing the errors in what was written about their home country? And what did they feel about the fact that this knowledge was contained in a manuscript about the Three Magi? What was the relationship in their minds between the black Magus and Ethiopia? In Europe, John of Hildesheim's *Book of the Three Magi*,[14] finished before 1375, was the primary literary basis for King Caspar as a black Ethiopian, and it also propounded the view that the emperor of Ethiopia was the descendant of and successor to the Three Wise Men who all died without heirs.[15] And one wonders too whether the names of Ethiopian 'dukes and princes' made them laugh because of the foolishness of using these terms in relation to Ethiopian elites (it was a favourite trick of the humanists to feign pretence that all social structures could be rendered in the terminology of ancient Rome) or whether the names and positions had been mangled in translation. Or were they homesick in Rome for

---

[12] Joan Barclay Lloyd, *African Animals in Renaissance Literature and Art* (Oxford, 1971), 29, and Francisco Alvares, *The Prester John of the Indies*, ed. C. F. Beckingham and G. W. B. Huntingford (2 vols., Cambridge, 1961), I, 128.

[13] Christopher Celenza, *Renaissance Humanism and the Papal Curia: Lapo da Castiglionchio the Younger's De curiae commodes* (Ann Arbor, MI, 1999), 177.

[14] For an English translation, see *The Three Kings of Cologne. An Early English Translation of the 'Historia trivium regum' by John of Hildesheim*, edited from the MSS, together with the Latin text, by Carl Horstmann (1886).

[15] Lazzarini, 'Un'ambasciata etiopica', 843–4 and Kaplan, *The Rise of the Black Magus*, 114 n. 226.

Ethiopia and therefore merely reacted happily upon hearing familiar names?

These two fleeting moments of laughter have allowed the introduction of this essay's main themes: European readings of the strangeness of African animals and artefacts, which stood in as representations of Africa; the role of African ambassadors in fleshing out European and African ideas of each other's worlds and connections between them; cultural assumptions and cultural difference in the fifteenth and sixteenth centuries (especially in this transcontinental situation); competing versions of global knowledge and of global Christianity; and the relevance of the prototype of the black Magus for sub-Saharan African ambassadors to Europe. The fifteenth and sixteenth centuries were crucial moments in the history of relations between Africa and Europe, and encompassed not only political and diplomatic encounters, but also the articulation of a whole host of cultural and religious assumptions. Catholicism was a key element in this relationship, and analysing the embassies sent by Christian sub Saharan African countries to Portugal and Italy in terms of cultural relationships repays investigation. Both sides had their misconceptions of each other, but they managed to interface on 'middle ground', and one possibility is that Catholicism provided this 'middle ground'.

An analysis of the cultural context to these embassies reveals how complicated the task of 'representing' Africa could be. The two Christian countries under discussion in this essay are Ethiopia (in East Africa) and the Congo (on the West coast of Africa), with two very different histories of Christianity and two very different histories of contact with Europe. Both countries were primarily interested in links with the pope because of his position as head of the Catholic church. Nearly all papal rituals stressed the majesty of the pope who possessed absolute power and was the Vicar of Christ, and all kings, emperors and their representatives had to kiss his feet in a symbolic gesture of 'adoration', similar to the way in which Roman emperors were once adored.[16] (In Portugal, by contrast, ambassadors were required to kiss the hand of the king.[17]) During the Renaissance magnificence in papal ritual increased, probably to reinforce the pope's power as head of a worldwide church, but it may also have been a response to increased magnificence from secular rulers.[18] For both reasons, and as European knowledge of the non-European world expanded and the papacy became more concerned to find new populations to Christianise and bring into the 'fold', many

---

[16] Peter Burke, *The Historical Anthropology of Early Modern Italy: Essays on Perception and Communication* (Cambridge, 1987), 173 and 175.

[17] Leite de Faria, 'Uma relação de Rui de Pina sobre o Congo escrita em 1492', *Studia*, 19 (1966), 223–303 at 271.

[18] Burke, *Historical Anthropology*, 181.

fifteenth- and sixteenth-century popes welcomed embassies from extra-European countries as a way of raising their profile. The exact reception accorded depended upon the personality and policy of individual popes, and upon precise world circumstances. Both the Congo and Ethiopia were also interested in links with Portugal, Congo because Portugal was the European power with which they had first come into contact and which they knew, and Ethiopia because Portugal was expanding to the East and was fast becoming the most important world power.

Ethiopia had been Christianised in the fourth century, and its church is one of the Oriental Orthodox churches (along with the Syrian, Coptic and Armenian churches), which had in common their rejection of the Council of Chalcedon in 451. Christianity was an essential part of its national and cultural identity, a defining feature that set it apart from all its surrounding Muslim neighbours, and by the sixteenth century renewed Muslim pressure certainly injected a sense of urgency into diplomatic and religious links between Ethiopia and the papacy. Ethiopian Christians were expected to practise circumcision, observe the food prescriptions set out in the Old Testament and honour Saturday as the Sabbath, and thus represented to Renaissance Europeans the 'strangeness' of African Christian practices. Leo X wrote to the emperor Dāwit II in May 1515 exhorting him to abandon the rite of circumcision as a precondition to Ethiopia entering the European Christian community. Only when the practice was abandoned could Ethiopia join with Portugal, the papacy and other kings to liberate Jerusalem, and only then would the pope send him a special nuncio bearing both spiritual and temporal gifts.[19] Needless to say, Ethiopia did not suspend circumcision. As the sixteenth century progressed, more and more emphasis was placed on religious conformity, and popes began to be far more demanding about the standardisation of religious norms. Matthew, the Ethiopian ambassador to Pope Paul III (1534–49), was formally interrogated in Rome about Ethiopian Christianity, and although his answers on most subjects conformed to Catholic precepts, he admitted to the controversial practice of circumcision while denying the often-raised medieval legend about Ethiopians practising baptism by fire.[20]

If one accepts Renaissance Aristotelian notions of civilisation, Renaissance Europe must have perceived a sharp contrast between Ethiopian civilisation, with its written culture and its long and distinguished tradition of chronicle-writing, and Congolese civilisation, with its oral and non-literate culture. The Congo only became

---

[19] Città del Vaticano, Archivio Segreto Vaticano [hereafter AV], Arm. XLIV, t. 5, fo. 108r.

[20] In his discussions with Paris de Grassis, Giovanni Battista Brocchi denied the existence of this practice, Città del Vaticano, Biblioteca Apostolica Vaticana [hereafter BAV], Vat. lat. 12270, fo. 89r.

Christianised in the fifteenth century, with the arrival of the Portuguese, and an elite of Congolese then became literate, able both to read and to write. Although writing one's name is in itself no proof of further ability to write, it does at least indicate a consciousness of literacy. Signatures survive, for example, of five Congolese envoys and students (and students certainly had to be literate in a meaningful way) in Lisbon in August 1514, four of whom were related to the Manicongo or 'king' of the Congo (one of them is D. Henrique, the first sub-Saharan African to be made a bishop, in 1518),[21] and a further five signatures are extant from September 1514, of Congolese who were returning to the Congo.[22] Envoys or ambassadors from other parts of Africa who were not able to write (for example, Pero Barroso, an interpreter from Benin who was in Lisbon in 1515) made a cross on the paper instead of signing.[23] In 1485 Diogo Cão and two of his companions engraved a stone marker at Ielala, about 160 kilometres from the mouth of the Zaire, with the Portuguese royal arms, a cross and an inscription recording the three names.[24] It is generally agreed that the ruler of Sogno, one of the six provinces of the Congo, was the first to convert to Christianity in 1491,[25] and later the Manicongo was persuaded to convert,[26] and some of his family, his elites and his subjects followed suit, taking the Christian names of the Portuguese royal family and Portuguese nobles. Portuguese royal recognition of their African royal and noble kin included the devising of Portuguese coats of arms for their African brother rulers and co-religionists – those for the Manicongo, for example, are preserved in the sixteenth-century Book of Nobility and Perfection of Arms in the Torre do Tombo in Lisbon.[27]

The Portuguese appropriation of the Congo and Portuguese overseeing of the country's religious structure should have ensured that Congolese Catholicism was closely modelled on European Catholicism, but although

---

[21] Lisbon, Instituto dos Arquivos Nacionais/Torre do Tombo [hereafter ANTT], Corpo Chronológico [hereafter CC] I, maço 15, doc. 110, and *Monumenta missionaria Africana: África Ocidental*, ed. António Brásio (series I, 15 vols., Lisbon, 1952–88), I (1471–1531), 288.

[22] Lisbon, ANTT, CC I, maço 16, doc. 10, and *Monumenta missionaria Africana*, ed. Brásio, I, 290.

[23] Lisbon, ANTT, CC I, maço 19, doc. 62, and *Monumenta missionaria Africana*, ed. Brásio, I, 342.

[24] *Portugal e os Descobrimentos: o Encontro de Civilações* (Lisbon, 1992), 102 (illustration) and 103.

[25] See João de Barros, *Ásia* (Lisbon, 1778), década I, liv. III, cap. IX, *Monumenta missionaria Africana*, ed. Brásio, I, 79–80, and Filippo Pigafetta, *A Report of the Kingdom of Congo and of the Surrounding Countries, Drawn out of the Writings and Discourses of the Portuguese Duarte Lopez* (1970), 43 and 72.

[26] Pigafetta, *A Report*, 73–6, and *História do Reino do Congo (MS. 8080 da Biblioteca Nacional de Lisboa)*, ed. António Brásio (Lisbon, 1969), 66–9.

[27] *Os Negros em Portugal – Séculos XV a XIX* (exhibition catalogue), Mosteiro de Belém (Lisbon, 1999), 182.

Portugal and the papacy continued to monitor every aspect, they could only do this from a distance, from Europe. So, for example, in 1595, the Congolese ambassador to Portugal, called António Vieira, who was a relative of King Alvaro II of the Congo, was closely interrogated about the state of religion in the Congo, even being quizzed about such apparently minor matters as the behaviour of the six local lay confraternities in the capital São Salvador.[28] He passed the exam with flying colours, but other sources indicate that Congolese Catholicism retained many of its pre-Christian aspects, which the Portuguese secretly condoned.

An Ethiopian embassy to the papacy is recorded in 1306,[29] but in the fifteenth and sixteenth centuries embassies became much more common, even though Muslim Egypt tried to stop or hinder all such traffic. Had they been allowed to reach their destination, embassies from the Congo to the papacy would also have become much more common in the sixteenth century after the Christianisation of the kingdom. A few were given instructions and many set off (for instance, Manuel, the brother-in-law of Nzinga Mvemba, or Afonso I, wrote to King João III of Portugal asking for an armed caravel to take him to Rome to offer obedience to the pope in 1540),[30] but none made it until the Portuguese Duarte Lopez finally arrived dressed as a hermit in Rome in 1589 after many adventures to find that he had become a subject of, and the country he 'represented' had become the possession of, Philip II, the king of Spain,[31] and that Sixtus V was unwilling to accede to his requests. The problem for Congolese ambassadors was that their route to Rome inexorably passed through Portugal (as they had to take ships to reach Europe and all the ships were Portuguese), but that once in Lisbon, the Portuguese were extremely reluctant to let the Congolese out of their sphere of influence and so kept them in Portugal.[32] This is what happened to the Congolese ambassador to Portugal, D. Pedro de Sousa, who was held in Lisbon in 1514 and not allowed to go to Rome with the famous Portuguese embassy to Leo X, headed by Tristão da Cunha.[33] Portugal guarded its power over the Congo jealously, and it is not coincidental that Congolese ambassadors started appearing in Rome only after Portugal's annexation by Spain in 1580.

[28] Città del Vaticano, BAV, Vat. lat. 12516, fo. 2r, and Città del Vaticano, AV, Fondo Borghese, serie II, 24, fo. 174r.

[29] J. R. S. Phillips, *The Medieval Expansion of Europe* (Oxford, 1988), 151–4; Edward Ullendorf and C. F. Beckingham, *The Hebrew Letters of Prester John* (Oxford, 1982), 8–9.

[30] *Monumenta missionaria Africana: África Ocidental*, ed. António Brásio, II (1532–69), 85–6.

[31] His instructions dated 15 Jan. 1583 are in *Monumenta missionaria Africana*, ed. Brásio, III (1570–99), 234–5. See also J. Cuvelier and L. Jadin, *L'ancien Congo d'après les archives romaines (1518–1640)* (Brussels, 1954), 128.

[32] François Baziota, *Ne-Kongo en Afrique centrale XVe–XVIIIe siècles* (Rome, 1971), 78–9.

[33] *Monumenta missionaria Africana: África Ocidental*, ed. Brásio, suplemento, XV, 33.

The second part of this essay will examine more closely the ways in which African ambassadors and embassies could 'represent' or be thought to represent Africa. In addition to giving representations of 'exotic' Africa as diplomatic gifts, the most obvious way is by representing the interests of their rulers and their countries. An embassy[34] could be composed of one individual or several, and ambassadors (with official credentials) should be distinguished from members of their trains or suites. In practice, official letters of instruction to ambassadors which were routine across much of Europe are sometimes lacking for ambassadors from sub-Saharan Africa, although significant numbers of official letters between Ethiopian emperors and popes,[35] between Congolese and Portuguese rulers[36] and between Congolese kings and popes,[37] are still extant and provide reasonable amounts of information about ambassadors and their aims. The stated aims of these embassies were often straightforwardly to make contact, or to offer obedience (egged on by European advisers, who were often religious, who said that was how Christian rulers in Europe behaved). Many ambassadors also seem to have been charged with checking aspects of Roman Catholic Christianity (e.g. the exact position of the pope[38] or how mass was conducted) and with trying to obtain relics and images of saints. Occasional ambassadors arrived in Europe to attend church councils. Ethiopian delegates (who turned out to be unofficial) headed by Pietro the deacon[39] attended the Council of Florence called by Eugenius IV, as did Andrea the abbot, the head of the Coptic delegation (which signed an agreement of union with the Catholic church). Their visit to Italy was recorded by Antonio Averlino, known as Filarete, in a double panel on the bronze doors of St Peter's, which were

---

[34] I am using the word embassy relatively loosely to encompass not only formal or official embassies, but also missions of a less formal nature.

[35] See, e.g., *Lettere tra i pontefici romani e i principi etiopici; secoli XII–XX*, ed. Osvaldo Raineri (Città del Vaticano, 2003).

[36] See, e.g., the letter dated 31 May 1515 from Afonso, king of the Congo, to Manuel I of Portugal, requesting a favour and supplying the names of two relatives he is sending to Lisbon as his representatives: in Lisbon, ANTT, CC I, maço 17, doc. 135, and *Monumenta missionaria Africana*, ed. Brásio, I, 333–4.

[37] See, e.g., the letter dated only 1512 from Afonso, king of the Congo, to Pope Julius II, offering obedience and giving the pope the names of his two ambassadors: in Lisbon, ANTT, CC II, maço 30, doc. 1, and *Monumenta missionaria Africana*, ed. Brásio, I, 270–1.

[38] Città del Vaticano, BAV, Vat. lat. 12270, fo. 90r, and Renato Lefevre, 'Cronaca inedita di un'ambasciata etiopica a Sisto IV', *Roma*, 18 (1940), 360–9 at 367.

[39] Enrico Cerulli, 'Eugenio IV e gli Etiopi al Concilio di Firenze nel 1441', *Rendiconti della R. Accademia Nazionale dei Lincei, Classe di scienze, morali, storiche e filologiche*, serie 6, IX (1933), 347–68 at 351–2, talks of the oration given by Pietro the deacon on 2 Sept. 1441 at his reception by Eugenius. An Italian version of this oration has been published in Franco Cardini, 'Una versione volgare del discorso degli "ambasciatori" etiopici al Concilio di Firenze', *Archivio storico italiano*, dispensa II (1972), 269–76 at 274–6.

Figure 1 Antonio Averlino (known as Filarete), 'Pope Eugenius IV Consigning the Decree of Union to Abbot Anthony, the Head of the Coptic Delegation at the Council of Florence', detail of panel from the central door of St Peter's Basilica, Città del Vaticano, bronze, completed 1445. Photograph: Bibliotheca Hertziana – Max-Planck Institut für Kunstgeschichte, Rome.

completed in 1445.[40] The first part of the panel records Eugenius IV consigning the decree of union to Abbot Andrea in Florence (Figure 1), and the second records the departure of the delegates (Figure 2) (but the scenes are generic rather than specific in terms of location, with the location being flagged by the word 'Florentie' underneath). Although only the Copts were involved in signing the decree of union, some of the same figures reappear in both scenes (including probably Pietro the deacon). Notice the stripes (stripes were the most frequently represented textile pattern in Ethiopian painting)[41] and the hand cross (a feature of Ethiopian

[40] See Michele Lazzaroni and Antonio Muñoz, *Filarete, scultore e architetto del secolo XV* (Rome, 1908), ch. 2: 'Averlino a Roma. Le porte di San Pietro (1433–1445)', 12–122 at 75, 78–9 and figs. 64 and 65.

[41] Michael Gervers, 'The Portuguese Import of Luxury Textiles to Ethiopia in the Sixteenth and Seventeenth Centuries and their Subsequent Artistic Influence', in Isabel Boavida, *The Indigenous and the Foreign in Christian Ethiopian Art: On Portuguese–Ethiopian Contacts in the Sixteenth and Seventeenth Centuries*, ed. Manuel João Ramos with Isabel Boavida (Aldershot, 2004), 121–34 at 127.

Figure 2 Antonio Averlino (known as Filarete), 'The Departure of the Coptic and Ethiopian Delegates from the Council of Florence', detail of panel from the central door of St Peter's Basilica, Città del Vaticano, bronze, completed 1445. Photograph: Bibliotheca Hertziana – Max-Planck Institut für Kunstgeschichte, Rome.

and Coptic Christianity). And in August 1561 Pius IV wrote a letter to the bishop of Hierapolis, asking him to encourage the Ethiopian emperor Mina to sent representatives to the Council of Trent.[42] But while some embassies had religious aims, other imperatives were more diplomatic and political. Both sides wanted what might have looked like the same thing – support in the fight against Muslim countries – but both wanted the other power to provide it. So all embassies from Ethiopia also had the task of trying to obtain papal and European financial, technological and psychological help against the Muslim threat in their region, just as all papal contacts with Ethiopia had the underlying motive of trying to enlist Ethiopian manpower against the Muslim threat on another flank.

The embassies themselves could take many forms – the most notable distinction is between those embassies from sub-Saharan Africa headed by or featuring Europeans (for example, Pietro Rombulo from Messina

[42] Città del Vaticano, AV, Arm. XLV, 20, fo. 14r–v. See *Epistolae ad Principes*, ed. Luigi Nanni (3 vols., Città del Vaticano, 1992–7), I, 412.

headed the Ethiopian embassy to Rome in 1450) and those headed by or featuring sub-Saharan Africans (for example, the Ethiopian Saga za Ab, known in Europe as Sagazabo, in 1527–33 or Ne-Vunda from the Congo in 1604–8) – but another important distinction was between ambassadors who were secular and those who held religious positions (for instance, the emperor of Ethiopia's chaplain called Antonio who headed the 1481 embassy to Sixtus IV or the Portuguese chaplain Francisco Álvarez who was Ethiopian ambassador to Clement VII in 1533). It was a delicate matter to decide who to send on these missions. There were obvious advantages to using Europeans rather than Africans as ambassadors to the papacy when the rules governing diplomatic etiquette were as rarified as they were at the papal court in the Renaissance, but the majority of Europeans who travelled to Ethiopia and the Congo (the only pool of potential candidates for appointment) were usually not of very elevated social status (they were often merchants or artisans), which was a considerable disadvantage.

There was also a difference of approach here between Ethiopia and the Congo, probably related to differences in social structure, and the Portuguese control of the Congo, as well as to direct and indirect familiarity with the papal court. Indigenous Ethiopian ambassadors were usually religious officials of high rank or trusted members of the imperial household, perhaps because the Ethiopians thought that European Christian powers could best be approached by men of religion. (This meant that they did not change into European clothes when in Europe but continued to wear their own religious dress). Indigenous Congolese ambassadors, on the other hand, were normally relatives of the king and could be cast in a much more 'noble' or princely light. As high-ranking royal relatives and courtiers, they donned expensive European clothes given to them by the Portuguese monarchs or popes on arrival at court. One other outstanding difference is noticeable between ambassadors from these two countries, for some Congolese ambassadors brought their wives, who represented yet another facet of Africa – African womanhood. For example, both Pedro de Manicongo and his unnamed wife were assigned sets of European court clothes in Lisbon by King João II in 1493,[43] and Damião de Góis commented on the many conversations in the second decade of the sixteenth century between King Manuel I and the Congolese ambassador, and on the way Queen Maria honoured the Congolese ambassador's wife.[44] It is highly unlikely that an Italian ambassador would have been accompanied on his embassy

[43] Lisbon, ANTT, CC I, maço 2, doc. 103, and *Monumenta missionaria Africana*, ed. Brásio, I, 154–5.

[44] Damião de Góis, *Chronica do Felicíssimo Rei Dom Emanuel* (Lisbon, 1566), part III, cap. XXXVII, and *Monumenta missionaria Africana*, ed. Brásio, I, 222.

by his wife in the fifteenth or early sixteenth centuries, and this is a startling example of African women being inserted into a role of political importance in Europe. The most famous fifteenth-century sub-Saharan African royal relative was 'Prince Bemoim' (Jelen, the *bumi* of Jolof), a Wolof from Senegambia and a member of the wider royal family,[45] who visited João II in Portugal in 1488.[46] João responded to his royal guests in royal fashion: Bemoim, his relatives and his retinue of forty were issued with European clothing suitable to their rank (to transform them outwardly into Europeans), and were allocated servants (to make their status clear). One chronicler praised Bemoim's impressive appearance and – rather ludicrously, as he had to speak through an interpreter – his oratory (considered one of the most fundamental Renaissance skills). While in Portugal Bemoim converted to Christianity and was baptised at a ceremony in the queen's bedchamber, taking the king's name João as his baptismal name; the king, queen and heir to the throne served as his godparents. A few days later he was dubbed a knight by his suzerain and given his own coat of arms before paying formal homage to the Portuguese king. However, Bemoim's subsequent fate – he was murdered on the return voyage to West Africa by a Portuguese noble Pero Vaz whom the king then declined to prosecute or punish – revealed that in fundamental ways King João II may not have recognised Bemoim's claim to be his Christian brother and kingly vassal.[47]

An interesting indicator of how the Portuguese behaved publicly towards eminent African visitors is provided by the fact that in the sixteenth century envoys and ambassadors from sub-Saharan Africa formed the largest group of Africans who were made knights in two of the very prestigious military Orders in Portugal – the Order of Christ and the Order of Santiago. D. Pedro de Sousa, the ambassador from the Manicongo to Portugal mentioned above, became a knight of the Order of Christ on 12 April 1512 (and one of two sets of clothes made for him in December 1515 included a black cloak or cape, black hose and a black cap,[48] which could have been his required dress as a knight of this Order). 'Jacome Abexi' (Giacomo the Abyssianian), the young nobleman related to the emperor of Ethiopia, sent with Matthew (Mateus) the Armenian

[45] Ivana Elbl, 'Prestige Considerations and the Changing Interest of the Portuguese Crown in Sub-Saharan Atlantic Africa, 1444–1580', *Portuguese Studies Review*, 10, 2 (2003), 15–36 at 27–8. As Bemoim's mother was not the principal wife of the king, Bemoim was considered 'illegitimate' in Portugal.

[46] P. E. Russell, 'White Kings on Black Kings: Rui de Pina and the Problem of Black African Sovereignty', in P. E. Russell, *Portugal, Spain and the African Atlantic, 1343–1490: Chivalry and Crusade from John of Gaunt to Henry the Navigator* (Aldershot, 1995), 151–63.

[47] Russell, 'White Kings on Black Kings', 157–62.

[48] *Monumenta missionaria Africana*, ed. Brásio, I, 345.

to Portugal to learn about diplomatic missions,[49] also became a knight of the Order of Christ on 2 April 1515.[50] And two out of three black Africans admitted as knights to the Order of Santiago during the sixteenth century were ambassadors: Luís Peres, *fidalgo* and lord chamberlain of the Manicongo, in 1550, and D. Pedro da Silva, an ambassador of the king of Angola, in 1579.[51] In an anonymous genre scene of the Lisbon waterfront dated *c.* 1560–80, there is a prominent depiction of a black knight of the Order of Santiago,[52] and the period from 1500 to 1580 when these four Africans were knighted was obviously a moment when African embassies and ambassadors to Portugal were being favourably received.

There were many routes whereby knowledge of or opinions on sub-Saharan Africa could have reached Europe. For instance, the 'converted' Muslim, Leo Africanus (Al-Hasan al-Wazzan),[53] wrote his great work of historical geography on Africa (*Della descrittione dell'Africa*) while living in Rome in the 1520s, under the patronage of Leo X, so it is reasonable to assume that Leo had access to its contents. This was translated into English by John Pory, and published with significant additions and interventions in 1600, under the title *A Geographical Historie of Africa*.[54] In both Italy and Portugal, there was far greater familiarity with Islamic North Africa than with the largely 'pagan' sub-Saharan Africa, and such knowledge as there was had sometimes (as in the case of Leo Africanus') been filtered through a North African lens. Certain Italian cities, such as Venice, had greater knowledge of Africa than others, such as Florence, because of longstanding contacts, and in general merchants were more interested and knowledgeable about the realities of contemporary Africa than kings and popes, whose understanding of African affairs was very likely to have been strongly influenced by classical and biblical sources.

[49] On this embassy, see Jean Aubin, 'L'ambassade du Prêtre Jean a D. Manuel', *Mare Luso-Indicum*, 3 (1976), 1–56.

[50] António Machado de Faria, 'Cavaleiros da Ordem de Cristo no século XVI', *Arqueologia e História*, 6 (1955), 13–73 at 63 and 50.

[51] Francis A. Dutra, 'A Hard-Fought Struggle for Recognition: Manuel Gonçalves Doria, First Afro-Brazilian to Become a Knight of Santiago', *The Americas*, 56 (1 July 1990), 93–4, nos. 13–14.

[52] Kate Lowe, 'The Stereotyping of Black Africans in Renaissance Europe', in *Black Africans*, ed. Earle and Lowe, 17–47 at 29 and fig. 3 (whole painting), and Annemarie Jordan, 'Images of Empire: Slaves in the Lisbon Household and Court of Catherine of Austria', in *Black Africans*, ed. Earle and Lowe, 155–80 at 159–60 and fig. 39 (detail of black knight).

[53] On Leo Africanus, see Dietrich Rauchenberger, *Johannes Leo der Afrikaner. Seine Beschreibung des Raumes zwischen Nil und Niger nach dem Urtext* (Wiesbaden, 1999), and Natalie Zemon Davis, *Trickster Travels: A Sixteenth-Century Muslim between Worlds* (New York, 2006).

[54] Leo Africanus, *A Geographical Historie of Africa Written in Arabicke and Italian by John Leo a More*, trans. John Pory (1600). See also the Hakluyt edition: Leo Africanus, *The History and Description of Africa and of the Notable Things Therein Contained*, done into English in the year 1600 by John Pory, ed. and with an introduction and notes by Dr Robert Brown (3 vols., 1896).

A by-product of African diplomatic 'representation' in Italy was an increase in the circulation of information about sub-Saharan Africa. One possible example of this can be seen in a map datable to before 1456 of 'Egyptus Novelo' included in a copy of a Latin translation of Ptolemy's 'Geography', now in the Bibliothèque Nationale in Paris.[55] The two halves of the map are derived from utterly different sources: the map of Egypt is in some senses a classically inspired Ptolemaic representation[56] while the map of Ethiopia is not Ptolemaic but derived from contemporary sources (so, for example, the rivers are well drawn and accurate and the mapping of the central region of the country is very detailed).[57] As the map had been drawn by the Florentine Pietro da Massaio, one hypothesis is that members of the Ethiopian delegation to the Council of Florence (1438–42) had been the source for the depiction of the Ethiopian section of 'Egyptus Novelo' in the Ptolemaic manuscript.[58] An interesting connection here is that this codex, along with a tapestry 'representing' Ethiopia (but it is not known in what way), had been sold in 1456 by a Florentine merchant Giovanni Artano to Alfonso d'Aragona of Naples.[59] Another example of information flow via Ethiopian nationals is the Camaldolese monk Fra Mauro of Venice's worldmap (*mappamondo*) of 1459 – Fra Mauro was a monk at S. Michele di Murano. His depiction of Ethiopia included parts that had been previously unknown, and he stated in a legend on the map itself that these new areas had been drawn by natives of Ethiopia with their own hands but that he had not been able to include all the new information.[60]

As far as Europe was concerned, the myths that had accrued around the legendary person of Prester John and his kingdom in the Indies impeded the absorption in Europe of 'correct' information about Ethiopia, as by the fourteenth century Prester John's kingdom had 'moved' from India to China to Ethiopia. Indeed, in many of the maps of Africa from the first half of the fifteenth century onwards, Prester John is represented as the principal ruler in Ethiopia. In the Portuguese cartographer

---

[55] Paris, Bibliothèque Nationale, Fonds latins 4802, fos. 130–1.

[56] Although Ptolemy said that north should go at the top of a map and here north is not at the top.

[57] The intention was to give most prominence to Ethiopia (south of the confluence of the Blue/White Niles).

[58] Laura Mannoni, 'Una carta italiana del bacino del Nilo e dell'Etiopia del secolo XV', in *Pubblicazioni dell'Istituto di geografia della Reale università di Roma*, serie B, I (Rome, 1932), 7–12 at 12.

[59] Giuseppe Mazzatinti, *La biblioteca dei re d'Aragona in Napoli* (Rocca S. Casciano, 1897), xxi.

[60] Tullia Gasparrini Leporace, *Il mappamondo di Fra Mauro* (Venice, 1956), plate X. Unfortunately, I have not been able to see P. Falchetta, *Fra Mauro's Map of the World with a Commentary and Translations of the Inscriptions* (Turnhout, 2006).

Figure 3 Diogo Homem, detail of Prester John, the ruler of Ethiopia, from the Queen Mary Atlas, 1558, British Library, Cotton MSS Additional MS 5415A, fo. 15v. Photograph: The British Library Board.

Diogo Homem's Queen Mary Atlas of 1558 now in the British Library,[61] the ruler of Ethiopia is represented as white, wearing clothes and a crown, and seated on a very elaborate Renaissance throne (Figure 3). The representation of the Manicongo from the same atlas shows him as black, with a crown and headcap, wearing clothes, on a throne, on a carpet (Figure 4). These two African rulers who had contacts with Portugal and Italy are the only two rulers of sub-Saharan Africa represented in this way in this atlas – the two other black African rulers (one of Mali and one of Nubia) are represented semi-naked, either standing or seated on a cushion – and they articulate the link between Christianity and civilisation in visual terms. All four kings wear gold crowns and hold staffs of office, so their power (as opposed to their level of civilisation) is not at issue.

The myth of Prester John was sustained by a very high level of disinformation which was fed into the European knowledge base – apocryphal letters claiming to have been written by him, and false ambassadors claiming to have been sent by him – as well as by the

---

[61] London, British Library, Cotton MSS Additional MS 5415A. This atlas was commissioned by Queen Mary of England (hence its name) for her husband Philip II of Spain. There is a facsimile edition of *The Queen Mary Atlas*, with a separate book of *Commentary* by Peter Barbour (2005); the ruler of Ethiopia appears on Map VIII of this, and of the Manicongo on Map VII.

Figure 4 Diogo Homem, detail of the Manicongo, the ruler of the Congo, from the Queen Mary Atlas, 1558, British Library, Cotton MSS Additional MS 5415A, fo. 114r. Photograph: The British Library Board.

priorities of humanists who set greater store on texts that contained information about Ethiopia by classical authors such as Ptolemy and Strabo than contemporary, eye-witness reports by merchants or travellers, or flesh and blood Ethiopians. Francesco Sforza, the bibliophile ruler of Milan in the mid-fifteenth century, was taken in by a false ambassador, and in classic Renaissance manuscript-hunting fashion wrote a letter to Prester John in 1459 asking if he had a copy of the text of Solomon's works which he longed to read and own.[62] The church in Ethiopia claimed a connection with biblical Israel through the queen of Sheba (an Ethiopian), and for a Renaissance Italian the prospect of locating lost manuscripts of Solomon's writings in Ethiopia would have been very beguiling.

The Prester John myth also had important implications for Ethiopian ambassadors in terms of terminology, for they were consistently described in documents and texts as *indiani* or Indians, even though they were known to come from Ethiopia. Ethiopians in Italy in the fifteenth and sixteenth centuries referred to themselves as *Abissini* or Abyssinians and (of course) never as *indiani*. Perversely, following Greek usage, throughout the Italian peninsula during the Renaissance the Italian and Latin words for Ethiopia and Ethiopian were used as generic terms for sub-Saharan Africa and sub-Saharan African rather than as specific terms (and this Latin usage also occurred on occasion in Portugal, so the Congolese in Lisbon are sometimes described as Ethiopians).[63] However, this incorrect usage was exactly mirrored in Ethiopian texts by Ethiopians using the generic term 'Franks' for Europeans.[64] This kind of 'blanket' naming or labelling based on an adherence to misinformation or tradition survived even when the potential for correcting it was readily available. In Renaissance Rome there was a constant presence of resident Ethiopians supported by the popes, who lived in a hospice near the church of Santo Stefano degli Abissini (or dei Mori), just to the north-west of the basilica of St Peter's in the Vatican,[65] and provided a base for pilgrims from their homeland to stay while in Rome, and in Ethiopia a small colony of Italians was recorded as having been resident at the emperor's court in Barata for twenty-five years when Giovanni Battista Brocchi from Imola arrived in Ethiopia probably sometime in 1480.[66] This lazy division by Italians and Ethiopians alike of foreigners into generic Africans or generic Europeans

---

[62] Girolamo d'Adda, *Indagini storiche artistiche e bibliografiche sulla libreria Visconteo-Sforzesca del castello di Pavia* (Milan, 1875), 118.

[63] Basílio de Vasconcelos, *Itinerário do Dr. Jerónimo Münzer* (Coimbra, 1932), 54.

[64] Taddesse Tamrat, *Church and State in Ethiopia, 1270–1527* (Oxford, 1972), 267.

[65] P. Mauro de Leonessa, *Santo Stefano Maggiore degli Abissini e le relazioni romano-etiopiche* (Città del Vaticano, 1929), esp. 171–91.

[66] Renato Lefevre, 'Note sulla penetrazione europea in Etiopia', *Annali Lateranensi*, 9 (1945), 361–407 at 396–9, and Renato Lefevre, 'Giovanni Brocchi da Imola e i suoi viaggi in Etiopia', *Annali Lateranensi*, 9 (1945), 407–44 at 430.

suggests that difference in skin colour overrode any other considerations of difference in language or origins.

In the third part of the essay, four aspects of the ceremonial culture of embassies from sub-Saharan Africa to the papacy will be considered in order to see what kinds of cultural assumptions were made on both sides, and whether the European knowledge base about Africa increased because of their visits. Diplomatic ceremonies at the curia were controlled by the papal masters of ceremonies, one of whom was Paris de Grassis (in post 1504–28), who in addition to keeping a diary also penned a still unpublished treatise on ambassadors to the Roman curia.[67] Perusal of its folios makes sobering reading. By definition, good papal masters of ceremonies were nit-picking and slightly obsessive individuals with excellent memories for detail, but the irascible Paris de Grassis's expectations with regard to ceremonial rituals placed foreigners – especially non-Europeans – at such a disadvantage that it was miraculous that any of them were ever permitted to enter the presence of the pope. In this treatise Paris de Grassis included a section on 'the orators sent by Prester John to the pope', in which he described the 1481 embassy to Sixtus IV, which by chance he had observed while still a youth (much of his information came from Giovanni Battista Brocchi who had acted as interpreter).[68] The first cluster of ceremonial concerns started with the entrance and reception of ambassadors, and their procession through the streets to their appointed lodgings. Ritual 'Europeanisation' was required even before entrance, and cultural assumptions about dress were very rigid. Paris de Grassis attempted to regulate exactly how ambassadors should be dressed as they entered (even specifying the colour of the inner and outer garments, the material and the length); in order for them to be dressed correctly, ambassadors from outside Europe had to be presented with European clothes.[69] The trajectory of Bemoim's transformation in Lisbon from African prince to European ambassador and Christian knight (via the acquisition of European clothes, European servants, European accoutrements, European skills and outward European religious conformity) was typical. Most ambassadors from sub-Saharan Africa who arrived in Rome were forced through at least some of these apparently civilising hoops; nor should it be forgotten that foreigners who did not 'Europeanise' were treated as figures of fun. Even after they had arrived at the Vatican, substantial hurdles could still remain. Ambassadors and embassies were rated according to their country of origin and the title of the ruler who had sent them, so that

[67] Città del Vaticano, BAV, Vat. lat. 12270: Paris de Grassis, 'Tractate de oratoribus Romane Curie'.

[68] Città del Vaticano, BAV, Vat. lat. 12270, fo. 89v.

[69] Città del Vaticano, BAV, Vat. lat. 12270, fos. 15r–16v.

imperial ambassadors required different treatment to royal ambassadors who in turn required different treatment to ambassadors from a republic. Across the Italian peninsula and in Western Europe the pecking order of rulers was already well established by the Renaissance, but the first, crucial task for an ambassador from a non-European country was to have his ruler's position or title translated into the appropriate Latin term (so, for example, the Ethiopian ambassadors to Sixtus IV in 1481 were awarded imperial status). An early sixteenth-century note in the Vatican archives addresses precisely this issue of whether the black so-called king of the Congo should be titled emperor, king or duke.[70]

A formal audience with the pope was obviously the most crucial of all components of an embassy to the papacy, and was the moment when the stated aims of the embassy should have been most apparent. One ambassador achieved much closer contact with a pope than just a formal audience. The first indigenous Congolese ambassador ever to reach Rome was Ne-Vunda, called Antonio Emmanuele Funta in Italian sources, a close relative of the Congolese king.[71] He had set off with a train of twenty-five, including his nephew, in 1604, and arrived in 1608 with only four alive. He was very ill on arrival on 2 January, was visited by Paul V on his sick bed on the evening of 5 January, and he died later that night, on the eve of Epiphany.[72] The aptness of the date was not lost on the Roman people, who according to Giovanni Paolo Mucanzio, one of the papal masters of ceremonies, saw the parallel between Ne-Vunda's arrival from the extremities of Africa to venerate the pope and offer obedience, and the journey of the Magi.[73] Paul V deliberately played on these echoes when he ordered that a death mask be taken of Ne-Vunda to provide a basis for a sculpted bust, and that Ne-Vunda's body be buried opposite the manger scene (*presepio*) in the church of S. M. Maggiore. In fact, representation of one of the Magi as black became common in Europe only from 1450 onwards, and was never much in use in Rome (where the first black Magus only appeared in *c.* 1519),[74] but the idea was appealing. Ne-Vunda's bust was sculpted by Francesco Caporale (Figure 5), and is now positioned in the baptistery (the monuments have all moved from

[70] Città del Vaticano, AV, Arm. XL, t. 50, n. 110: 'Sopra la cosa del re negro qual chiamano re de Congro ad me pare che purché se restrenga ad Congro se possi chiamare imperatore, re et duca secondo informi la parte.'

[71] See Fabio Colonna di Stigliano, 'Il monumento del negro in Santa Maria Maggiore e l'ambasciata congolese a Roma del 1608', *Roma*, 3 (1925), 109–21 and 154–69, and '*Cose dell'altro mondo*'. *L'ambasceria di Antonio Emanuele, Principe di N'Funta, detto 'il Negrita' (1604–1608) nella Roma di Paolo V*, ed. Luis Martínez Ferrer and Marco Nocca (Città del Vaticano, 2003).

[72] His progress can be followed in the *avvisi* in Città del Vaticano, BAV, Urb. Lat. 1076, part I.

[73] Città del Vaticano, AV, Fondo Borghese, serie I, 721, fo. 192r.

[74] Kaplan, *The Rise of the Black Magus*, 103 and 118.

Figure 5 Francesco Caporale, bust of Ne-Vunda, the Congolese ambassador to the papacy, porphyry, 1629, Santa Maria Maggiore, Rome. Photograph: The University of London.

Figure 6 Medal depicting Ne-Vunda's reception by Paul V, 1608. Photograph: The University of London.

their original positions). He is dressed in a Roman toga, but he also carries a quiver of arrows on his back (records reveal that in fact he was dressed in 'Spanish' fashion), a strange conjunction of the classical and the primitive. At this moment, Ne-Vunda was being used to project a very particular representation of Africa. Even though he had been seen in Rome, and the sculpture incorporated the features of his death mask, the Africa he 'represented' was still an imaginary and incorrect classical and biblical Africa rather than a real and authentic contemporary Africa. Ne-Vunda's visit was also celebrated in a medal of him having an audience with Paul V (Figure 6), an audience that never took place in that form. Renaissance popes from the early fifteenth century onwards had chosen to portray themselves and important events in their reigns in medals, so it is interesting that Ne-Vunda's papal audience had been chosen as significant. Roman news-gatherers on Ne-Vunda's arrival also noted with amusement that he only had 'seashells for money'[75] – the general purpose monies in the Congo were indeed certain shells[76] – but that the pope would pay for everything he needed.

The third matter of crucial importance for the reception of an embassy was that appropriate gifts were brought, for gifts too signified very clearly a country's position in the diplomatic league table. A rare glimpse of gift exchange from an Ethiopian perspective is afforded by an Ethiopian text originally written in the sixteenth century entitled *Homily on the Wood of the True Cross* that describes the presents given by Venice to the Ethiopian ambassadors in 1402.[77] Several of these presents seem to reappear as gifts in other contexts at other times, so it is well worth tracing their story in outline. According to the Ethiopian text, during the reign of the emperor Dāwit I (1382–1413), two European merchants arrived at the Ethiopian court. The emperor asked what had happened to the True Cross found by Helena in the time of Constantine, and was told that 'the European kings had divided it up amongst themselves in little pieces', he subsequently sent ambassadors to Europe to acquire a piece of the Cross. When they arrived in Venice, the doge arranged for a piece to be sent via Alexandria to Ethiopia, along with other relics and presents. In 1509 the empress Eleni of Ethiopia sent an Armenian ambassador to the king of Portugal who carried as a gift 'a cross made from the same wood on which Our Lord was crucified in Jerusalem, and of which a portion was sent to us'. In her accompanying letter she described how the wood had been separated in two pieces, one of which was sent and one of which was kept.[78] It seems likely that a smaller section of this second piece (in conjunction with a gold cross) was sent by the Ethiopian emperor Dāwit II with his ambassadors Francisco Álvarez and Şaga za Ab who left in 1527 for Rome via Portugal. And in January 1533 in Bologna this gold cross was finally presented by Álvarez to Pope Clement VII in a public consistory, and presumably the piece of the True Cross was with it.[79] So this relic[80] would have travelled from Venice to Ethiopia to Portugal and back to Rome in the space of 130 years in a highly ritualised sequence of circular gift-giving. What does

[75] Città del Vaticano, BAV, Urb. Lat. 1076, part I, fo. 6r.

[76] John Thornton, 'Early Kongo Portuguese Relations: A New Interpretation', *History in Africa*, 8 (1981), 183–204 at 187.

[77] Osvaldo Raineri, 'I doni della Serenissima al re Davide I d'Etiopia (MS Raineri 43 della Vaticana)', *Orientalia christiana periodica*, 65 (1999), 363–448.

[78] Sergew Hable-Selassie, 'The Ge'ez Letters of Queen Eleni and Libne Dingil to John, King of Portugal', in *IV Congresso internazionale di studi etiopici* (2 vols., Rome, 1974), I, 547–66 at 554 and 557.

[79] Renato Lefevre, 'L'ambasceria di David Re d'Etiopia a Clemente VII (1533)', *Accademie e biblioteche d'Italia*, 34 (1966), 230–48 and 324–38 at 236–9.

[80] Cf. Tamrat, *Church and State*, 267.

this signify? It has been suggested that unwanted diplomatic gifts given to Florence or Venice were sold at auction after the relevant embassy left town, and even that visiting princes or ambassadors sold the gifts they had been given back to the city shortly after the ritual had taken place.[81] But here the opposite has taken place – a truly revered gift has later been given away in order to claim parity of status through gift-giving.

Three other gifts from the 1402 embassy are worthy of mention. The first was liturgical – a silver chalice with effigies of the twelve apostles, inscribed with the words of the mass – which was almost certainly later given to Francisco Álvarez by Dāwit II in November 1520 as a personal present.[82] The second represented the new technology of Europe – a mechanical clock that struck the hour 'without benefit of human hand', described in minute detail in the Ethiopian text;[83] clocks such as this had been made in Italy since the first half of the fourteenth century. The third is an oddity, for Venice sent to the emperor of Ethiopia, the ruler of a country with diverse climactic and geographical regions, but more noted for its droughts than its summertime tropical monsoons (which are also typical), gifts of clothes to wear 'when it rained'.[84]

The fourth part of ambassadorial visits to Rome was concerned with formal access to religious sights and artefacts. Veneration of relics was an integral part of a visit to Rome, and ambassadors and envoys from sub-Saharan Africa were given exceptional access, possibly in an attempt to induce awe. In October 1441 Eugenius IV wrote a letter from Florence to the canons and chapter of the basilica of St Peter in Rome, asking them to show the Veronica (the piece of cloth believed to be imprinted with Christ's face) to Andrea the abbot of Eygpt, and Pietro the deacon of Ethiopia, who had attended the Council of Florence. Although he was muddled about their positions (he called them both ambassadors of the emperor Constantine of Ethiopia known as Prester John) and about the aim of their missions (he claimed to think that they had both come to ask for union with the Western church), Eugenius's reasons for wanting them to be given this exceptional access were clear – he wanted them to be 'edified', and he wanted by granting this papal sign of great favour to further incline them in the direction of unity.[85] The Veronica was normally displayed only on certain set occasions such as the Sunday following Epiphany, Easter Sunday and Ascension Day. The 1441 visitors were also shown many other relics, such as the heads of the apostles Peter and Paul,

[81] Richard Trexler, *Public Life in Renaissance Florence* (New York, 1980), 325.
[82] Alvares, *The Prester John*, I, 298 (ch. 81), and see Marilyn E. Heldman, 'A Chalice from Venice for Emperor Dāwit of Ethiopia', *Bulletin of the School of Oiental and African Studies*, 53, 3 (1990), 442–5 at 443–4.
[83] Raineri, 'I doni', 373.
[84] *Ibid.*, 372.
[85] Città del Vaticano, AV, Reg. Vat. 360, fo. 120v.

and the head of St John in S. Giovanni in Laterano.[86] By chance, the Ethiopian ambassadors in Rome in 1450 were not only fortunate enough to visit during a Jubilee year but were treated to the spectacle of the canonisation on 24 May of the great Franciscan preacher, San Bernardino of Siena, by Nicholas V in St Peter's. Their presence was remarked upon by another preacher, Giacomo della Marca, who was sitting near to them.[87] So it appears that while African knowledge of Europe may have increased as a result of these embassies, European knowledge of Africa remained unsatisfactorily mired in traditional preconceptions and misunderstandings.

The question of who acted as interpreters or translators for these embassies is a crucial one, especially in the context of navigating cultural difference and furthering the circulation of knowledge and understanding of sub-Saharan Africa in Europe. Access to the necessary knowledge (whether of language or etiquette) was essential if everything were not to be 'garbled' in translation'. If a European who could translate into Latin or the relevant vernacular were available or indeed were to lead the mission, there was no problem. Occasional glimpses of how translation was managed spatially can occasionally be found. Paris de Grassis records that whenever Sixtus IV was in church during the stay of the Ethiopian ambassadors in 1481, the head of the embassy, Antonio, stood on the pope's right and Giovanni Battista Brocchi stood on the pope's left, translating for him – which means that translation took place across the person of the pope.[88] The presence in Rome of the small Ethiopian community and Ethiopian hospice at S. Stefano should have ensured availability of interpreters in Rome itself, but the reputation of the community was not always high, so trustworthy Ethiopians who could interpret into Italian and Latin were at a premium. But how did interpreting square with the fact that 'eloquence . . . was the hallmark of the ambassador'?[89]

European ambassadors may have been preferred on occasion to indigenous ambassadors in Ethiopia and the Congo not only because they could speak the requisite languages, but also because they understood the rules governing the writing of formal letters and knew how to write to popes and kings. Francisco Álvarez in his book on the Portuguese embassy to Ethiopia describes in extraordinary detail the genesis of the two letters sent by Dāwit II to Clement VII which were eventually (after over eight years in transit) read to the pope in a consistory in Bologna in 1533. In 1524

---

[86] Città del Vaticano, BAV, Vat. lat. 6823, fo. 64v, and Città del Vaticano, Vat. lat. 5255, fo. 155v.

[87] Dionisio Pacetti, 'Le prediche autografe di S. Giacomo della Marca (1393–1476) con un saggio delle medesime', *Archivium franciscanum historicum*, 35 (1942), 296–317, and 36 (1943), 75–97 at 94–5.

[88] Città del Vaticano, BAV, Vat. lat. 12270, fo. 90v; Lefevre, 'Cronaca inedita', 367.

[89] Mallett, 'Ambassadors and their Audiences', 235.

Dāwit said he wished to write to the pope of Rome, and asked for help, and Álvarez agreed. The content of the letter was relayed orally from the emperor to his chief chaplain to 'the monk who is going to Portugal as ambassador' (that is, Sagazabo) and finally to Álvarez. Álvarez wrote his letter, and the process was reversed as it was translated into Ge'ez and sent back to Dāwit, who was very pleased 'and amazed because it had not been taken out of books'. Dāwit ordered his learned priests to study in their books and search for what more could be put into a letter, and a separate one was constructed by them.[90]

Not only did these two letters reach their destination but the process whereby they were then translated back into Portuguese, then Latin and finally Italian is known, and they were preserved by being printed almost immediately – March 1533 – in a small pamphlet by Jacob Keymol from Flanders.[91] It was at this 1533 reception of the Ethiopian ambassadors from Portugal and Ethiopia by Clement VII that the Italian humanist Paolo Giovio[92] obtained, in addition to the material for the digression on Ethiopia that he included in his *Histories of his Time* (other material came from the head of the Ethiopian community of S. Stefano), a copy of a portrait of the Ethiopian emperor Dāwit II,[93] also known by his baptismal name as Atanadi Dengel,[94] or Lebna Dengel ('incense of the Virgin').[95] Giovio penned a textual description of the emperor in his work, adverting to the skin colour of his face ('like that of a quince roasted over ashes', in a typically Italian reference to food) and to his plainly 'not curly hair in the manner of black Africans',[96] and the two combined fixed the 'authentic' image of the physiognomy of the ruler of Ethiopia for Italians.

The two letters from Dāwit II to Clement VII are very revealing. Dāwit states that he is sending ambassadors to Rome to 'kiss the foot of the pope' 'as the other Christian princes, to whom I am inferior neither in power

---

[90] Alvares, *The Prester John*, II, 417–18 (ch. 115).

[91] See Città del Vaticano, AV, Arm. XLI, t. 1, n. 129, where Clement VII grants Keymolen the privilege of printing these letters.

[92] Paolo Giovio was also responsible for the translation of the Ethiopian letters from Latin into Italian. See Renato Lefevre, 'Divagazioni di poeti e di eruditi sul regno di prete Gianni', *Annali Lateranensi*, 8 (1944), 55–89 at 69.

[93] Lefevre, 'Divagazioni', 78.

[94] This name is inscribed on a late sixteenth-century miniature in the Kunsthistorisches Museum in Vienna, which is a copy after the painting from the Giovio collection in the Uffizi in Florence.

[95] His baptismal name was Lebna Dengel and his thronal name was Wānag Sagād, 'revered by lions'. See Jeremy Lawrance, 'The Middle Indies: Damião de Góis on Prester John and the Ethiopians', *Renaissance Studies*, 6, 3–4 (1992), 306–24 at 307.

[96] *Paoli Iovii Novocomensis Episcopi Nucerini historiarum sui temporis* (Basel, 1567), 866: 'rotundo ore mali cotonei sub cinere tosti colorem exprimente' . . . 'capillo non plane more Aethiopum intorto'.

nor in religion, are accustomed to do'.[97] This phrase protesting equality is repeated later in the letter, and one wonders whether this sense of inferiority was genuinely Dāwit's or whether it was a layer of concern inserted by Álvarez. Dāwit also referred to letters from Eugenius IV in his possession, and made clear his religious beliefs (almost his religious credentials) in order to convince the pope that he was a 'true' Christian. A fundamental part of Ethiopian and Congolese 'representation' of self concerned their Christianity, and Ethiopian and Congolese ambassadors and envoys were consistently charged with protesting this to suspicious kings and popes. The second letter, written by Dāwit's own team of scholars, adopted a very different tone. 'Why', he asked the pope reproachfully, 'have you not sent any messenger to us so that you could ascertain with more certainty how we were living and how we were faring, as you are the shepherd and I am your sheep?'[98] At another point Dāwit bemoaned his exclusion from the circle of Christian kings, complaining that Portugal used to send legates and ambassadors, but no longer did so, nor did any other Christian king, and adverting once again to letters from Eugenius IV, and even to a 'book' of Eugenius which he owned. The final section of the letter is the most poignant: he told the pope that he was surrounded by Muslims, and asked why the Christian countries did not stick together, as the Muslims did, enjoying great fraternal peace, but instead indulged in injurious controversies and refused to help each other.[99] This outsider's view of the Reformation from a sub-Saharan African Christian ruler is startling for its global perspective on what is usually considered a European problem, just as Dāwit's criticisms of the pope's lack of proper consideration of him as a Christian prince force a reassessment of assumptions about the relationship between the two positions. Multiple translations (and transformations) cannot blunt the import of the message.

The Álvarez story is exceptional in its detail, but several letters in Portuguese (some displaying creole 'grammatical irregularities')[100] from D. Afonso, king of the Congo, to popes and Portuguese kings survive, written by Afonso's Congolese secretary, João Teixeira.[101] These too manage to communicate their important messages, even if they did not always abide by European grammatical rules. But both

---

[97] L'ambasciaria di David Re dell'Etiopia al Santissimo S. N. Clemente Papa VII insieme con la obbedienza al prefato Santissimo S. N. resa (Bologna, 1533), sigs. civ and ciir.

[98] Ibid., sig. ciiir.

[99] Ibid., sig. dir.

[100] Creoles typically draw all their vocabulary from one language but have a grammatical structure that is atypical.

[101] See, e.g., Monumenta missionaria Africana, ed. Brásio, II, 38–40, and John Thornton, Africa and Africans in the Making of the Atlantic World, 1400–1800, 2nd edn (Cambridge, 1998), 213–14.

processes – multiple translation and composition by a non-native speaker – were unsatisfactory, because the nuances of meanings became blunted or because incorrect grammar allowed Europeans to adopt a position of superiority, as African letters also 'represented' Africa.

'Representing' a real, contemporary Africa in Renaissance Italy and Portugal was a complicated business. Not only were classical, biblical and medieval versions of Africa still alive and kicking, but also encounters between African ambassadors and Renaissance European rulers were shaped by global forces, national, royal and papal conventions and traditions, different belief systems, individual personalities and strongly held cultural assumptions. These could be as benign as misunderstandings about the existence of texts by Solomon, as disingenuous as the insistence that ambassadors in Europe must wear European clothes or as insidiously damaging as notions about relationships of superiority and inferiority. The very existence of ape and zebra skins and the thought of using shells as a form of money induced laughter in Renaissance Italians, yet time and again sub-Saharan Africans cut through the thickets of rhetoric surrounding European actions and showed themselves to be extremely astute commentators on the European scene ('the European kings had divided up the True Cross amongst themselves in little pieces'; why did the Christian countries indulge in injurious controversies when they should have been presenting a united front against the Muslim threat?). The advent of Portuguese imperialism and a globalised Christianity to some extent increased European and African knowledge of each other's worlds and of the connections between them, in part through the exchange of embassies and ambassadors, but it also exposed the raw edges of transcontinental cultural assumptions and cultural differences, which these Renaissance encounters did little to heal. African ambassadors, like African gifts, African Christianity, African letter-writing, African dress and African currencies, were commandeered in Renaissance Europe to 'represent' not just their own rulers or their own countries but a whole continent of the European imagination.

Transactions of the RHS 17 (2007), pp. 129–56 © 2007 Royal Historical Society
doi:10.1017/S0080440107000564 Printed in the United Kingdom

HOW SCIENTIFIC CONVERSATION BECAME SHOP TALK*

By James A. Secord

READ 26 JANUARY 2006

ABSTRACT. The expansion of print and the rise of specialist disciplines from the early nineteenth century are usually associated with a decline in informed conversation about the sciences and other forms of learning among the aristocracy, gentry and professional classes. Yet an extensive body of evidence suggests that the sciences remained a vital part of conversational culture in England at least through the 1860s. Ultimately, however, discussing specialist knowledge at parties became condemned as 'talking shop'. This was not so much the result of changes within science, as is usually assumed, but was instead a byproduct of the increasing differentiation of roles throughout society. By the early twentieth century, scientific practitioners had created new places for broad-ranging talk about their subjects, most characteristically in the tea rooms attached to university laboratories.

With the English, conversation is a languid silence broken by occasional monosyllables, and by the water flowing every quarter of an hour from the tea urn.

E. Jouy, 'Conversation', in *Encyclopédie Moderne*, ed. M. Courtin (Paris, 1823–32)[1]

Writing about talking is a paradoxical activity. The apotheosis of print in the nineteenth century has led other forms of communication to seem feeble and ephemeral. This is especially true in science, where print has dominated ideas of what it means to make a contribution to knowledge. Historians have assumed that scientific talk is ornamental and supplementary, mattering only on the way to producing a published result, or as nothing more than a remnant of a fading oral culture. 'Words are but wind', as one etiquette manual noted in 1861, 'and when spoken leave no mark behind.'[2]

---

* An extended version of this essay is published in *Science in the Marketplace: Nineteenth-Century Sites and Experiences*, ed. Aileen Fyfe and Bernard Lightman (Chicago, 2007), ch. 2. I am grateful for comments from Patricia Fara, Aileen Fyfe, Jan Golinski, Ludmilla Jordanova, Larry Klein, Bernie Lightman, Margaret Meredith, Don Opitz, Simon Schaffer, Anne Secord and Paul White.

[1] Translated in Orlando Sabertash [John Mitchell], *The Art of Conversation, with Remarks on Fashion and Address* (1842), 67.
[2] Anon., *Etiquette for Ladies* [1861], 44.

Oral performance, however, has been and remains at the heart of the making of knowledge. Although little has been written on the nineteenth century, scientific talk has been extensively examined in other settings. One body of literature is focused on the salon culture of Paris, London and other European cities of the eighteenth century, when leading figures came together in salons and coffee houses for discussions of natural philosophy along with literature, politics and the arts.[3] The other is the scientific laboratory of the twentieth century. Beginning in the 1970s, anthropologists and sociologists recorded the discourse of technicians, experimenters and others as part of a process of understanding contemporary science in the making.[4]

By comparison the nineteenth century has been an uneasy borderland. This failure to understand scientific talk in this period is in large part because so many studies have depicted it in terms of decline from the supposedly golden age of conversation in the eighteenth century. On the positive side, this stress on polite civility, coffee houses and salons has enabled historians of Enlightenment natural philosophy to recover the intellectual life of an era that had been dismissed as an awkward pause between the scientific and industrial revolutions. Yet an idealised image of the eighteenth century as a conversational golden age is far from unproblematic.[5] Most significantly, the political implications of enlightened conversation have typically been understood in terms of social theorist Jürgen Habermas's concept of a bourgeois public sphere, arising in the late seventeenth and eighteenth centuries, and based on rational discussion between private individuals in a social realm free of state control. On this conception, the nineteenth century appears as a period of fragmentation and commodification, when the public sphere was transformed under the pressures of the emerging industrialised mass media. Habermas aimed to use history to sketch an ideal type of rational public discourse, and his account is thus primarily a social critique rather than a history.[6] Although Habermas's views have been decisively

3 P. Fara, *Pandora's Breeches: Women, Science and Power in the Enlightenment* (2004); G. V. Sutton, *Science for a Polite Society: Gender, Culture, and the Demonstration of Enlightenment* (Boulder, CO, 1995); M. Terrall, 'Salon, Academy, and Boudoir: Generation and Desire in Maupertuis's Science of Life', *Isis*, 87 (1996), 217–29; A. N. Walters, 'Conversation Pieces: Science and Politeness in Eighteenth-Century England', *History of Science*, 35 (1997), 121–54.

4 H. Collins, *Gravity's Shadow: The Search for Gravitational Waves* (Chicago, 2004); B. Latour and S. Woolgar, *Laboratory Life: The Social Construction of Scientific Facts* (Beverley Hills, 1979); M. Lynch, *Art and Artifact in Laboratory Science: A Study of Shop Work and Shop Talk in a Research Laboratory* (1985); S. Traweek, *Beamtimes and Lifetimes: The World of High Energy Physicists* (Cambridge, MA, 1988).

5 B. Cowan *The Social Life of Coffee* (New Haven, 2005).

6 J. Habermas, *The Structural Transformation of the Public Sphere: An Inquiry into a Category of Bourgeois Society*, trans. T. Berger (Cambridge, MA, 1989 [1962]); C. Calhoun, *Habermas and the Public Sphere* (Cambridge, MA, 1992).

criticised, eighteenth-century conversation continues to hold a revered place in our own culture, in large part as a nostalgic reaction against the forces of modernity and technological progress.[7]

My aim, in contrast, is to put conversation back at the centre of our historical understanding of science in the nineteenth century. Rather than charting the transformation of an Enlightenment ideal, I will look at the ways in which scientific talk was managed and how this changed. Science is of particular significance in this context, as it has been hailed on one hand as a model for unconstrained rational discussion, and on the other lamented as a force for specialisation leading to the fragmentation of public intellectual life. In tackling the issues, I will deal with a variety of different settings for talk, from papers delivered at scientific meetings to the rituals of courtship. My focus will be on informal conversation in the clubs, salons and soirées of the English social elite. This was a world characterised by the few hundred elite families that constituted 'Society' and dominated the annual Season. Among these circles, conversation – defined as the unplanned, easy talk of the well bred – was central to sociability.[8] Conversation, as I will suggest, remained central to science, although what could be said to whom, and under what circumstances, was transformed. The conventions of late Georgian and early Victorian science gave way in the final decades of the nineteenth century to a situation in which expertise played very different roles.

The story sketched in this essay is built upon a reassessment of what has usually been labelled 'gentlemanly science', a phrase that can better be rendered as 'polite science'. The term 'polite science' makes sense for reasons of gender, as many practitioners were women;[9] but more fundamentally it brings out the significance of broader ideals of civil society and social deference that underpinned the pursuit of knowledge in England throughout much of the nineteenth century. The ethos, etiquette and attitudes of those engaged in scientific pursuits have been closely studied for the late seventeenth and eighteenth centuries, but far less thoroughly for the nineteenth. Historians of Victorian science have devoted a great deal of attention to gentlemen since the path-breaking work of Jack Morrell and Arnold Thackray, but only more recently have they begun to analyse the practices of gentility.[10] In

[7] S. Miller, *Conversation: A History of a Declining Art* (New Haven, 2006).

[8] L. E. Klein, *Shaftesbury and the Culture of Politeness: Moral Discourse and Cultural Politics in Early Eighteenth-Century England* (Cambridge, 1994), 3–14.

[9] A. B. Shteir, *Cultivating Women, Cultivating Science: Flora's Daughters and Botany in England, 1760–1860* (Baltimore, 1996).

[10] J. B. Morrell and A. Thackray, *Gentlemen of Science: Early Years of the British Association for the Advancement of Science* (Oxford, 1981). Recent discussions include F. Green Musselman, *Nervous Conditions: Science and the Body Politic in Early Industrial Britain* (Albany, NY, 2006); P. White, *Thomas Huxley: Making the 'Man of Science'* (Cambridge, 2003); A. Winter, *Mesmerized: Powers*

consequence, the continuing significance of polite sociability for the aims and practice of science has often been minimised, with gentlemanly status simply reinforcing the dominance of a relatively modern-looking core of experts.[11] This too easily leads to a division between 'specialist' and 'popular' science that is inappropriate to understanding a period when people differing in gender, rank and depth of expertise not only talked about science but in doing so contributed directly to its making.

Talking and publishing

To understand polite science and the significance of conversation within it, we need to begin by examining the broader relationship between oral performance and publishing.[12] It is still too often assumed that the publication patterns of science took on a quintessentially modern form with the foundation of the Royal Society's *Philosophical Transactions* in the 1660s as a means for exchanging information among those engaged in the pursuit of natural knowledge.[13] Yet throughout the eighteenth and the first half of the nineteenth century, the routes to making public a novel finding were as many and diverse as the range of practitioners engaged in natural philosophy and natural history. Take a list of what became identified as major discoveries and see where they were first announced. Some were made public in lectures or demonstrations of new instruments, others in letters to friends or for publication in the *Gentleman's Magazine* and in newspapers, some in books of travel or philosophy.[14] Still others were shared among a small circle of friends and patrons, as with the botanist Robert Brown's work on particulate motion or the canal surveyor William Smith's findings about the role of fossils in determining the order of strata.

---

of Mind in Victorian Britain (Chicago, 1998); and R. Barton, '"Men of Science": Language, Identity and Professionalization in the Mid-Victorian Scientific Community', *History of Science*, 41 (2003), 73–119.

[11] M. Rudwick, *The Great Devonian Controversy: The Shaping of Scientific Knowledge among Gentlemanly Specialists* (Chicago, 1985), 15–16.

[12] For a geographical perspective on this issue, see D. Livingstone, 'Text, Talk and Testimony: Geographical Reflections on Scientific Habits: An Afterword', *British Journal for the History of Science*, 30 (2005), 93–100, at 96–7.

[13] Charles Bazerman's pioneering study, *Shaping Written Knowledge: The Genre and Activity of the Experimental Article in Science* (Madison, 1988), thus leapt from the seventeenth to the twentieth century. Bazerman has gone some way to examine the intervening period in *The Language of Edison's Light* (Cambridge, MA, 1999), as have A. G. Gross, J. E. Harmon and M. Reidy in *Communicating Science: The Scientific Article from the 17th Century to the Present* (Oxford, 2002). A. Johns, 'Miscellaneous Methods: Authors, Societies and Journals in Early Modern England', *British Journal for the History of Science*, 33 (2000), 159–86, offers a more realistic view of the *Philosophical Transactions*.

[14] J. Golinski, *Science as Public Culture: Chemistry and Enlightenment in Britain, 1760–1820* (Cambridge, 1992); S. Schaffer, 'Scientific Discoveries and the End of Natural Philosophy', *Social Studies of Science*, 16 (1986), 387–420.

These publication patterns were part of a shared culture involving a wide variety of practitioners, from learned theologians and genteel women to quarry workers and skilled artisans.[15] The networks which brought these groups together were founded on prevailing ideals of a hierarchical order of gender, rank and status. Novelty was not identified with discovery events announced in scientific papers, a genre which became defined only during the later nineteenth century, but depended instead on a broad spectrum of communication. Contributions ranged from newly observed nebulae and rare mosses, to philosophical and theological frameworks for understanding nature. The work of science passed between various domestic settings and public meeting rooms, taverns and theatres. Collecting, travelling, experimenting and observing were important activities, but they were always valued in a system grounded in heredity and hierarchy.

Presentation in print was only one moment, and not necessarily the most significant, in the broader process of the making of a matter of fact within polite science. If we look at the groups central to the ideals of natural philosophy and natural history in this period, notably the aristocracy, high gentry and traditional professions, we find that knowledge was communicated primarily though the spoken word. Certain knowledge was intimate knowledge, grounded in private conversation, discussions at meetings and lectures by celebrated men. At Oxford and Cambridge the professors of science of the eighteenth century published little: enlightened university life was about local reputation and high table conversation – not about rushing into print or joining the world of commerce. Those who did publish extensively, such as Newton's successor William Whiston, were often on the margins of university life; after a series of theological scandals, he moved to London and made a living through his books and lectures. Publishing was only one part of the broad spectrum of ways to establish a position as a possessor of knowledge.

In medicine, too, physicians gained reputation not so much by publishing technical works on spa waters or the classification of diseases; but primarily through performance at the bedside, with skill in medical consultations demonstrating true mastery. Physicians needed Latin learning and traditional medical knowledge as signs of gentility: to focus too single-mindedly on publication could harm a practice, by highlighting those aspects of medicine that made it a less desirable career than other professions such as the law, the clergy and the military.[16] To stress new

[15] D. Miller, 'The Revival of the Physical Sciences in Britain, 1815–1840', *Osiris*, second series, 2 (1986), 107–34; A. Secord, 'Corresponding Interests: Artisans and Gentlemen in Nineteenth-Century Natural History', *British Journal for the History of Science*, 27 (1994), 383–408; Shteir, *Cultivating Women*.

[16] N. Jewson, 'Medical Knowledge and the Patronage System in Eighteenth-Century England', *Sociology*, 10 (1974), 369–85.

science-based research of the kind carried out in France, as Thomas Wakley did in founding the *Lancet* in 1823, was a new and radical idea.[17]

In an intellectual culture in which oral performance held such high status, one could reach the pinnacle of scientific success with virtually no publications at all. The most notable case is that of the naturalist Sir Joseph Banks. President of the Royal Society and leader of British science for several decades, Banks published almost nothing. The flora from his Pacific travels was never issued (it was too expensive even for the tiny audience who traditionally would have underwritten such works), nor did he publish a book on his Icelandic travels or his researches into plants. Instead, his reputation was founded on his collections and library, his experience as a traveller and his status as a gentleman. He maintained his position not through publishing, but through personal contacts and correspondence. Banks and his sister Sarah Sophia welcomed numerous visitors to his great house on Soho Square, and his vast library, which held his books and collections, became a place to meet, eat and talk for those with natural history interests.[18] Conversation was central to this way of doing science.

From this perspective, the mathematician Charles Babbage's notorious polemical *Reflections on the Decline of Science in Britain* (1830) missed the point in decrying the large number of Fellows of the Royal Society who had not published a paper in its *Transactions*. Publishing in this way was a sign of merit, but by no means the only one. Status could derive from the possession of a fine collection of mineral specimens or dried plant specimens; a position as a patron of science; or through extensive reading and travels.

The foundation of specialist societies in London, starting with the Geological Society of London in 1807, is often taken as marking a fundamental shift in the pursuit of science, and a challenge to what David Miller has called 'the Banksian learned empire'.[19] Although there was real conflict, it is important to recognise just how much those advocating a new order shared with their opponents. Although publication was given a higher priority, it remained embedded within a gentlemanly culture that placed a high value on face-to-face contact. Most of the new specialist societies grew out of informal meetings of enthusiasts in taverns and the premises of publishers. Their rooms were located in London's West End, near the leading metropolitan clubs. The most radically innovative of the

[17] A. Desmond, *The Politics of Evolution: Morphology, Medicine and Reform in Radical London* (Chicago, 1989).
[18] J. Gascoigne, *Joseph Banks and the English Enlightenment: Useful Knowledge and Polite Culture* (Cambridge: 1994).
[19] D. Miller, 'Between Hostile Camps: Sir Humphry Davy's Presidency of the Royal Society of London, 1820–1827', *British Journal for the History of Science*, 16 (1983), 1–47.

new groups, the Geological Society of London, had been founded as a 'little talking Geological Dinner Club', and although it soon expanded its aims, the subject as a whole remained focused on verbal discussion and conversational contact.[20] Its first president, George Bellas Greenough, published only one short book and devoted most of his life to compiling maps and organising his impressive personal collection. Like-minded gentlemen could meet in the Society's rooms at Somerset House on the Thames; membership was expensive and women, as in other clubs, were not allowed. Or the members could visit, often with wives and sisters, Greenough's mansion in Regent's Park, which was purpose-built by the architect Decimus Burton for natural history research. These were the places where visiting foreigners really learned about what was going on in geology. Scientific practitioners inhabited a familiar landscape of upper-class metropolitan intellectual life, embedded in the regular calendar of Society and the Season. Annual charts, widely distributed and displayed, showed the main schedule of scientific meetings running from November through June.[21] This was when professional men were in town and when most books were published. Once parliament opened in the new year, the town experienced its largest influx of aristocrats and people of fashion: this was when most private parties were given, when the opera was in season, and when tailors and dressmakers were at their busiest.[22]

Of course, societies such as the Geological, Astronomical and Linnean viewed publishing papers read at their meetings as one of their chief aims. But it is significant that until the 1840s quarto transactions were the main forum for publication – a luxurious format with fine paper, wide margins, good spacing between the lines, and a stately publication schedule.[23] These were works fit for a gentleman's library. To supplement these, most of the societies also issued proceedings, which recorded the basic contents of the papers read at each meeting. Their purpose, however, was as much to tell those who had not been at the meetings what they had missed as it was to communicate findings within the wider European community

[20] M. Rudwick, 'The Foundation of the Geological Society of London: Its Scheme for Cooperative Research and its Struggle for Independence', *British Journal for the History of Science*, 1 (1963), 325–55, at 328.

[21] W. J. Brock and A. J. Meadows, *The Lamp of Learning: Two Centuries of Publishing at Taylor & Francis* (1998), 46–7.

[22] The best discussion I have found on the timing of the Season for the early period is the discussion of Mayfair in 'The Social Character of the Estate: The London Season in 1841', in *Survey of London: Volume 39: The Grosvenor Estate in Mayfair, Part I (General History)* (1971), 89–93; for the later nineteenth century, see L. Davidoff, *The Best Circles: Society, Etiquette and the Season* (1986 [1973]).

[23] M. Rudwick, 'Historical Origins of the Geological Society's *Journal*', in *Milestones in Geology: Reviews to Celebrate 150 Volumes of the Journal of the Geological Society*, ed. M. J. Le Bas (1995), 5–8.

of learned specialists.[24] Priority was not defined as being primarily a matter of publication until the middle decades of the century. That was when discoveries such the planet Neptune and the composition of water emerged as subjects of fierce partisan rivalry.[25] The stress on publication was accompanied by the rise of new, heroic ideas of authorship, with discovery attributed to individual men of science whose celebrity was marked by their appearances in print.

Many aspects of the relation between publication, oral performance and scientific practice usually thought to be characteristic of the eighteenth century thus remained in place for much longer than is often assumed. Notably, the verbal presentation of a paper – even when not accompanied by immediate discussion – remained central to the presentation of new scientific work. Right through the 1840s, the great moment for any paper at the Geological Society was not when it appeared in print, but when it was read and debated at one of the meetings.[26] On his return from the *Beagle* voyage, Charles Darwin was struck by the way in which publishing in geology seemed secondary to verbal performance. 'Geology is at present very oral', he told a friend in 1846, '& what I here say is to a great extent quite true.'[27]

Even the publication patterns of Charles Babbage, the astronomer John Herschel, the geologist Adam Sedgwick and other scientific reformers bear this out. Within the metropolitan setting for intellectual life, they were seen as 'great men', characters of exceptional ability and talent. Their characteristic writings were not articles in specialist journals, although they wrote many of these; instead, they were known for encyclopaedia essays, observational records, reflective treatises and speeches at the Royal Institution of London (f. 1799) and the British Association for the Advancement of Science (f. 1831), which rapidly emerged as key sites for oral performance in the new sciences. Contemporaries saw such men as possessing genius or talent not so much through publications, but through their persons. Their position was signalled by their status as 'lions', whose presence could give intellectual depth and sparkle to a social gathering.[28] Conversability was one of the key attributes of the gentleman.

The more formal, institutional platforms for oral scientific performance tended to be reserved for men, although women engaged fully in certain

[24] Rudwick, *Devonian Controversy*.

[25] D. Miller, *Discovering Water: James Watt, Henry Cavendish and the Nineteenth-Century 'Water Controversy'* (2004).

[26] J. Thackray, *To See the Fellows Fight: Eye Witness Accounts of Meetings of the Geological Society of London and its Club, 1822–1868* (Faringdon, 2003).

[27] Darwin to J. M. Herbert, [3 Sept.? 1846], in *The Correspondence of Charles Darwin*, ed. F. Burkhardt *et al.*, III (Cambridge, 1987), 338.

[28] J. Secord, *Victorian Sensation: The Extraordinary Publication, Reception, and Secret Authorship of* Vestiges of the Natural History of Creation (Chicago, 2000), 410–16.

kinds of fieldwork, experiment and conversation. These could lead to an international reputation, especially in subjects (such as mineralogy and botany) dominated by private collections. In European natural history circles of the 1820s, Charlotte Murchison was better known as a conchologist than her husband Roderick was as a geologist.[29]

Polite science

The importance of informal associations and conversation in establishing reputation is well illustrated by the case of Mary and William Somerville after they moved to London in 1816.[30] Married in 1812, they belonged to a circle of learned couples who became central to metropolitan science. Alexander and Jane Marcet – the latter's *Conversations on Chemistry* (1806) had recently appeared – were key figures, as were other couples such as the Katers, the Murchisons and the Youngs. Mary Somerville was a self-taught mathematician, who had been encouraged as a young woman in Edinburgh partly through the networks of military practitioners during the wars with Napoleonic France. Her second husband, William Somerville, was an experienced traveller who had served as an army physician in North America and in South Africa.

For the Somervilles, science offered a vital niche in urban society. They participated in a lively intellectual culture centred on informal gatherings that involved both men and women. They collected minerals, made observations, discussed new books and welcomed visiting foreigners. 'All kinds of scientific subjects were discussed', Mary Somerville recalled, 'experiments tried and astronomical observations made in a little garden in front of the house.'[31] When William's army position was abolished after the end of the Napoleonic Wars, he and Mary travelled to the Continent, where they could live more cheaply until a new post turned up. Here they were welcomed to similar gatherings in the best scientific circles of Paris and Geneva. The Somervilles were not aspiring amateurs, nor potential patrons (even with Mary's substantial inheritance from her first marriage, they did not have the money for that); rather, they were valued participants in an enterprise which was open to many different kinds of practitioners. The scientific activities pursued by the Somervilles after

---

[29] M. Kölbl-Ebert, 'Charlotte Murchison', in *The Dictionary of Nineteenth-Century British Scientists*, ed. B. Lightman (4 vols., Bristol, 2004), 1440–2.

[30] The first half of following section draws on my general introduction in volume I of the *Collected Works of Mary Somerville* (Bristol, 2004). For more on Mary Somerville, see K. A. Neeley, *Mary Somerville: Science, Illumination, and the Female Mind* (Cambridge, 2001); E. C. Patterson, *Mary Somerville and the Cultivation of Science, 1815–1840* (Boston, MA, 1983); and esp. C. Brock, 'The Public Worth of Mary Somerville', *British Journal for the History of Science*, 39 (2006), 255–72.

[31] M. Somerville, *Personal Recollections, from Early Life to Old Age* (1873), 130.

their return to London in 1818 grew out of this predominantly domestic milieu. In mineralogy, for example, they devoted their efforts to what all serious mineralogists considered as the science's core activity: they formed a cabinet, filled with superb specimens given by friends and purchased on their travels. Their house was filled with paintings by Mary, and with books on literature, art and science.

The Somervilles were thus at the very heart of Regency science in London. This was not simply because of their social status – they were high gentry, but not in a position to purchase either the best specimens or to employ others in scientific work. And during the 1810s and 1820s, their status was certainly not based on their reputations as original discoverers or writers. Mary Somerville had published prize-winning contributions to the *New Series of the Mathematical Repository* both before and after her marriage to William, but she did this under a pseudonym ('A Lady'). She was, rather, known for her mathematical skills by reputation. The primary significance of her pseudonymous puzzle-solutions did not derive from publication, but rather their status as marks of participation in a network of practice that ranged from working men to John Herschel and, in 1819, the thirteen-year-old John Stuart Mill.[32]

Although Mary Somerville's status as a genteel woman might seem to involve special issues when publication was at stake, this is true only in part. The case of William Somerville shows that many of the same concerns applied to both sexes. When they married, he was a seasoned traveller, a friend of the poet Sir Walter Scott, and the first European to visit parts of the Cape Colony. Using his position as a medical man, he had conducted researches on the much-debated anatomy of the female sexual organs of the Khoi-khoi, a subject that soon came to be much in the news through the exhibition of Sara Baartman, the so-called 'Hottentot Venus'.[33] He gave a paper to the Royal Society of London, which was published in the *Medico-chirurgical Transactions* in 1816, translated into Latin to limit its readership. The illustrations were too explicit to be published in this context and could only be viewed in the Royal Society's library, where the manuscript of his paper remains to this day.[34] Although this article was all that William Somerville ever published, he became a full

---

[32] These problem-solutions, which predate her first experimental paper by fifteen years, are included in the first volume of Mary Somerville's *Collected Works*.

[33] S. Qureshi, 'Displaying Sara Baartman, the "Hottentot Venus"', *History of Science*, 42 (2004), 233–57; L. Schiebinger, *Nature's Body: Gender in the Making of Modern Science* (Boston, 1993); and R. Holmes, *The Hottentot Venus: The Life and Death of Saartjie Baartman (Born 1789– Buried 2002)* (2007).

[34] W. Somerville, 'Observationes quaedam de Hottentotis', in *Medico-chirurgical Transactions*, 7 (1816), 154–60. A translation is available as 'On the Structure of Hottentot Women', in *William Somerville's Narrative of his Journeys to the Eastern Cape Frontier and to Lattakoe, 1799–1802*, ed. Frank Bradlow (Cape Town, 1979).

participant in the learned life of London and was elected a Royal Society fellow in 1817.

It was, in fact, with the aim of meeting William and gaining access to Chelsea Hospital that the opinionated American physician Charles Caldwell presented himself at the Somervilles' house in the winter of 1821–2. Like many foreign travellers, he recorded numerous customs that natives took for granted. Caldwell was especially interested in conversation, and left in the company of Somerville's wife while his host attended to his patients, Caldwell engaged her in talk. They began by discussing 'the polite literature of the day', a subject upon which she seemed completely at ease. Noticing some volumes on natural history in an opened bookcase, he found that she knew far more about mineralogy than he did. A volume of Pierre Simon Laplace's abstruse masterpiece, the *Méchanique Céleste*, suggested astronomy as a subject and in this 'she conversed with such a familiarity and compass of knowledge as might have led to a belief that she had just returned from a tour among the heavenly bodies'. After realising that she was also a skilled experimentalist and an artist of some skill, he asked the crucial question: 'who are you?' 'I am Mrs. Somerville, sir', she purportedly replied. 'I know that, madam, but who were you before you became Mrs. Somerville?'[35]

Mary Somerville then is reported to have said that she had been 'a little Scotch girl', and 'a pupil' of the Edinburgh natural philosopher John Playfair. In Caldwell's novelised memoir, the reader has been moved from a commonplace conversational opening about literature, through a series of revelations of increasing understanding about science, and then is brought down again by a remark that was simultaneously modest but also revealed Somerville's connection to contemporary centres of expertise. The entire narrative depends on the fact that it reports an encounter with Somerville, when she was well known in London but before she had become famous in the United States; it also depends on the implication that the reader has low expectations of the conversation of the women of England.

Caldwell clearly said as much to Mary Somerville, and a few days later she sent him an invitation to a 'conversation party of ladies' at her home. The gathering was explicitly designed to prove the conversational powers of women in general and of English ones specifically. Here, at a single evening party, were Elizabeth Fry, Elizabeth Lamb, Maria Edgeworth and two of Edgeworth's sisters.

> And when the introduction was over, my kind cicerone said to me playfully, but in an undertone, [']I have caught you; prepare yourself; you are about to have female

[35] *Autobiography of Charles Caldwell, M.D. with a Preface, Notes, and Appendix*, ed. H. W. Warner (Philadelphia, 1855), 378–80.

conversation enough to convince you that the ladies of England can talk as well as those of your own country – a truth which you seem to doubt'. . .

And, in a moment, she disappeared, and 'left me alone in my' – no, not in my 'glory' – but in my half dismay, at the task of entertaining half a dozen of talk-loving ladies. 'But,' said I to myself, 'they are all, I hope, so anxious to hear the vibrations of their own tongues, that they'll talk and entertain each other, and I shall have nothing to do but listen.'

Very soon, however, I discovered my mistake.[36]

One by one, the women conversed with Caldwell in such a way as to convince him that Mary Somerville was not exceptional: English ladies could converse with all the propriety, skill and interest of American ones. Other than her husband, Caldwell was the only man present.

Caldwell noted that none of his interlocutors at this party, other than his hostess, had spoken to him on deep or scientific subjects; but that was not a reflection of the interests of women such as Fry or the Edgeworths, who were very conscious of moving in circles where such issues were regularly discussed. A typical evening party of the kind they frequented is described in a letter Maria Edgeworth wrote to her step-mother while staying at the country house of the agricultural improver Sir John Sebright:

> Mrs. Somerville and I were sitting on the opposite sofa all night and Dr. Wollaston sitting before us talking most agreeably and giving us a clear account of the improvement of refining sugar which Mr. Howard who established his patent for the same just before his death has left five thousand a year to his children – a good reward for one invention! – for an improvement in a common process. Observe it is on an article of universal consumption.[37]

There was, in fact, a striking continuity between the kind of topics that could be discussed at such intimate gatherings and the contents of the conversational genre of science books that became such a dominant feature of the educational literature of the 1820s and 1830s. For example, William Hyde Wollaston's lively description of sugar-making became the basis for a passage in Edgeworth's improving children's book, *Harry and Lucy Concluded* in 1825.[38] The most famous of these scientific dialogues, Jane Marcet's *Conversations on Chemistry*, first published in 1806, grew out of actual conversations with a 'friend', probably her husband Alexander Marcet, the Swiss chemist, mineralogist and physician.[39] The book also stressed that the experiments had been carried out by the author at home, thus demonstrating that science was a suitable part of domestic life.

---

[36] *Ibid.*, 381–3.

[37] M. Edgeworth to F. A. Edgeworth, 16 Jan. 1822, in M. Edgeworth, *Letters from England*, ed. Christina Colvin (Oxford, 1971), 322.

[38] For the reference, see *ibid.*, 322.

[39] J. Marcet, *Conversations on Chemistry. In which the Elements of that Science are Familiarly Explained and Illustrated by Experiments* (2 vols., 2004, [1806]); for Marcet, the best starting point is S. Bahar, 'Jane Marcet and the Limits to Public Science', *British Journal for the History of Science*, 34 (2001), 29–49.

Works such as those by Marcet and Edgeworth became a major feature of the publishing scene in the 1820s and 1830s. The title – *Conversations* – that came to be most closely, but not exclusively, associated with the genre,[40] clearly involved a claim that scientific knowledge could be a polite accomplishment.

The etiquette of science

Even at the beginning of the century, not all science would have been deemed appropriate among mixed company or in general discussion. This was the tension surrounding the notion that, in principle, science was available to all. Some subjects were simply unfashionable. Mathematics, other than in the form of puzzles and conundrums, was generally seen as too obscure: Babbage was regularly quizzed for his use of abstruse mathematical analogies in everyday speech.[41] Phrenology appears to have been out of bounds in most London circles from the 1830s, after phrenological bores had been widely parodied and pilloried in the press. Major General John Mitchell, author of a pseudonymous semi-satirical *Art of Conversation* (1842), described his surprise on hearing an English lady express interest when an Italian marquis asks her if she has heard of phrenology:

> 'The Italians,' continued my companion, 'know so little of these things themselves that they think other people equally ignorant; it was therefore kind of him to give us the information.' 'Then you would have voted an Englishman, who should have lectured you on this exploded old subject, a regular bore?' 'To be sure I would, and would have cut him and his lecture fast enough.' 'I am glad to hear it,' said I, 'for it shows how much more you really expect from your own countrymen than from all these foreigners, much as you praise and admire them.' 'Hem,' said Lady C., 'I wish you would employ your philosophy in getting me a good partner for the next quadrille.'[42]

Other subjects were in bad taste. It was improper to pose certain kinds of direct question: ask a physician what his specialty was, and he might be forced to tell the company that he was a male midwife.[43]

Certain topics were seen as opening the possibility of political or religious controversy. This was definitely the case with evolutionary debate in most circles before publication of *Vestiges of the Natural History of Creation* in 1844, and in some afterwards.[44] Even among men of science, open expression of heterodoxy was often seen as bad manners. Take the following exchange between the leading London physiologist William

---

[40] A. Fyfe, 'Introduction', to Marcet, *Conversations*.

[41] Journal entry for 8 Jan. 1832, in *Life, Letters, and Journals of Sir Charles Lyell, Bart.*, ed. K. M. Lyell (2 vols., 1881), I, 363–4.

[42] [Mitchell], *Art of Conversation*, 21–2.

[43] *Etiquette for Gentlemen: With Hints on the Art of Conversation*, 30th edn (1847), 48.

[44] Secord, *Victorian Sensation*, 155–66.

Sharpey, the mathematician Augustus De Morgan and the ambitious government geologist Andrew Ramsay, who recorded it in his diary in 1848:

> 'You geologists' said Sharpey 'shock our religious feelings dreadfully, you make so light of all established chronologies as regards the age of the world.' I was not aware' quoth I, [']you had any religious feelings, or I might have managed my expressions better.' 'Oh' said he 'its not that, but you see we are of all sorts here, some of us have religious feelings, & others have none' waving his hand to De Morgan. 'Well' said I 'I can't stop to make an expression always that will please all, & must speak the plain truth.' 'I don't see the necessity' growled De Morgan 'if it be heterodox'!!!45

The most common problem was pedantry: sparkling conversation could be hard to combine with the close study and intense devotion demanded by an independent scientific vocation. This could lead men of science to seem monomaniacal, self-absorbed, small-minded or eccentric.46 Learning, no matter how profound, was 'unwelcome and tiresome' unless accompanied by good breeding and a proper sense of occasion.47 An army friend who had known Roderick Murchison in his foxhunting days lamented his turn towards geology: 'an excellent fellow and a most agreeable comrade' now seemed able to talk only of dull grauwacke and the 'Silurian system'.48

Aware of the problem, those engaged in science recognised that conversation was only one kind of talk, and carefully distinguished between different kinds of spoken discourse. What might be said in an annual presidential address differed from what was appropriate for a report of new research; the verbal sparring used in the Geological Society's parliamentary-style meeting room was not the same as private chat in the corridor beforehand. Worries that the Society's lively debates might be misconstrued led to defences that they were 'conversations'. Even the most expert practitioners sometimes refrained from talking about science at all. Gathering together until two in the morning in Lord Cole's rooms after the anniversary meeting, the gentlemanly Charles Lyell and his friends drank 'fines inflicted of bumpers of cognac on all who talked any 'ology'.49

Early Victorian novels often feature men of science obsessed with priority and insignificant detail. A classic example is the chapter 'The

---

45 A. Ramsay, diary entry for 1 Feb. 1848, Imperial College Archives, KGA Ramsay 1/10, fo. 20r.

46 S. Shapin, '"A Scholar and a Gentleman": The Problematic Identity of the Scientific Practitioner in Early Modern England', *History of Science*, 29 (1991), 279–327.

47 *Etiquette for All, or Rules of Conduct for Every Circumstance in Life: With the Laws, Rules, Precepts, and Practices of Good Society* (Glasgow, 1861), 14.

48 Dowager Duchess of Argyll [I. Campbell], *George Douglas, Eighth Duke of Argyll, K. G., K. T.: Autobiography and Memoirs* (2 vols., 1906), I, 349.

49 Thackray, *To See the Fellows Fight*, 81.

Man of Science' in Charles Kingsley's *Alton Locke* (1850). The episode involves the novel's eponymous hero and a clerical professor of natural history at Cambridge, but the caricature was intended to criticise the conversational faults of men of science more generally. The man of science proposes to carry out an experiment on Alton Locke, to see if a common working man can be turned into a naturalist.

> '"And what have you read on these subjects?"' he asks.
> I mentioned several books: Bingley, Bewick, 'Humboldt's Travels', 'The Voyage of the Beagle', various scattered articles in the Penny and Saturday Magazines, &c., &c.
> 'Ah!' he said, 'popular – you will find, if you will allow me to give you my experience – '.

That experience turns out to be a complete knowledge, based on thirteen years' study, of a single obscure reptile from the Balkans. The man of science claims that the fashionable world was 'overstocked with the *artem legendi* – the knack of running over books, and fancying that it understands them, because it can talk about them'. In the end, Alton Locke does not find mastering the details of science so difficult after all: his mentor's attempt to denigrate learning by calling it 'popular' has failed the test of experience.[50]

The case of Mary Somerville brings the increasing dangers of pedantry into clear relief. Her most widely read books, especially *On the Connexion of the Physical Sciences* (1834), were neither for narrow specialists nor for novices only; they were reflective treatises targeting an inclusive readership, based on her experiences in London in the 1810s and 1820s. As time went on, and especially after she became a potential 'lion' after publication of the *Mechanism of the Heavens* in 1831, she seems increasingly to have regulated her scientific talk, avoiding displays of knowledge except in conversations with those she knew to have an interest. People who met her hoping for a feast of witty repartee went away disappointed. As the celebrated talker Sydney Smith said in 1843, 'as to herself I could never get anything out of her beyond what you might get from any sempstress. She avoids all depth in converse – and no pretty superficial – very amiable no doubt.'[51] Clearly Somerville feared being seen as a bizarre specimen, a bluestocking. As a young girl, Julia Clara Byrne remembered being terrified of a mathematical grilling from the author of the *Mechanism of the Heavens*, though recognising that her concern was groundless, 'as no one could be less pretentious in manner, or more amiable and gentle in conversation'.[52]

Somerville's own writings were explicitly part of the vast effort that went into facilitating talk about science. Good conversation was not

---

[50] C. Kingsley, *Alton Locke, Tailor and Poet. An Autobiography*, new edn (1883 [1850]), 179–84.

[51] M. Edgeworth to H. Butler, 3 Dec. 1843, in Edgeworth, *Letters*, 601.

[52] J. C. Byrne, *Gossip of the Century* (2 vols., 1892), I, 260.

chit-chat, gossip or small talk, it had to be planned for and carefully orchestrated. This is evident in the extensive machinery of review journals that emerged during the nineteenth century. These served as an adjunct to the literature of conduct, suggesting to readers what might be appropriate to say about particular books. The reviews selected passages and quoted them at length, pointing out 'beauties' and phrases that might be useful in discussion. Etiquette manuals were usually despised for communicating rules that everyone was supposed to know but not follow slavishly; but everyone read periodical reviews. Reading informed opinion about the latest books was part of the process of preparing for conversation.

From the 1830s onwards, a flood of etiquette manuals aimed at nouveaux-riches from the middle classes attempted to codify the rituals of conversation. These manuals tended to lay down formal rules, stressing that manners were the mask that made society function.[53] Initially this literature recommended science as a key element in the social game. As one evangelical guide told young ladies preparing for the marriage market, botany and botanical conversation were especially favoured topics: 'even in the winter there are mosses and lichens, the very study of which is almost enough for a lifetime'.[54] The recommendation of botany as a feminine study was a commonplace (as in Mrs Sarah Ellis's best-selling books), but it is revealing to see an approach recommended that could lead to deep expertise. The recommendation here is not only of the pursuit of an ornamental knowledge of flowering plants, easily accessible and easily obtained, but also of the potential of botany as a lifelong interest, involving difficult subjects such as the cryptogams. Expertise about plants was particularly likely to be shared between women and men.

Etiquette manuals aimed at aspiring gentlemen recognised the role that the sciences could play in socialising with the opposite sex. The more cynical authors even encouraged male readers to exploit these as tactical openings and chat-up lines; an interest in the heavens could be the first step towards a seduction. *Etiquette for Gentlemen: With Hints on the Art of Conversation* (1847) told young men to think through topics and tactics before attending parties. Science could have a much more useful role than was often assumed.

> It is a common practice with men to abstain from grave conversation with women. And the habit is in general judicious. If the woman is young, gay and trifling, talk to her only of the latest fashions, the gossip of the day, etc. But this, in other cases is not to be done. Most women who are a little old, particularly married women, – and even some who are young, – wish to obtain a reputation for intellect and an acquaintance with science. You therefore pay them a real compliment, and gratify their self-love, by conversing occasionally upon grave matters, which they do not understand, and do not

---

[53] M. Morgan, *Manners, Morals and Class in England, 1774–1858* (Houndmills, Basingstoke, 1994); see also A. St George, *The Descent of Manners: Etiquette, Rules and the Victorians* (1993).
[54] *The English Gentlewoman: Or, Hints to Young Ladies on their Entrance into Society* (1845), 18.

really relish. You may interrupt a discussion on the beauty of a dahlia, by observing that as you know they take an interest in such things, you mention the discovery of a new method of analysing curves of double curvature. People who talk only trifles will rarely be popular with women past twenty-five.[55]

From this worldly-wise point of view, women had to feign an interest in scientific knowledge, while men had to humour them by pretending that their interest was genuine.

Shop talk

Moving a conversation in a single step from the most ornamental parts of botany to the most complex realms of mathematics was not really a recommended strategy: it was a joke. The example does, however, illustrate the ambiguities conversation about science was beginning to pose in a society increasingly organised around formal rules rather than tacit agreement. The central distinction involved aspects of a topic suitable for all, and those that could be brought up for discussion among those engaged upon it as a paid professional career. Not least, this marked a widely regarded distinction between women and men. As one of the manuals put it, 'Professional men must carefully avoid professional wit, as well as professional subjects, unless when called upon to bring forward some peculiar case or illustration; for general society tolerates no university, mess-table, or law-court stories.'[56]

This became known as the problem of 'shop talk', which emerged as a major concern from the 1850s, when periodical essays, novels and etiquette manuals highlighted the difficulties of dealing with integrating a large influx of professionals, business men and industrial entrepreneurs into the higher ranks of society. The term had originated as slang, with 'shop' or 'shoppy' signifying talk of commerce or business. It carried strong class overtones, for to introduce money and finances into everyday conversation was bad form and a sign of low origins. As Fanny Trollope wrote in her industrial novel, *The Life and Adventures of Michael Armstrong, the Factory Boy*, 'the gay fatherly phrase, "Don't talk of that, for God's sake, my dear! – it smells of the shop", has turned away many innocent eyes from contemplating that, which had they looked upon it, could hardly have endured so long'.[57] Shop brought the politics of the machine into the salon.

During the first half of the century, scientific talk might be pedantic or inappropriate in other ways, but it was not 'shoppy'. This is because a knowledge of nature was not considered the province of a specific

[55] *Etiquette for Gentlemen*, 51.
[56] [Mitchell], *Art of Conversation*, 110.
[57] F. Trollope, *The Life and Adventures of Michael Armstrong, the Factory Boy* (1840), 137–8.

profession or business pursued for pay. In fact, the lack of connection to 'trade' had long been one of the chief attractions of science as a topic for general conversation. Early in *Conversations on Chemistry*, Jane Marcet had one of the characters doubt the worthiness of chemistry as a subject for general conversation on the grounds that it was part of the trade of pharmacy. The authoritative Mrs B, however, corrects this misconception. Chemistry was a significant aspect of human learning, appropriate for all, while pharmacy 'properly belongs to professional men, and is therefore the last that I should advise you to study'.[58] On the same grounds, attendance at scientific lectures could be encouraged, even when these were part of a medical course – as long as women and other members of the general public skipped those parts that were concerned with therapeutics or the more intimate aspects of human anatomy.[59]

From the 1860s, the increasing dominance of the professions in intellectual life was one of the factors leading to a broadening of the debate about 'shop talk' beyond medicine, the law and similar fields. An article in the *Cornhill Magazine* for 1865 cautioned the new class of literary professionals against assuming that talk of literature was inherently of general interest.

> But what we wish to impress upon the literary class is that such writing is shop, and just the same in principle as the parish talk of parsons, or the barrack talk of soldiers... In a word, the outside public cares not for professional topics except when they rise above the lower level of the workshop into that broader region where they are to some extent common property. In the case of literature this region is wider, and extends lower than in the case of other professions. But literature, too, like them, has its mere mechanical sphere, its 'shop', in fact; and this, we say, can be interesting only to the workmen.[60]

This broader definition was being applied to areas from philosophy and philology to geography and geology. An article in the *Saturday Review* for 1875, for example, mentioned Egyptian antiquities and the origin of language as having potential for shop talk.

The blurring of boundaries is subtly brought out in Charles Dickens's *Our Mutual Friend* (1864–5). The indolent solicitor Mortimer Lightwood apologises for using 'the phraseology of the shop' in employing the term 'client' to refer to Mr Boffin. His excuse is that Boffin is likely to be the only client he shall ever have, and hence is 'a natural curiosity probably unique'. Although the apology for shop talk is wholly unnecessary in the circumstances, it leads Lightwood to develop an analogy that does go into another kind of jargon, that of natural history. Not only is Boffin 'The natural curiosity which forms the sole ornament of my professional

---

[58] Marcet, *Conversations*, I, 2–3.

[59] A. Secord, 'Botany on a Plate: Pleasure and the Power of Pictures in Promoting Early Nineteenth-Century Scientific Knowledge', *Isis*, 93 (2002), 28–57, esp. 40–5.

[60] [T. E. Kebbel], 'Shop', *Cornhill Magazine*, 11 (1865), 489–94, at 494.

museum'; but Boffin's secretary also becomes 'an individual of the hermit-crab or oyster species, and whose name, I think, is Chokesmith – but it doesn't in the least matter – say Artichoke'.[61] Lightwood has worried so much about the rules of etiquette in talking about the law, that he fails to avoid shop about science.

As the polite science characteristic of the period up through the 1840s disappeared, the opportunities for using science in conversation among the social elite began to change. New discoveries and inventions remained suitable topics for discussion, but they were more closely tied to current affairs as reported in the daily newspapers and weekly press. In many circles, for example, Darwin's *On the Origin of Species* began to be widely debated only after Paul du Chaillu returned from Africa with his gorillas.[62] Such spectacles offered novelty and general interest in a form that was self-consciously aimed at a non-specialist audience. Controversial, difficult or specialised subjects could to be repackaged for ready use as specific 'topics', with a stress on the telling anecdote and the remarkable story. News events became increasingly central to introducing science and other forms of knowledge into public discussion. This can be seen in a cartoon from *Punch*, in which a young woman drawn by John Leech as self-consciously 'pretty' tells a young man attempting to engage her in conversation that she has already talked enough of the gorilla, the rebuilt Crystal Palace at Sydenham and the other regular topics of the day. She is thereby labelled as 'A HORRID GIRL' who has deprived an awkward admirer of his planned conversational openings.[63] *Punch* became the great repository of bemused reflection on the problem of shared knowledge, as everyone could laugh at social gaffes that were just a bit more ridiculous than those going on all around them.

The sciences were by no means the only area affected by fears that Society, as it admitted new classes of experts, would be swamped by shop talk. In fact, the elite social world became more segmented and specialised, with specific occasions organised to appeal to the various 'sets' – artistic, literary, sporting, political. These are brilliantly depicted in a number of entertaining surveys of the contemporary scene, notably George Augusta Sala's *Twice Round the Clock* (1859) and Richard Doyle's *Bird's Eye Views of Society* (1864). Both men were survivors of the competitive world of journalism and keen observers of metropolitan life. Their books gave readers a sequence of panoramic views of the highly diversified settings of mid-Victorian London society: 'At Home' musical evenings; political banquets, art sales, clubland dinners and so forth. Doyle's

[61] C. Dickens, *Our Mutual Friend* (n.d.), 357.
[62] H. Rushing, 'The Gorilla Comes to Darwin's England' (MA thesis, University of Texas at Austin, 1990).
[63] 'Horrid Girl', *Punch*, 1 June 1861, 226.

Science and Art Converfazione.

Figure 1 'Conversazione: Science and Art', part of a series of engravings illustrating the increasingly distinctive spheres of mid-Victorian society. Richard Doyle, *Bird's Eye Views of Society* (1864), 45–6. Private collection.

'Conversazione: Science and Art' (Figure 1) shows a room packed with 'all kinds of novel, curious, interesting, and instructive objects': antiquities, microscopes, telescopes, portraits, batteries, diving bells and weapons of war. The scientific soirée, which appears to have originated in France and was imported by Babbage in the 1820s, became one of the chief ways in which scientific discussion could take place on a more sustained basis within polite society.[64]

Such occasions were attractive to the wider social world in that they offered a carefully mediated way of encountering scientific novelties. For those pursuing studies in the laboratory, field and museum, they increasingly provided opportunities for explaining science in a setting that was, in effect, halfway between a lecture and an informal conversation. As Doyle's cartoon shows, the role of the practitioner in these settings had changed: there is more overt didactic presentation and a stress on celebrity and individual discoverers. There are many women present, but they are part of the audience, with the exception of a lone 'female savant' talking to no one, identifiable by 'a decided tendency she has to part her hair on one side', standing alone in the middle of the right hand side of the picture. She does not belong to any of the groups of women

[64] S. Alberti, 'Conversaziones and the Experience of Science in Victorian England', *Journal of Victorian Culture*, 8 (2003), 208–30; Secord, *Victorian Sensation*, 410–21.

taking a look through the telescopes or other stereoscopes; but neither is she engaged in the more specialised talk enjoyed by the scientific men. The implication is that learned women do not fit in to this new form of diffusing popularised science. As the accompanying text notes, the men of science 'chat to one another, exchanging ideas, or criticising some new invention, or drinking tea'. The esoteric quality of their talk is signalled by their strange appearance: 'Some with a half mild, half wild, slightly eccentric look, others eager and thoughtful, a good many with spectacles and long hair.'[65]

The talk of such celebrities, even those without long hair, was seen to be worth recording. Those who knew the leading men of science well recognised the skill it took to manage conversations on topics that were increasingly seen as specialised and esoteric. A widely acknowledged master in such social settings was the lower-middle-class schoolmaster's son, Thomas Henry Huxley. Darwin thought him 'the best talker I have known', remarking that he was skilled in adjusting his conversation to the listener, retaining his fierce anti-clerical polemics for print or for conversation with intimates.[66] Huxley's son's biography made a special point of describing his style of conversation. A friend sent the following recollection:

> I was in some trepidation, because I didn't know anything about science or philosophy; but when your mother began to talk over old times with my wife, your father came across the room and sat down by me, and began to talk about the dog which we had brought with us. From that he got on to the different races of dogs and their origin and connections, all quite simply, and not as though to give information, but just to talk about something which obviously interested me. I shall never forget how extraordinarily kind it was of your father to take all this trouble in entertaining a complete stranger, and choosing a subject which put me at my ease at once, while he told me all manner of new and interesting things.[67]

Such eulogies, often found in late Victorian and Edwardian lives and letters, were effectively recommendations about how a man of learning could be a moral example to others in his consideration for the needs of others.[68] Huxley simultaneously encouraged his visitor to relax and showed that there was nothing to be feared about scientific conversation after all. In preserving such exchanges biographers felt that they were recording a style of talk that was disappearing.

Notably, it was in the waning years of the Victorian era that antiquarians developed the myth of the early eighteenth-century coffee-house as the apotheosis of civil conversation.[69] Certainly Huxley felt that

[65] R. Doyle, *Bird's Eye Views of Society* (1864), 45–6.
[66] *The Autobiography of Charles Darwin, 1809–1892*, ed. N. Barlow (1958), 106.
[67] *Life and Letters of Thomas Henry Huxley*, ed. L. Huxley (2 vols., 1900), II, 429.
[68] White, *Thomas Huxley*.
[69] Cowan, *Social Life of Coffee*.

the intellectual tone of high Society was declining. In an essay written just before his death in 1895, he raged against the 'refined depravity among the upper classes', who were taking in spiritualism and superstition rather than science. He spoke against the 'half-cretinised products of over-civilisation', who had become soft and weak-minded.[70] In this vividly imagined world of fin-de-siècle decadence, there seemed little place for the kind of serious, morally informed discourse on science that Huxley had attempted to bring into the highest realms of metropolitan social life.

Although Huxley's reaction was extreme, the final decades of the nineteenth century do mark a significant change in the relations between elite Society and what was rapidly becoming known as 'the scientific class'. As Stefan Collini has pointed out, this is the period when 'academic' began to be used in a pejorative sense, as 'not leading to a decision; unpractical; theoretical, formal, or conventional'.[71] In many of the trend-setting groups, the detailed pursuit of science became relatively unfashionable, replaced by a new emphasis on pleasure and partying for its own sake. Leonore Davidoff has shown in *The Best Circles* that Society became focused on the rituals of presentation to the queen, the marriage market and renewing the upper classes with American and industrial money – and less the matrix for discussing politics and ideas. Parties became more elaborate, with fantastic costume balls, more relaxed sexual attitudes and a stress on witty repartee.[72] As Lady Dorothy Nevill disapprovingly recalled at the end of her life:

> In the old days Society was an assemblage of people who, either by birth, intellect or aptitude, were ladies and gentlemen in the true sense of the word. For the most part fairly, though not extravagantly, dowered with the good things of the world, it had no ulterior object beyond intelligent, cultured and dignified enjoyment, money-making being left to another class which, from time to time, supplied a select recruit for this *corps d'élite*. Now all this is changed, in fact, society (a word obsolete in its old sense) is, to use a vulgar expression, 'on the make'.[73]

Although her contrast is drawn too sharply, many commentators deplored the loss of moral earnestness as the century drew to a close. The social elite continued to learn (and talk) about scientific, technological and other 'improving' issues, but with a few distinguished exceptions,[74] this

---

[70] A. Desmond, *Huxley: Evolution's High Priest* (1997), 227, and B. Lightman, '"Fighting even with Death": Balfour, Scientific Naturalism, and Huxley's Final Battle', in *Thomas Henry Huxley's Place in Science and Letters: Centenary Essays*, ed. A. Barr (Athens, GA, 1997), 323–50.

[71] S. Collini, *Public Moralists: Political Thought and Intellectual Life in Britain* (Oxford, 1991), 223–4.

[72] Davidoff, *The Best Circles*, 59–70.

[73] D. Nevill, *The Reminiscences of Lady Dorothy Nevill*, ed. R. Nevill (1906), 355, quoted in H. Perkin, *The Rise of Professional Society: England since 1880* (1989), 65.

[74] There were, of course, notable practitioners of science among particular families within the social elite, such as the Balfours and the Rayleighs (for this, see D. Opitz, '"Behind Folding

was increasingly not through contact with original investigators, but through articles by science journalists and professional writers. Topics for conversation were taken not from long articles in the *Quarterly* and *Edinburgh*, but from short punchy pieces in the dailies and weeklies. In effect, the best circles increasingly had their own 'shop', focused on high fashion, topical sensation and social ritual. Not surprisingly, commentators around this time acknowledged that within certain limits shop was 'the best talk of all', as it simply meant conversation informed by an understanding of the subjects under discussion.

Laboratory conversation

For their part, men of science at the end of the century increasingly sensed that the best conversations were to be had with those who possessed similar training. The typical practitioner was frequently pursuing science for pay, either as an academic, on behalf of the state, or as a professional writer.[75] The new breed of academically trained practitioners tended to look not to genteel Society for models of behaviour, but to middle-class ideals of propriety, or even to alternatives in scientific bohemia. One sign of this, found in many late Victorian scientific lives and letters, is the way in which biographers lamented what appeared as their subjects' inordinate fondness for rank. Charles Lyell, Roderick Murchison and Mary Somerville seemed to belong to a different scientific world, one in which was seen to have paid undue obeisance to social rank.

Even Huxley's mastery of social chit-chat with the great, as we have seen, was considered as remarkable and worth recording. Such connections could be hugely important for public support and the funding of science. A quiet word in the corridors of the Athenaeum or Reform club could be worth hours of lobbying at Westminster; ties maintained through family or college connections could smooth over differences about the religious consequences of (say) evolution or materialism. But the generation of scientific men who came to power in the 1880s, however patient they might be in conversing with novices and potential patrons, thought of substantive scientific talk as occurring much more exclusively in their places of work. Memories of talk in general social settings are

Shutters in Whittinghame House": Alice Blanche Balfour (1850–1936) and Amateur Natural History', *Archives of Natural History*, 31 (2004), 330–48, and S. Schaffer, 'Physics Laboratories and the Victorian Country House', in *Making Space for Science: Territorial Themes in the Shaping of Knowledge*, ed. C. Smith and J. Agar (Basingstoke, 1997), 149–80. These important instances of 'country-house science' need to be balanced with an understanding of the role of science within upper-class households more generally, and especially in metropolitan settings – the possibilities for what could be called 'town-house science'.

75 Collini, *Public Moralists*; T. W. Heyck, *The Transformation of Intellectual Life in Victorian England* (1982). On the move towards professional life in England more generally, see Perkin, *Rise of Professional Society*.

taken over by recollections of lively exchanges at the laboratory bench or in the field.

Younger scientists found such interactions intensely liberating. Talk of this kind, in their view, was just one of the many benefits that flowed from their campaign for professional careers. From this perspective, discipline boundaries were not Foucauldian prisons, but ways of maximising pleasurable occasions for the free exchange of ideas and a recognition of shared understandings.[76] At the most general level, proponents of science argued that the Enlightenment ideal of conversation as rational discussion among equals was realised most completely at the lab bench.

One sign of the new order was the increased significance of tea in the making of science. The situation in Cambridge, where the tensions of introducing science into a genteel culture of learning were especially acute, gives a good idea of the issues. Throughout most of the nineteenth century, tea had usually been served at evening parties. Some professors invited everyone around to their house or college rooms, part of the way in which scientific issues were part of more general patterns of academic life. John Stevens Henslow and his wife Harriet Jenyns Henslow hosted evening events of this kind in their home which the young Charles Darwin regularly attended.[77] Tea in the afternoon, an innovation introduced into London aristocratic houses during the 1840s,[78] does not appear to have become a university tradition for several decades. When new laboratories began to sprout up on the New Museums site during the 1870s and 1880s, they had no common rooms or facilities for refreshment.

So it was only in 1879 that the Cavendish professor, Lord Rayleigh, began to sponsor laboratory teas as a way of combining a relaxing break with possibilities for free discussion. It was an informal occasion, using a teapot with a broken spout. His wife Lady Rayleigh often attended, as did his sister-in-law Eleanor Sidgwick, who worked on determining the fundamental units of electricity.[79] As Rayleigh's son recalled, others in the laboratory soon joined in, so that tea afforded 'a valuable opportunity for intercourse and exchange of ideas on scientific subjects'.[80] Afternoon tea, a fashionable innovation of the Victorian aristocracy, was thus reinvented by Lord and Lady Rayleigh as a means for ensuring that scientific discussion did not just focus on specific experiments, but retained the openness considered essential to innovation. At first the teas were held in the professor's rooms, but early in the twentieth century those engaged

[76] R. E. Kohler, 'The Constructivists' Tool Kit', *Isis*, 90 (1999), 329–31.

[77] J. Browne, *Charles Darwin: Voyaging* (1995), 123.

[78] J. Pettigrew, *A Social History of Tea* (2001).

[79] P. Gould, 'Women and the Culture of University Physics in Late Nineteenth-Century Cambridge', *British Journal for the History of Science*, 30 (1997), 127–49.

[80] R. J. Strutt, *John William Strutt, Third Baron Rayleigh* (1924), 128–9.

Figure 2 Parody coat of arms for the Botany School in Cambridge, with rampant helianthuses facing a cup of tea. *Tea Phytologist*, 23 Jan. 1934, vol. x, no. 1, p. 1. University Archives, BG 66. By permission of the Syndics of Cambridge University Library.

in planning new facilities began to set aside staff rooms and other spaces for scientific talk.[81]

Many of the new research schools that developed in these years crystallised as much around the tea-room as the lab bench or field. A good example is archaeology, where new ideas which made the department famous from the early decades of the twentieth century were hatched over tea.[82] In 1908 the students at Cambridge's Botany School dubbed their magazine the *Tea Phytologist*, a spoof on ecologist Arthur Tansley's *New Phytologist*, founded six years before.[83] In a mock coat of arms from the 1934 issue (Figure 2), the teacup took its rightful place as the central symbol of modern scientific practice. Parodying the University's own celebrated motto, it proclaimed 'Hinc lucem et pocula theae' ('from here, light and cups of tea').[84] Informal scientific talk did not decline in the new circumstances of the twentieth century: but it moved into new places and assumed new forms.

---

[81] A. E. Munby, *Laboratories: Their Planning and Fittings* (1921).

[82] P. J. Smith, 'A Splendid Idiosyncrasy: Prehistory at Cambridge, 1915–50' (Ph.D. thesis, University of Cambridge, 2004).

[83] H. Godwin, 'Early Development of *The New Phytologist*', *New Phytologist*, 100 (1977), 1–4, at 3.

[84] *Tea Phytologist*, 23 Jan. 1934, vol. x, no. 1, p. 1; see also the issues for 27 Nov. 1939, vol. x + 1, no. 1, p. 1, and Mar. 1984, vol. T42 no. 24T, p. 1. The motto was a variant on the University's famous maxim, 'Hic lucem et pocula sacra', literally translated as 'from here, light and sacred draughts'.

Conclusion

There is no easy divide apparent in any part of this story between 'popular' and 'expert' science. The marketplace for science has always involved exchange, and never simply passive consumption. In the late Georgian and early Victorian era, the talk of the scientific elite had been an integral part of the conversational practice of polite society. This was even true of accounts of original research, as indicated by the case of the Geological Society and similar groups in London's West End clubland. By the end of the century, the situation had changed. Practices in science still drew upon those of polite society, but often in distinctive settings such as the laboratory tea room. As I have suggested, rituals associated with the genteel world of polite conversation became key elements in the academic research schools that dominated science in the late nineteenth and twentieth centuries. Such borrowings are no less significant or pervasive just because they were less obvious.

There could be a temptation to read the story I have told as yet another indication of the impact of specialisation and professionalisation within science. And clearly the creation of new roles, new academic structures and new forms of paid careers is part of what made the 'scientist' a less likely dinner companion in a Mayfair townhouse in 1900 than his counterpart three-quarters of a century earlier.

Science, with its arcane terminology and finely honed disciplinary categories, has often been depicted as a leading force in breaking down the possibilities for a coherent intellectual culture.[85] In *Absent Minds*, Collini shows how central the issue of specialisation became to debates about the character of intellectual life in early twentieth-century Britain.[86]

Yet as Collini also points out, discussions of the subdivision of labour in the pursuit of knowledge have characteristically been accompanied by a sense of decline: the world of the generalist is always the world we have lost. Accusations of scholasticism and over-specialisation are as old as knowledge itself, and are certainly not peculiar to late Victorian and Edwardian Britain.[87] If anything, the arrival in domestic settings of science-based technologies such as electric lighting made the topicality of science more evident than ever before.[88] Moreover, the emergence of science as a paid career was the outcome of a campaign, by Babbage and others, to associate the pursuit of knowledge with the gentlemanly

---

[85] Heyck, *Transformation*.

[86] S. Collini, *Absent Minds: Intellectuals in Britain* (Oxford, 2006), 451–72.

[87] S. Shapin, *A Social History of Truth: Civility and Science in Seventeenth-Century England* (Chicago, 1991).

[88] G. Gooday, 'Illuminating the Expert–Consumer Relationship in Domestic Electricity', in A. Fyfe and B. Lightman, eds., *Popular Science: Nineteenth-Century Sites and Experience* (Chicago, 2007).

status long enjoyed by those in the existing professions of medicine, the military and the law. It was not intended to break the link between science and gentility, but to strengthen it. There is no reason, then, to see the drive for professionalisation within science as the primary reason for the transformation in practice I have sketched here.

Instead, the growing tensions in talking about science towards the end of the nineteenth century can best be understood as part of more general changes in the social organisation of elites in Britain. These changes had as much – probably more – to do with the specific needs of genteel society than with any changes in the comparatively small-scale world of science. During the agricultural depression of the 1870s through the 1890s, new money from America and the wealthy commercial classes had to be brought into the marriage market, and this made learned company at the dinner table potentially awkward. Men of science were increasingly excluded from the highest social circles not because their knowledge was more specialised than it had been, but because the purpose of conversation among the elite had been transformed.

Paradoxically, then, men of science began to gain the professional status some of them had craved, at the very moment that status was losing its cachet as an entry into genteel society. The new plutocrats, increasingly focused on creating a potent fusion between power and wealth, welcomed the money flowing into late Victorian and Edwardian London from the United States; but they did not have much of a taste for what appeared to be another American import, the 'scientist'. The word had been invented at a meeting of the British Association for the Advancement of Science in the 1830s, but became regularly used in Britain only from the 1890s.[89] With a few exceptions, the fashionable world did not embrace the growing class of experts associated with industry, state education and government bureaucracy. The unwritten rules of talk had changed. To discuss the electron theory or fossil botany at ordinary dinners and soirées, other than when these subjects were in the news, was (with rare exceptions) seen to be talking shop.

The taboo reached its apotheosis around the time of the debate over the novelist C. P. Snow's *Two Cultures* of 1959, which in many ways was a meditation on scientific conversation. Snow puzzled about the kinds of subjects deemed appropriate for discussion at London parties and Cambridge high tables. 'Oh, those are mathematicians', he reported one college head as saying, 'We never talk to *them*.' Snow was appalled that so many otherwise well-educated people could complacently admit that they knew nothing of non-parity conservation or the second law of thermodynamics. The problem, in his partisan diagnosis, involved a divide between science and all the other main institutions of British

[89] White, *Thomas Huxley*, 4–5.

public life, from the Westminster establishment to the haunts of the self-proclaimed literary avant-garde in Chelsea. The distance from those places to Imperial College and the Science Museum in South Kensington was the conversational equivalent of an ocean, 'as though the scientists spoke nothing but Tibetan'.[90] The separation, Snow suggested, had been bad at the start of the twentieth century, but in the intervening decades it had only become worse.[91] Snow's book created a controversy that has continued for half a century, although the situation it described has since been transformed out of all recognition through television, the internet and the impact of science on everyday life. The 'two cultures' debate was itself one sign that things were beginning to change, as the problem of how to talk about science emerged as the topic of lively conversation it remains today.

---

[90] C. P. Snow, *The Two Cultures*, ed. S. Collini (Cambridge, 1993), 2–3.
[91] *Ibid.*, 17.

Transactions of the RHS 17 (2007), pp. 157–83 © 2007 Royal Historical Society
doi:10.1017/S0080440107000576   Printed in the United Kingdom

THEODORE VACQUER AND THE ARCHAEOLOGY OF MODERNITY IN HAUSSMANN'S PARIS*

By Colin Jones

READ 20 OCTOBER 2006 AT THE UNIVERSITY OF HERTFORDSHIRE

ABSTRACT. Théodore Vacquer (1824–99) was an archaeologist who excavated, directed excavations in and visited all archaeological sites in Paris between the 1840s and his death. In the latter part of his career, he served as assistant curator at what became the Musée Carnavalet, specialising in the Roman and early medieval history of the city. Taking advantage of the reconstruction of the city in the nineteenth century associated with the work of Paris prefect, Baron Haussmann, he was able to locate far more of Roman Paris than had been known before. His findings remained the basis of what was known about the Roman city until a new wave of archaeological excavations after 1950. Vacquer aimed to highlight his discoveries in a magnum opus on the history of Paris from earliest times to AD 1000, but he died with virtually nothing written. His extensive archive still exists, however, and provides the substance for this essay. The essay seeks to rescue Vacquer from the relative obscurity associated with his name. In addition, by setting his life and work in the context of the Haussmannian construction of Paris as the arch-city of modernity it aims to illuminate the history of archaeology, conservation and urban identity in nineteenth-century Paris.

The subject of this essay is the life and work of a Parisian nobody. It concerns in particular the eyes of that Parisian nobody: what they saw and what we can know of what they saw. The nobody in question is Théodore Vacquer, a man whose whole life was lived under the star of anonymity, isolation and non-achievement. He was a failed engineer and a failed architect. A highly ambitious author who wrote copiously behind closed doors, he published next to nothing. 'Reticent to the point of secrecy' was the judgement of one acquaintance (an admirer, moreover); he was also 'whimsical to the point of peculiarity'. His quirkily rebarbative character was such that even his friends referred to him as 'a wild boar' and 'a permanently rolled-up hedgehog'. His desperately unglamorous

* I am grateful to the audience of the essay, when read at the University of Hertfordshire, for their comments. I have given versions of the essay at numerous other venues, and been rewarded by much help and many new ideas. I also wish to thank in particular Malcolm Todd, Didier Busson, Bonnie Effros and Josephine McDonagh for their help and encouragement. Cartography is by Edward Oliver.

Figure 1 Théodore Vacquer. From M. Vasseur-Depoux, *Catalogue des manuscrits des bibliothèques publiques de France. T. LIX. Bibliothèque historique de la ville de Paris* (Paris, 1975).

portrait (Figure 1) reveals an awkward posture, the rough, embarrassed hands of a workman rather than an intellectual and, half hidden from view by his spectacles, a veiled, oblique, reticent gaze.[1]

---

[1] Vacquer seems to have slipped the attention of just about all historians of Haussmann's Paris. I stumbled across him and his archive while writing *Paris: Biography of a City* (2004). There is a brief but well-informed account of his life by his friends F. G. de Pachtère and C. Sellier: 'Théodore Vacquer, sa vie, son oeuvre. Le fonds Vacquer à la Bibliothèque de la Ville de Paris', *Bulletin de la Bibliothèque des travaux historiques*, 4 (1909), which is the introduction to the catalogue of his manuscripts in the Bibliothèque Historique de la Ville

Théodore Vacquer was a Parisian archaeologist who spent all his life in the city excavating, viewing and reflecting upon its past. And his career covered the period in which Paris was refashioned under the inspiration of Baron Haussmann, Emperor Napoleon III's prefect of the Seine from 1853 through to 1870. Paris rebuilt, boulevardised and mythologised became over that period the archetypal city of modernity, visually celebrated as such in the canvasses of Impressionist and Post-Impressionist painters.[2] Vacquer's life also coincided, we might note, with the period in which archaeology was emerging as a professional discipline, and in which protection of heritage (*patrimoine*) was becoming the object of governmental priority.[3] The thrust of this essay will be to argue that the life of this forgotten and neglected figure allows us – paradoxically, most often by dint of his failures rather than his successes – to explore intersections between archaeology and modernity, history and myth, past and future, record and imagination, and memory and amnesia in the history of nineteenth-century Paris, crucible of urban modernity. Ultimately – a century after his virtually unremarked death – this Parisian 'nobody' is a somebody whose life and writings have much to teach us.

Théodore Vacquer was born in Paris in 1824, in the Sorbonne neighbourhood at the heart of the present-day Fifth Arrondissement. The latter encompasses within its limits most of Roman Paris, or Lutetia, which would prove to be his lifelong obsession. He was a true *titi parisien* – his family was city-bred, and he was educated in the city. He failed the entrance examination for the Ecole Polytechnique up on the Montagne Sainte-Geneviève in the late 1830s, and thereupon

de Paris [hereafter BHVP]. The epithets I have used and and the photograph are drawn from this article, which draws on oral as well as a wide range of now unfindable manuscript materials (see esp. p. 10). The admirer is Seymour de Ricci, in a brief note, 'Paris à l'époque romane', in the *Revue archéologique* (1914), 112. For the present article, I have used in particular Vacquer's autobiographical sketches to be found in Carton 248 of the Fonds Vacquer. The latter was re-catalogued in the 1970s and the class-marks indicated by Pachtère and Sellier were altered. For the current organisation, see M. Vasseur-Depoux, *Catalogue des manuscrits des bibliothèques publiques de France. T. LIX. Bibliothèque historique de la ville de Paris* (Paris, 1975).

[2] On the Haussmannisation of Paris, the bibliography is too vast to recount in a footnote. See esp. D. Jordan, *Transforming Paris. The Life and Labors of Baron Haussmann* (1955); D. H. Pinkney, *Napoleon III and the Rebuilding of Paris* (1958); F. Loyer, *Paris Nineteenth-Century: Architecture and Urbanism* (1988); J. Gaillard, *Paris, la ville, 1852–70: l'urbanisme parisien à l'heure de Haussmann* (Paris, 1976); A. Sutcliffe, *The Autumn of Central Paris. The Defeat of Town Planning, 1850–1970* (1970); and N. Evenson, *Paris: A Century of Change, 1878–1978* (1979). See too G. Haussmann, *Mémoires*, ed. F. Choay (Paris, 2000).

[3] For an overview of these inter-related issues, see F. Choay, *The Invention of the Historic Monument* (Cambridge, 2001); The section on 'Le Patrimoine', in *Les lieux de mémoire*, ed. P. Nora (3 vols., paperback re-edn, Paris, 1997 – work in this series first appeared in 1984), II (esp. A. Chastel, 'La notion du patrimoine'); E. Gran-Aymerich, *Naissance de l'archéologie moderne, 1789–1945* (Paris, 1998); A. Schnapp, *La Conquête du passé. Aux origines de l'archéologie* (Paris, 1995); D. Poulot, *Une histoire du patrimoine en Occident, XVIIIe–XXIe siècle* (Paris, 2006).

renounced plans to become an engineer, so as to train as an architect. It was on a building site in 1841 that he witnessed the discovery of stone sarcophagi from the Merovingian period – a moment which he described in terms of an epiphany. 'One day, I noticed on a building site that the earth that the workers were bringing up to the surface contained debris from the Roman period. Several days afterwards, there appeared admirable Roman substructures, whose form and state of conservation were excellent.'[4] But Vacquer did not stop there. He returned home and compared these findings with the record of the city's past as it was recounted in current historical work on the early history of Paris. The most up-to-date scholarship – Dulaure's *Histoire de Paris*, for example[5] – at once revealed itself to Vacquer as 'both incomplete and erroneous'. Vacquer left his armchair and went out hunting for other vestiges of a misrecorded Parisian past. 'Up to now', he later noted, 'the history of Paris had been written by the fireside.' But things looked different, Vacquer was excited to learn, in the field. 'I saw that every day and in all neighbourhoods the navvy's spade was laying bare and destroying ancient sites.' His vocation as an architect was abandoned. He now vowed to follow all building work as best he could, with the aim of recording findings and where possible rescuing relics. He soon discovered, moreover, that he was falling into the habit of directing his attention by preference 'on Roman-occupied areas', 'often to the detriment of areas built on in the Middle Ages'. This would be, he projected, 'his life's work'.[6]

This was a good time to be evolving into the proto-archaeologist of Roman Paris. For at this time, thanks mainly (though not entirely) to Prefect Haussmann, more of the central parts of Paris were being dug up than had ever been dug up before. Emperor Augustus had famously re-made Rome in the image of a great empire, and Haussmann's master, Napoleon III, charged him with the same task for his own imperial capital. It is probably true that historians have tended to follow Haussmann's own lead and make him (with Napoleon III) almost entirely responsible for this transformation. As Nicholas Papayannis has recently pointed out, the idea of rational urban planning on which the Haussmannian project was based dated back to the Enlightenment (and in some respects even earlier).[7] Haussmann's predecessor as Prefect of the Seine from 1833 to 1848, Count Rambuteau, trialled many of the processes which Haussmann was

    4 Pachtère and Sellier, 'Vacquer', 2; BHVP 248, fo. 301v. In the biographical account, I am drawing essentially on these sources unless otherwise stated.

    5 J. A. Dulaure, *Histoire physique, civile et morale de Paris*, 2nd edn (Paris, 1825).

    6 Pachtère and Sellier, 'Vacquer', 2ff; BHVP 248 esp. fo. 301.

    7 N. Papayannis, *Planning Paris before Haussmann* (2004). See too *La modernité avant Haussmann: formes de l'espace urbain à Paris, 1801–56*, ed. K. Bowie (Paris, 2001). For the continuation of his legacy after 1870, see Sutcliffe, *The Autmn of Central Paris*; Evenson, *Paris: A Century of Change*; Loyer, *Paris Nineteenth-Century*; Jones, *Paris: Biography of a City*, etc.

to employ. And 'Haussmannisation' continued unabashed well into the Third Republic down to the outbreak of the First World War.

Yet Haussmann did most to fuse together the range of ideas and practices into an irresistable force for root-and-branch urban transformation. It was, moreover, mainly his diggers that changed the medieval heart of Paris, which had always been a fundamental part of the age-old image of the city. Since the time of Philip Augustus in the thirteenth century, Paris had grown outwards, creating concentric circles around a central, irreducible, historic core. The latter remained relatively unaffected even as the city's fringe went through multiple evolutions, new building and wide streets rarely penetrating the invisible carapace which seemed to protect that inner heart. The Île de la Cité, for example, where Julius Caesar had located the city of the Parisii whom he had defeated in the Gallic Wars, was in Vacquer's youth one of the filthiest, most overcrowded and generally disgusting parts of old Paris.[8] From around mid-century, however, it was transformed by techniques which were extended throughout these central zones of the city and which tore up the old surface. It was not only the case that Haussmannian techniques metamorphosed old Paris, with its winding, narrow and clogged up streets, its insanitary miasmatic atmosphere, its all-too-contagious political radicalism and turned it into the ordered city of open spaces, flowing boulevards and rationalised infrastructure. They also thereby revealed an ancient substratum. On the latter, Vacquer set to work: all 'demolition of foundations, [and the building of] channels for sewers, water mains and gas pipes' were grist to the Vacquerian mill. 'The earth is a book', he noted confidently, 'for he who can read it.'[9]

In 1866, after nearly two decades of ceaseless excavation, Vacquer's semi-official activities were recognised by his appointment as inspector of the Service historique de la ville de Paris. It was probably around this time that he determined to write up his copious findings as a prized work of scholarship, his life's work, as he told himself. He could by now draw on an unruly mountain of documentation. Throughout his career, Vacquer took notes and made sketches on site. These were often on scraps of paper and (literally) the backs of envelopes and restaurant menus, and they utilised his own shorthand conventions. He could feel proud that in the years during which Baron Haussmann had refashioned Paris as a new city, the prized city of modernity, he himself had located a lost one, namely, Lutetia. The Roman baths had long been known – though

---

[8] The classic treatment of this theme is L. Chevalier, *Laboring Classes and Dangerous Classes in Paris during the First Half of the Nineteenth Century* (1973). The Île de la Cité certainly lay within Lutetia, but there is now some contention among archaeologists that the capital of the Parisii where Caesar first encountered the tribe was further along the river at Nanterre.

[9] Pachtère and Sellier, 'Vacquer', 7; BHVP 248, fo. 301v.

they had often been mistaken in fact for the palace of the fourth-century AD Roman Emperor, Julian the Apostate. But, as Vacquer's worknotes attest, through extensive observation and excavation he also identified for the first time the late Antique rampart on the Île de la Cité, the Roman streetplan, a theatre on the Rue Racine, a forum and associated buildings on the Rue Soufflot, cemeteries out beyond the Luxembourg gardens and in the south-east of the city close to the Gobelins, and an amphitheatre by the Rue Monge. Virtually all of this was literally *terra incognita* for a millennium-worth of Parisians.[10] The scale and significance of Vacquer's findings on the Roman city simply cannot be underestimated.

Vacquer was, however, never to complete the manuscript in which he planned to do justice to all he had found. From 1872 his studies were linked in with work for the Museum of the City (now better known as the Musée Carnavalet) where he was appointed associate curator (*sous-conservateur*). His growing role in conservation and museum work, particularly in cataloguing the Carnavalet's Gallo-Roman collections, squeezed out time he could devote to writing up his voluminous findings. His only publications amounted to brief worknotes on different archaeological sites, which were mainly published in little-read local history journals.[11] His evenings and weekends were spent poring over his manuscripts, scribbling amendments and addenda, amassing further materials, classifying and reclassifying his discoveries. The never-ending scale of his task, as new finds continued to be made (the digging of the Paris Metro was just under way in his final years), discouraged him too: 'by its very nature', he noted, his cherished volume 'can in some ways never be complete'.[12] Personal demons seemed to be haunting him, and he agonised ceaselessly over the act of writing. He never in fact got beyond the preface to his planned opus magnum, and endlessly revisited it, tinkering and retouching his text rather than embarking on the book's substantive contents. The death of his wife in 1898, and administrative reorganisation at the Carnavalet which forced him into retirement, seemed to demoralise him. He now passed his days reading listlessly in public libraries. The perpetually rolled-up hedgehog would die in 1899, his work unfinished and his name so little known that hardly an obituarist could be found to

---

[10] For the archaeology of Roman Lutetia, the key text is D. Busson, *Carte archéologique de la Gaule: 75. Paris* (Paris, 1998), esp. Busson's introduction. See too P. Velay, *From Lutetia to Paris. The Island and the Two Banks* (Paris, 1992); P. de Carbonnières, *Lutèce, Paris ville romane* (Paris, 1997); P. M. Duval, *De Lutèce oppidum à Paris capitale de la France* (1993); and D. Busson, *Paris ville antique* (Paris, 2001). The first work drawing extensively on the Vacquer papers – but also on oral testimony of the man was F. G. de Pachtère, *Paris à l'époque gallo-romaine (Etude faite avec l'aide des papiers et des plans de Th. Vacquer)* (Paris, 1912: still worth consulting).

[11] The extensive bibliography in Busson's *Carte archéologique* (40) lists a dozen pieces by Vacquer, extending overall to less than fifty pages.

[12] BHVP 248, fo. 301v.

record the passing of the 'mysterious' Vacquer,[13] let alone evaluate his importance. The nearest his work got to having immediate posthumous influence was when his friend and collaborator Pachtère used his work-notes to compose a map of Lutetia – a subject to which I will return at the end of this article.[14]

On his death, Vacquer's papers passed into the possession of the historical services of the city (and his colleagues and acquaintances there were little short of stupefied at what his papers revealed of the extent of Vacquer's secretive discoveries).[15] The Vacquer archive came to be housed in the *Bibliothèque historique de la ville de Paris*, on the Rue Pavée in the Marais. There we can still consult them. There are nearly a hundred boxes in all, containing about 10,000 pieces. There is no Ariadne's thread, nor even an Umberto Eco nor a Julian Barnes, to serve as guide to a labyrinthine corpus which increasingly strikes the hapless researcher as the disordered, capillary byway of a somewhat deranged mind. This delphic archive has acquired the appearances of a palimpsest, a crazy quilt of pencilled jottings, quilled scribblings, newspaper snippets, picture postcards, water-coloured topographies and indeterminate sketchings. Indeed the Fonds Vacquer has achieved the form of an archaeological site itself, and its different parts can only be accessed through, and only take their meaning from, a process of historical sedimentation.

Today, archaeologists of Roman and Merovingian Paris are the most assiduous frequenters of the Vacquer archive, scholars puzzling away at even a single one of the hundred boxes so as to get some fleeting glimpse of how Roman Lutetia might have revealed itself to the eyes of Théodore Vacquer.[16] If they take the trouble to consult the oracle, it is because they realise that those eyes were not simply the first to view most of the vestiges of Roman Lutetia. Vacquer was also the only scholar to have seen many of these things with the eyes of erudition. He was, as he modestly avowed to himself, 'merely the editor of what existed and what I have seen'.[17] Wretchedly, this was an 'editor' who never published.

Since his death, Théodore Vacquer has thus become a sphinx, an eyeless riddle. Archaeology's inbuilt penchant for destroying evidence as it proceeds must take part of the blame here: we can consult the manuscript sources of Vacquer's historian contemporaries, but not the material remains over which he pored. In addition, Haussmannisation

---

[13] Cf. the title of one of the few journalistic notices on Vacquer's death, 'Un mystérieux sondeur de Paris antique', cited in Pachtère and Sellier, 'Vacquer', III.

[14] See below, p. 179.

[15] Seymour de Ricci, 'Paris à l'époque romane', 112.

[16] See e.g. S. Legaret, 'L'interprétation des dossiers de Vacquer: essai de méthode', *Cahiers de la Rotonde*, 2 (1979) – mostly in fact devoted to unpicking carton 63 from the Fonds Vacquer.

[17] BHVP 248, fo. 310.

itself contributed to our present ignorance: for, as we shall see, little of what Vacquer found was accounted sufficiently monumental by city authorities or by the French state to be accredited as worthy of preservation and memorialisation. Vacquer received little or nothing in terms of public appreciation for his efforts, which only encouraged this constitutionally uncommunicative and maddeningly reticent man to turn in further on himself. As a result he took most of his unrivalled knowledge of Lutetia to his grave with him and never put into words what his eyes had seen.

While archaeologists obsess over Vacquer, historians ignore him altogether. What, simply, has never been done is to place this extraordinary figure and his life work into the history of the nineteenth century, rather than of Antiquity. Rather than seeing the Vacquer archive as an eye-glass on to ancient Lutetia, the remainder of this article will approach Vacquer's archaeological endeavours as a means of exploring the history and the myths of the city of modernity that nineteenth-century Paris prided itself on being – the city, that is, where Théodore Vacquer lived, prospered, saw – and failed in all he attempted.

It is important to register from the outset the place of myth in this story of proclaimed modernity. In his book, *Paris, City of Modernity* (2000), Patrice Higonnet analysed a whole miscellany of Paris's self-mythologisations – Paris as revolution, fashion, pleasure and so on – and how these play into an over-riding myth of Paris as the quintessential site of modernity.[18] This rich study has no space, however, for consideration of how Paris might have mythologised its own history – a startling omission, in fact, not least in that Paris has had a mythic history almost as long as it has had a past. Indeed, its history is inseparable from its self-mythologisations.

The grounds on which Paris's mythologisation was longest based was genealogical, or, rather, *faux*-genealogical.[19] From the seventh century onwards, a myth of origins had accorded the Franks a Trojan ancestry, and from the ninth century Paris was fittingly Trojanised. One early standard version of the myth saw a certain Francion fleeing a blazing Troy and settling in Sycambria before moving to the Rhine frontier whence he and his followers invaded Roman Gaul in the fourth century AD. Another variant argued that the origins of the Roman name of Paris – Lutetia – were derived from Leucothea, a marine goddess cited in Homer. Another claimed that the city was 'like' (*par*) the city of Issius (*Isius*) – and indeed something of a cult around the alleged Greek goddess Issius

[18] P. Higonnet, *Paris, Capital of the World* (Cambridge, MA, 2000). I thank Professor Higonnet for a helpful conversation on this topic.
[19] M. Barroux, *Les origines légendaires de Paris* (Paris, 1955); and J. P. Babelon, *Paris au XVIe siècle* (Paris, 1986), ch. 1. Also useful is *Paris et ses historiens aux XIVe et XVe siècles*, ed. A. Le Roux and L. M. Tisserand (Paris, 1867). For the wider mythologisations of France see esp. C. Beaune, *The Birth of an Ideology: Myths and Symbols in Late-Medieval France* (Oxford, 1991).

was still evident at the abbey-church of Saint-Germain-des-Prés which retained until the sixteenth century what was alleged to be her wizened effigy.[20] Despite the increasingly recondite absurdity of its variants across the Middle Ages and Renaissance, the Trojan myth served clear dynastic purposes: by deriving from Troy, which was thought to have been founded half a millennium before Rome, the Capetian kings of Trojan Paris could claim genealogical and hence ideological precedence over both Roman popes and Holy Roman Emperors. There was something faintly comic about such hubristic pretension: for Lutetia had been little more than a small, provincial Roman city, which even within Gaul had been overshadowed by Lyon, Nîmes, Arles and many others.

This kind of genealogical reading of Paris's mythic past became even less convincing in the seventeenth and eighteenth centuries under the pressure of shifts in modes of historical analysis, but some of its variants continued to find favour. The story that Paris pre-dated the arrival of Julius Caesar in the Gallic Wars provided comfort for the notion of Gaulish origins. But it was above all the emergence in the nineteenth century of the notion of Paris as the mythic city of the future rather than the past which put paid to such approaches. The quiet demise of genealogical accounts of the city's long-standing mythic past was a relatively unnoticed casualty of the establishment of the notion of Paris as city of modernity. The myth now looked forward rather than back. It was still of course a myth.

The process of mythopoeia by which Paris and modernity were fused together had, as its visionary seers, the poet Charles Baudelaire, the 'painters of modern life' (Manet, Monet, Renoir, Pissarro, etc.), and belatedly the philosopher, Walter Benjamin. Its principal technician, as we have suggested, was Baron Georges Haussmann.[21] Baudelaire and his explicator, Benjamin, subscribed to Haussmann's vision of the modern city as a vortex where bodies and commodities ceaselessly circulate in a dazzlingly atemporal whirl of mobility, novelty and exchange. Whether travelling in one of the new omnibus services or else merely strolling in the Haussmannian city, the unrestrained, percipient rambler – the *flâneur* in fact – would find his steps and eyeline directed by the new streets and boulevards on the public monuments now showcased in isolated splendour.[22] Some of these monuments dated from the nineteenth

[20] Babelon, *Paris au XVIe siècle*, 27–8.
[21] See esp. T. J. Clark, *The Painting of Modern Life. Paris in the Art of Manet and his Followers*, revised edn (Princeton, NJ, 1999); R. L. Herbert, *Impressionism: Art, Leisure and Parisian Society* (1988); Walter Benjamin, *The Arcades Project* (Cambridge, MA, 1999); and K. H. Stierle, *La capitale des signes. Paris et son discours* (Paris, 2001). One should note that Benjamin, archaeologist of capitalist modernity, showed no interest whatever in the city of Paris's archaeological record.
[22] The literature on the *flâneur* is vast. The works cited in n. 21 are a starting-point.

century – the Arc de Triomphe, the obelisk Gares du Nord et de l'Est and so on. But others were ancient monuments which were placed in a new context. These tended only to survive if they could be remoulded so as to play a part in the Haussmannian cityscape, their historic aspect largely subsumed under the functionalist, a-historic trappings of the city of modernity. Monuments, first, were cut free from their surrounding medieval or post-medieval overbuilding, according to rules of *dégagement* formulated by proponents of urban renewal in the Enlightenment.[23] Second, many monuments were updated and modernised. And third, their elevation was sometimes altered in the interests of the overall planning demands of the modern city.

We see these three processes at work in the case of Notre Dame cathedral on the Île de la Cité, where Vacquer cut his teeth as an archaeologist in the 1850s. Closely crabbed and confined by a jumble of largely undistinguished housing and the crumbling remains of former church buildings, the cathedral was progressively cut free from its surrounding pulp so that it could stand in splendid isolation. Under the scrupulous eye of arch-conservationist and architect, Emmanuel Viollet-le-Duc, incrustations from the sixteenth and seventeenth centuries were ruthlessly excised, to allow the gothic idiom to dominate; the adjacent Hôtel-Dieu demolished outright to improve the monument's all-round visibility; and new statues and gargoyles commissioned in the approved gothic manner. Important here too was the six-fold increase in the size of the square in front of the cathedral, the ancient Parvis de Notre-Dame. This was now generously opened out, completely altering the experience of viewing the site, and bringing it into line with modernist Haussmannian creations. In addition, considerable work was undertaken to level the soil around the square. If one today descends the steps leading to the archaeological crypt on the Place du Parvis-Notre-Dame, one encounters some six metres lower than the existing street level, the medieval street leading along to what were steps up to the cathedral's west front. Much of the Île de la Cité in fact was packed with soil under Haussmann so as to be a metre or more higher than the ancient terrain.

The fate of the Parvis de Notre-Dame is a reminder that the work of Haussmannisation involved the levelling of the historic terrain on which the city had been built. Historians have often stressed how Haussmannisation entailed the building of a massive sewer system and the development of catacombs for the relocated cemeteries of the central zones of the city. Yet these subterranean constructions did not have such a profound effect on the visible historic tissue of the city as the more

---

[23] For *dégagement* as a staple principle of urban renewal through *embellissement*, see, besides Papayannis, *Planning Paris*, J. L. Harouel, *L'embellissement des villes: l'urbanisme français au XVIIIe siècle* (Paris, 1993); and *L'urbanisme parisien au siècle des Lumières*, ed. M. Le Moel (Paris, 1997).

subtle kind of levelling evident in the Île de la Cité – a process to which the Vacquer archive bears ample witness. Haussmannisation involved not simply the excavation and remodelling of Parisian land-surface, and the replacement of crooked roadways by rectilinear boulevards. Haussmannian vistas worked best across levelled, flattened space. And the legibility of Paris as the city of modernity entailed a profound remodelling of the city's depths and heights, and the consequent erasure of much of its historic density by a process of systematic elevation and depression of topological features which had hitherto played significant parts in the city's history.

The city had originally been located on a marshy bog in a meander of the river Seine – the name Lutetia probably derived from *lutum*, Latin for mud or muck. That muck now had to be drained, certainly, but it could also be relocated altogether. Merovingian settlement on the Right Bank had clustered around small hillocks – or *monceaux* – which were now brought down in size, leaving only the vaguest of traces of a millennium's worth of history. Today one may cast one's eye at the steps leading up to the churches of Saint-Gervais in the Marais and of the nearby Saint-Jacques-de-la-Boucherie, little suspecting that those steps are the last remaining vestiges of two such *monceaux*, erased from the landscape by Haussmann's bulldozers.[24] Then, again, when one looks up the Avenue de l'Opéra towards the Opéra-Garnier, it takes imagination to visualise the fortified ramparts, the towering midden-heaps and two ramshackle windmills which had to be removed so as to give the enduring modernist impression of monuments viewed across a wide horizontal expanse. In the case of the Opéra, one can do more than visualise in fact, for there are photographic records of the process of change. Haussmann rather championed the new medium of photography as a means of indicating the extent of his achievement and used it to highlight a 'before and after' approach to the city. The notion of *le Vieux Paris* only made sense as a product of the city's modernisation. The function of the city's history was to glorify the present and the future, and to act as a memento of a past that had been mercifully discarded.

The boulevardisation and modernisation associated with the creation of the new city, involving the sweeping away of medieval and post-medieval debris and the flattening of the terrain, uncovered what lay below the surface. Not least, it lay bare the material remains of a civilisation scarcely known hitherto – save through the scanty documentary record – namely, Roman Paris, Lutetia, the focus of Théodore Vacquer's life and energies. In a very real sense, then, we can

[24] For an episode in 1111 based on the independent power base of the comte de Meulan on the St Gervais *monceau*, see R. H. Bautier, 'Paris au temps d'Abelard', in *Abelard en son temps* (Paris, 1981), 40ff.

understand Vacquer as Haussmann's doppelganger. He was literally the archaeologist of Haussmannian modernity. Haussmann operated through erasure of topological features and the material culture and vestigial traces of a discardable past: Vacquer made of those very processes of destruction and reconstruction the substance of his life and work. He, he alone, saw those things happen, he and he alone could piece the jigsaw together.

In order to assess Théodore Vacquer's role in these processes of modernisation, it is helpful to understand something of Parisian historiography in the nineteenth century – and in particular the emergent notion of heritage, or *patrimoine*.[25] The foundation of the Ecole des Chartes in 1821 had helped to stimulate the documentarist, Rankean study of national history. In addition, the emphasis of early nineteenth-century liberal historians on the role of the communes within that national past inevitably focused much attention on the history of the nation's capital city. In 1830, Guizot established the French Commission on Historical Monuments, which reconnected with work of inventorisation and classification of urban monuments that had started in the 1790s but fallen into decay.[26] From 1833, the Commission had its own inspectorate and a skeletal bureaucracy. It proceeded by listing monuments of historic or aesthetic significance, and, where necessary, supplied guidelines on their restoration.

By the 1830s, there were signs of a growing wish to explore the history of the city not only through the archival record but also through analysis of the existing built environment. There was even a sense in which this might be even more instructive than archival research. Particularly outspoken in this respect was the great novelist and poet, Victor Hugo, a fierce opponent of excessive clearance. His paean to the Middle Ages, the novel *Notre-Dame de Paris* (1829) had already launched a 'war on demolition', which he would doggedly pursue for the next half century and more, in a veritable conservationist campaign in journalistic, public and occasional writings, spiced with occasional bursts of bombastic humour. Though he was still in a minority as regards the need for conservation, he shared with his opponents the view that what counted most were public monuments of high aesthetic or historical significance. He and his conservationist allies, like the Commission for Historic Monuments, all prized highest medieval building, and in particular the gothic style. The Commission in particular had a pecking order which valorised politically and artistically significant buildings prior to the Renaissance. This meant that the architecture of the sixteenth, seventeenth and eighteenth centuries was often ruthlessly

[25] See the works cited above, n. 3.
[26] From *Lieux de mémoire*, ed. Nora, II, see esp. D. Poulot, 'Alexandre Lenoir et les musées des monuments français', L. Theis, 'Guizot et l'institution de la mémoire', and A. Fermigier, 'Mérimée et l'inspection des monuments historiques'.

sacrificed and virtually never defended. At the other end, Vacquer's traces of the pre-gothic also tended to lose out.[27] The often sparse and invariably unmonumental low-grade public ruins and domestic buildings for the most part, drawn from what was a third-rate Roman conurbation, which were his stock in trade, lay well outside the conservationist purview.

Théodore Vacquer saw his role as informing the public and the state about the Gallo-Roman and early medieval period which was overshadowed so extensively by the high Middle Ages. From the 1840s, Adolphe Berty was collecting data on medieval and Renaissance buildings in work which would produce multi-volumed publication after 1866 as the *Topographie historique du Vieux Paris*.[28] Vacquer set about bridging the gap between Berty and his associates on one hand, and on the other the emergent scholarship on the prehistoric period, which was the focus of Eugène Belgrand (the paleolithic scholar was also Haussmann's lieutenant, and was largely responsible for the engineering achievement behind the creation of the Paris sewer system).[29] Vacquer sought to fill the gap between the Middle Ages and the prehistoric era. He eschewed the prehistoric era, but ran out of interest in Paris after the year 1000. This made him unusual – a characteristic trait – since this was when most other scholars began.

A further influence on Vacquer was the life and work of Viollet-le-Duc, mentioned above. Viollet-le-Duc was the ardent champion of the gothic, and the principal theorist of historical restoration in nineteenth-century France. His views exuded an aggressive historicism which girded the notion of restoration with the mystique of artistic creation. 'To restore an edifice', he famously argued, 'is not to maintain it, repair it or refashion it; it is to reestablish it in its complete state which may never have occurred at any given moment.'[30] The restorer should be able to work from the functionality of parts to capture the idea of the whole. It is Viollet-le-Duc who was responsible for the restoration of the medieval city of Carcassonne and the chateau of Pierrefonds, producing buildings which seem more to prefigure Walt Disney than literally to depict what these sites ever looked like at any moment in the Middle Ages. Viollet-le-Duc also

[27] The antiquarian writer Jollois produced a *Mémoire sur les antiquités romaines et gallo-romaines de Paris* in 1840 which did something to stimulate interest in early medieval Paris, but failed to turn the tide.

[28] Berty's work was published in fragments and was never complete or comprehensive. For an example, see his *Histoire générale de Paris. Topographie historique du Vieux Paris. Région du Louvre et des Tuileries* (Paris, 1866).

[29] E. Belgrand, *La Seine. I. Le bassin parisien aux âges préhistoriques* (2 vols., Paris, 1869). Cf. BHVP 248.

[30] E. Viollet-le-Duc, *Dictionnaire raisonné de l'architecture française* (10 vols., Paris, 1867–70), VIII, 14. On this highly influential figure see B. Foucart, 'Viollet-le-Duc et la restauration', in *Lieux de mémoire*, ed. Nora, II.

restored the basilica of kings out at Saint-Denis and was responsible for the restoration of the Sainte-Chapelle on the Île de la Cité – work which came in places dangerously close to medievalist pastiche. His reconstruction of Notre-Dame was also notorious in this respect. His plans included his serious proposal to erect a spire on each of the cathedral's two towers, on the ground that the building's architects had originally planned this eventuality – it was in due time decided that the towers could not bear the weight.[31] Over in England, John Ruskin was developing a very different version of what could and should be involved in the restoration of historic monuments.[32] Ruskin had some followers in France – but not many. The ideas of Viollet-le-Duc enjoyed a hegemony in the French world of restoration right down to the end of the nineteenth century, thus ensuring that ideas of historical restoration merged somewhat confusedly with imaginative and artistic creativity. As we shall see, this approach influenced Vacquer.

Many of these strands came together over an archaeological dispute in Paris in the 1870s and early 1880s, which constituted a defining moment in Vacquer's odyssey and a signal marker in the history of Parisian conservation, and in some senses in the history of Parisian memory too. It is an episode which we might call the the 'Battle of the *Arènes*' ('Battle of the Arena'). The dispute focused on the Roman amphitheatre – the *Arènes de Lutèce*, as it came to be called – built in the second century AD over towards what is nowadays the Jardin des Plantes in the Fifth Arrondissement.[33] The *Arènes* were probably only operational for a century or more, before growing insecurity within the Roman Empire led to their falling into disuse. Although the English student Alexander Neckham recorded the continued existence of the monument in the twelfth century, shortly afterwards much of the masonry was probably carted off to provide substance for the city wall of Philip Augustus, constructed between 1190 and 1215. So remote was memory of Lutetia by this time, so askew any sense of the Parisian past, moreover, that chroniclers recorded that Parisians were using stone from walls which had been constructed to defend the city against invasion by Saracens. After this, the *Arènes* remained as a place-name, but no visible sign of the former monument was evident. It was buried under one of those hillocks, those *monceaux*, which, as I have suggested, were so anathematic to Haussmannian horizonality.

---

[31] See the illustration in *Lieux de mémoire*, ed. Nora, I, 1624.

[32] For a comparative glance at Ruskin, see Choay, *The Invention of the Historic Monument*, 92ff.

[33] Formigé, *Les Arènes de Paris* (Paris, 1918). The works cited above, n. 10, provide more recent analyses.

It was in the 1860s, during the building of the Rue Monge, one of the outer network of boulevard-like streets which Haussmann had started to establish on the Left Bank, that the relics of the Roman arena were suddenly uncovered. The levelling of a *monceau* on which had stood the convent of the Augustines of Notre-Dame, sequestered by the state in 1860, revealed substantial Roman remains. Vacquer was soon on hand to confirm that what was now visible were the remains of the northern half of a very substantial arena, and he went on to manage this early phase of excavation. The *Arènes* accorded far more closely with the notion of the monumental than anything Vacquer had discovered so far. It was a find that was too significant to be merely covered over by the trappings of Haussmann's modernity or dismissed as insufficiently monumental. He also must have been encouraged that public interest was growing too, stimulated by new discoveries (skeletons, medallions, jewellery, stone carvings, etc.) widely reported in the press.

Yet Vacquer had an opponent far more in tune with the Haussmannian Zeitgeist than the prickly antiquarian – namely, an omnibus company. It had been the latter which, on digging down nearly twenty metres, had discovered the Roman remains. The company managers were not interested in conservation: they wanted the old convent site to be converted into an omnibus depot. Napoleon III visited the site in person in 1870, but deferred a decision on it, not least because of the likely high cost of full restoration. Baron Haussmann was by then, moreover, politically on the run, hounded by press and political opponents over alleged financial malversations. It must have been one of the last decisions he made, prior to his dismissal, to refuse permission to restore and conserve. Citing the *avis défavorable* accorded the site by the Commission of Historical Monuments, Haussmann gave the green light to the omnibus company.

Thus far, the story seems to constitute a nice modernist parable, then – and a cautionary tale for conservationists. The latter had proved to be disastrously divided, and had not put up a sufficiently powerful public case for the preservation of the most monumental pre-medieval remains ever to be uncovered in the city. If Vacquer was disappointed, to some extent he had himself to blame: he was said to have been irritatingly quarrelsome with fellow-conservationists. In any case, the opening of the Franco-Prussian War and the ensuing sieges of Paris hardly provided an encouraging context for public campaigning. The overthrow of the Second Empire was hardly the most propitious moment for attracting support for imperial remains. The conservationists could only take some small pleasure from the fact that German bombs lobbed into the city during the Prussian siege destroyed a number of huts belonging to the omnibus company.

New roadworks and street clearance continued in the vicinity of the bus depot in following years. A decision in the early 1880s to open a side street off the Rue Monge led to the demolition of another convent in the area. Digging down, the builders found what was evidently the other part of the arena. A public campaign was started almost at once, and worked with newfound energy.[34] This time there was no omnibus company in play, and no Haussmann to say no. The struggle was tough. But a turning point was reached in July 1883, when the now venerable Victor Hugo wheeled magnificently into action, issuing a public letter to the city council in support of conservation:

> It is not possible that Paris, the city of the future, should renounce the living proof that it was a city of the past. The arena is an ancient mark of a great city. It is a unique monument. The municipal council which destroys it would in some manner destroy itself. Conserve it at any price.[35]

Three days later, the city council purchased the land containing the remnants of the arena. It was rescued from housing development, and plans for its full display were only inhibited by the need to lay bare the full extent of this 'ancient mark of a great city', as Victor Hugo had put it.

The Haussmannian parable of 1870 had thus received a conservationist riposte. The year 1883 was a cautionary tale not for conservationists but for modernisers. The incident seems to have been a pivotal part of a set of developments relating to conservation which were unfolding at an accelerating tempo.[36] The city authorities began to adopt a more sensitive and responsive attitude towards its own heritage – an approach which was helped by a kind of anti-Haussmannian backlash in planning circles during the Fin de Siècle. The straight line of the boulevard which had been the avatar of Haussmannian modernity was increasingly qualified by a taste for the curvilinear, the neo-rococo, the picturesque and the more organic morphology of *art nouveau*. This measured (if never complete) shift away from High Haussmannism was popular too. The campaigners who in 1883 had laboured hard to get the media and the public on their side were now actually pushing against an open door. A number of lobbies emerged as effective fighters for the conservationist cause, and highlighted appeals to public support.

The emergence of effective public lobbies would be crowned by the establishment in 1898 of the Commission du Vieux Paris – a semi-official body which is still in existence and which has proved a doughty fighter for a more historic awareness of the city's built environment. The Commission du Vieux Paris played a key role, for example, in changing the protocols of the Commission of Historic Monuments in a way

---

34 See the materials at BHVP 518: 'Campagne pour la sauvegarde des Arènes'.

35 Cited in de Carbonnières, *Lutèce*, 101.

36 On this phase of the movement for Parisian conservation, the work of Anthony Sutcliffe is particularly useful: *The Autumn of Central Paris* and *Paris: An Architectural History* (1993).

which highlighted the desirability of conserving buildings surrounding a major monument – rather than just cutting it free from its aesthetically 'inferior' context. Although France was painfully slow to adopt the kind of rescue archaeology which became the norm in England and many other European countries over the middle decades of the twentieth century, it is probably true to say that no notable destruction of ancient historic sites on the scale and significance of the Arènes farrago has occurred since then.[37] Generally speaking, from the 1880s, the Haussmannian reflex in Paris has had to find ways of accommodating discourses of heritage and historicity.

There was, however, to be a further twist in the tale of the *Arènes*. With excavations now steaming ahead, and with public opinion primed to expect great things, it became apparent that there was very little of value actually located at the site. The scale of the arena pit – around a hundred metres in diameter, making it the second largest in the whole of Roman Gaul – had excited wild hopes. In fact, it soon became blindingly obvious to the archaeologists involved that nothing on the scale of the magnificent amphitheatres of Arles and Nîmes was going to emerge. Partly this was because the most impressive part of the monument lay under (and had been destroyed under) the famous 1870 bus depot. The original builders of the amphitheatre had deployed the topography of the site to advantage, using what had been an upward slope on the Rue Monge to erect some thirty rows of seats facing west. These had all gone. Worse, it was now discovered that on the eastern side there was no banked seating at all: on that side was located a stage for theatrical performances – making the *Arènes* a mixed theatre-arena of a kind found elsewhere in Roman Gaul. What with the Haussmannian destruction of the 1870s, the removal of stone in the thirteenth century to build the Philip Augustus wall, plus age-old attrition on the site, there was extremely little about which to get excited. 'In order to preserve the arena', noted one somewhat alarmed official, 'it would first be necessary to show that the arena exists; experience seems to me to demonstrate the opposite.' 'As a monument', he concluded, 'there is nothing there any more.'[38]

The city official in question was aware of the eager anticipation of the general public, and feared that the destruction of what little remained would trigger accusations of vandalism which the municipal authorities wished to avoid. In the event, the affair was quietly laid to rest with no public fanfare, as excavations continued at a snail's pace. The existence of a circular wall two metres high encircling the arena pit was identified, excavated – and then to all intents and purposes constructed. Ten rows of

---

[37] The demolition of the Second Empire market buildings at Les Halles in the 1970s comes closest.

[38] BHVP 521: 'Rapport sur les fouilles et la conservation des ruines des arènes de la rue Monge', fo. 119.

seats were also put in place on the southern edge of the site. This was far less than the thirty rows which archaeologists had identified as once being here – but whose reconstruction would have required the demolition of a sizeable chunk of the Rue Monge. Much of the work of (re)construction was only completed in 1915–16, in the midst of a war when issues other than *patrimoine* were on the minds of government and people alike and when memory of the old Battle of the *Arènes* was fading into insignificance.

In this remarkable record of archaeological fiasco, one would expect to find our friend Théodore Vacquer. In fact, he was notable mainly by his absence. His bad behaviour towards visitors to the site of the *Arènes* in 1870, whom he was said to have terrorised with the unbridled rage of a wild boar, was such that he was henceforth banned from most excavations. The man who had indeed discovered the site in 1869–70 was only on the sidelines in the 1880s. In the last years of his life, the grumpy antiquarian refused even to mention the name of the *Arènes*, and became angry and dismissive if anyone brought it up in his presence – to the extent that a fellow curator at the Carnavalet warned him not to give the impression that he was siding with the enemies of conservation.[39] Just as the monument itself was being recovered for Parisian memory, he preferred to forget the whole thing. His embittered, unmanageable character meant that he was increasingly excluded from significant excavations in Paris. He preferred to sulk in his tent – and to do (or, in the case of his magnum opus, not to do) other things.

In his unpublished manuscripts, Vacquer himself gave a revealing explanation for his silence over the *Arènes*, and his growing disenchantment with the discipline of archaeology to which he had devoted his life.

> Virtually all the relics and monuments that I have made known would have been destroyed and forever unknown without me. I have acquired the fullest certainty in that no other archeologist except I has ever turned up a excavations and worked them. It was only the *Arènes* [he added resentfully] which attracted attention and which the curious and the world of savants were interested in.[40]

The hidden archaeologist of Haussmannian modernity, the 'editor', as he called himself,[41] of Paris's pre-medieval past, thus chose to remain hidden, preferring private satisfaction to public éclat. In lines which reveal something of his mental turmoil, he struggled to justify his position of principled invisibility, of keeping effectively to himself all that his eyes had seen.

> If I have [crossed out: always] avoided publicising my discoveries as I went along, this was so as to avoid [crossed out: my attracting] generally despoliatory rivalries, and so as not to attract the curious onto sites where I was kindly tolerated [later addition: and where I kept myself more or less invisible]. Had other people, lacking in experience

---

[39] Pachtère and Sellier, 'Vacquer', 10 and n.
[40] BHVP 248, fo. 302v.
[41] See above, p. 163.

and showing indiscreet and embarrassing zeal, come there as a result of my presence, they would have caused me to be thrown out alongside them by architects and building contractors who have no time for archaeology.[42]

'Archaeologists show us' – and this is now another archaeologist speaking, in this case the great archaeologist of Parisian memory – 'that nothing is forgotten, nothing is destroyed and that the meanest circumstance of life, as far from us as can be imagined, has marked its furrow in the immense catacombs of the past in which humanity recounts its life.'[43] This quotation from Proust is an interesting one in which to insert the anti-hero of this essay. The curious Battle of the *Arènes* may well have been, as I have argued, a turning point in terms of public appreciation of heritage. But it was a turning point around which our shy hedgehog stubbornly refused to turn. He felt out of place in the modern world of public heritage campaigning, or incorporative *sociétés savantes*, and of writerly rivalries. Much about Vacquer's commitment to archaeology in his youth had marked him out as a pioneer. But by the 1890s the rest of the world was catching him up – even regarding him as a remnant as archaic as his subject-matter. When in 1841 he had had his Merovingian epiphany, archaeology was simply not taught in any major establishment of higher education or learning. Now the discipline had already established itself in the Ecole des Chartes, the Louvre, the Collège de France, the Ecole Pratique des Hautes Etudes and the Sorbonne, and was professionalising, fast.[44]

In any case, it must have become increasingly evident to this constitutional loner that the postponement of writing his great work on Gallo-Roman Lutetia – a subject for which no one either then nor since has been more fitted – was a postponement *sine die*. He had always struggled to write: he preferred a trowel to a pen in the hand. Latterly, his workload at the Carnavalet was a convenient pretext for hiding something akin to writer's block. He published nothing, he stated, 'so as not to deflower anything'.[45] He preferred to keep his powder dry and his scholarly virginity intact in his study, where he spent his time simply going over his notes, adding further layers of meaning and punctilious corrections to their already palimpsestic indecipherability.

Vacquer's life thus shows us how wrong Proust really was: in archaeology, much *can* be forgotten and much *can* be destroyed, and in order to be a mediator of memory an archaeologist needs to leave

[42] BHVP 248, fo. 310v.
[43] Cited in P. Velay and J. Godeau, *Les premiers mots de Paris* (Paris, 1997), 27.
[44] M. C. Grenêt-Delacroix, 'Etat et patrimoine sous la Troisième République. De l'amateur au professionnel dans la gestion du patrimoine national', in *L'esprit des lieux. Le patrimoine et la cité*, ed. D. Grance and D. Poulot (Grenoble, 1997).
[45] BHVP 248, fo. 310v.

traces of his activity which are intelligible to those who follow. If not, then the eyes of the archaeologist – the eyes of Théodore Vacquer in fact – will remain forever those of a sphinx.

Yet despite their ungiving, quizzical nature, the eyes of Théodore Vacquer can help us, I believe, to explore the links between remembering and forgetting, between memory and amnesia, between myth and modernity, which lie at the heart of this article. When we visit or revisit the *Arènes de Lutèce* – as I fear, as a result of this chapter, we really must – it might also help us to reflect on what is a 'site of memory'. The idea of 'sites of memory' has had tremendous vogue in recent years, grounded in the multi-volumed, multi-authored work edited by Pierre Nora, *Les lieux de mémoire*.[46] When one reads Nora and his team one is struck not only by how many such sites were in fact monuments based in Paris – and which largely conform to a Haussmannian aesthetic: made (or, as in the case of Notre-Dame cathedral, as we have suggested, re-made) in the course of the long nineteenth century; best seen at a distance, from the optic of the straight line and across horizontally ordered (and, as I have suggested, horizontalised) space.[47] The *Arènes de Lutèce* simply do not conform to this pattern at all. Perhaps this is why Nora and his crew ignore it. The *Arènes* constitute a very unusual Parisian – and *ergo* very un-Haussmannian and un-modernist – monument. It is complicatedly encrusted within a tangle of side-streets and a small public park. There are no modernist, Haussmannian framings. The site is dominated visually by the backs of the houses facing on to the Rue Monge; and dominated aurally by the excited yelling of children in the nearby Ecole Maternelle. The place has become in essence a playground. The passing tourist may hear the occasional concert here, but one is far more likely to come across local children playing a scratch game of soccer, lobbing *boules* or engaging in hide-and-seek. The failure of the *Arènes* as a monument of modernity and as a site of memory has released it so it could become a locus of neighbourhood sociability – infantile, juvenile, parental, romantic. The tourists may in consequence stay away – but *tant pis* (or even *tant mieux*). This is after all a site of memory which Parisians have managed to forget, not once but twice in their history. It is a site of memory which is barely a site at all in the Haussmannian sense, and in which memory jostles along quite comfortably with amnesia. In sum the *Arènes de Lutèce* suggest that there are more ways of parsing the term *lieu de mémoire* than are imaginable in the world of Pierre Nora and his eruditely Cartesian *confrères*.[48]

---

[46] *Lieux de mémoire*, ed. Nora.

[47] E.g. the Eiffel tower, the Pantheon, Notre-Dame cathedral, the Louvre, the Palais-Bourbon, the Collège de France, Sacré-Coeur de Montmartre, Parisian statues.

[48] Critical appreciations of this project include B. Taithe, '*Monuments aux morts?* Nora's *Realms of Memory* and Samuel's *Theatres of Memory*', *History of the Human Sciences*, 12 (1999), and

The failure of the *Arènes* to be incorporated into Paris's mythologising myths about itself over the nineteenth and twentieth centuries seems also to be linked to more fundamental issues about the Parisian, and indeed the French, past. The national trauma which the Franco-Prussian War of 1870 had inflicted had damaging effects on the fundamental conceptualisation of Vacquer's life-time project. His wish to write on Paris's pre-medieval past – Gaulish, Gallo-Roman, Merovingian, Carolingian – was now out of tune with the times. The post-1871 historical establishment rekindled Germanophobia in polemics which replayed some of the older Enlightenment debate over 'Germanist' and 'Romanist' readings of the past. The tendency now was to valorise the contribution of the Gauls or the Gallo-Romans to French history, and to downgrade estimation of Germanic influences, Frankish, Merovingian or Carolingian.[49] This was true of the great national histories of Lavisse, Fustel de Coulanges and Camille Jullian and others just as it was of much of the conservation lobby (including Viollet-le-Duc in fact). It is difficult not to imagine the depth of Vacquer's disillusionment as he read such men who erected this caesura over the French past in a way which made his projected volume on Paris anachronistic – all the more in that such men consistently fetishised historical documents while underrating or even ignoring outright archaeological findings. At his death archaeology was becoming the Cinderella discipline among the 'ancillary sciences' of a highly 'textualist' tradition of history-writing.[50]

Vacquer's discomfiture linked too to broader issues regarding Parisians' view of the Roman phase of their own history. It may seem perverse to suggest that Paris has any problem with *Romanitas* generally. The downgrading of Germanic influence on the French past after 1871 was accompanied by benign readings of Roman influence. Furthermore, from the Renaissance onwards, Roman antiquity has provided many of the building models, the monumental templates and the urban grids which have made Paris what it is. Unsurprisingly too, over the course of the centuries poets and writers are far more likely to compare Paris with Rome than with any city. This was certainly the case in the nineteenth century, according to Pierre Citron's wonderfully (if quaintly) encyclopaedic computations: in his list of literary citations where Parisian comparisons are made, Rome stands way out in front, ahead of Athens

H. T. Ho Tai, 'Remembered Realms: Pierre Nora and French National Memory', *American Historical Review*, 106 (2001).

[49] See the excellent article by Alain Schnapp, 'France et Allemagne: l'archéologie en jeu dans la construction nationale', *Mélanges de l'Ecole française de Rome*, 113 (2001); and K. Pomian, 'Francs et Gaulois', in *Lieux de mémoire*, ed. Nora, II.

[50] Cf. O. Buchsenschutz and A. Schnapp, 'Alésia', in *Lieux de mémoire*, ed. Nora, III, 4132ff.

and Jerusalem – with Babylon and Sodom and Gomorrah staunchly bringing up the rear (so to speak).[51]

What is less clear – and therefore all the more striking – is the extent to which Paris's debt to *Romanitas* seems to have excluded positive valuation of the city's own ancient history within the wider community. Napoleons I and III showed far more interest in ancient Rome than ancient Lutetia.[52] Napoleon III was even an ardent enthusiast for archaeology: he engaged in enthusiastic quest to locate the site of the battle of Alesia in which Julius Caesar had defeated the Gauls under Vercingetorix, and inaugurated the Musée des Antiquités Nationales at Saint-Germain-en-Laye in 1867. Yet ultimately he preferred an omnibus depot to a Roman ruin at the heart of his capital city.[53] Ancient Lutetia weighed exceeding light in the imperial scales: after all, Lutetia had been a provincial small town, with a small-town history, no major monuments worth exploiting and a Trojan foundation myth far too wacky to be recycled. It was as though some Freudian family romance was in play, in which every Parisian (except of course poor Théodore Vacquer) was ashamed of the ignoble status of Lutetian genealogy and sought out a myth of substitution which would equip the modern city with an altogether nobler – if totally imagined – parentage. Paris was really the child of Rome, not of Lutetia.

Even had Théodore Vacquer managed to bring his magnum opus successfully to fruition, one has leave to doubt whether it would have made much difference. Given the reluctance of his peers to accept a Lutetian heritage, it seems very unlikely. As we have suggested, the nationalist ideology which gripped post 1870 history-writing looked askance at archaeological findings unconducive to Gallophilic national myth. The same was true in addition of the myth of the transhistorical modernity of the city of Paris which developed over the nineteenth century alongside a notion of *le Vieux Paris*. Neither had time nor much respect for Lutetia. Despite Victor Hugo's support for the *Arènes* in 1883, his life-time achievement was rather to foster a view of ancient Paris as grounded in the gothic – a mood which the photographers of Parisian modernity like Marville and Nadar inscribed into Parisian memory in their representation of tangled medieval streets and gothic shadings.[54] In twentieth-century Rome, in contrast, archaeologists would cut through medieval debris like butter through a knife so as to reach the imperial

---

[51] P. Citron, *La poésie de Paris dans la littérature française de Rousseau à Baudelaire* (2 vols., Paris, 1961), II, 112.

[52] Classical and neo-classical references for the First Empire are picked up well in the relevant volume of the series, *Nouvelle Histoire de Paris*: J. Tulard, *Le consulate et l'empire*, 2nd edn (Paris, 1983). For Napoleon III's fascination with the battle-site of Alesia, see Buchsenschutz and Schnapp, 'Alésia'.

[53] See above, p. 171.

[54] For early photography and the city, see S. Rice, *Parisian Views* (1997).

substratum: for Rome's idea of itself was not grounded in the Middle Ages but in Antiquity.[55] The situation as regards Paris was very different. In order to see the most impressive Roman monument in Paris – the Roman baths – one has actually to enter the Museum of the Middle Ages![56] Once Parisian archaeologists had reached the Roman substratum in the nineteenth century they found it difficult – such was the prioritisation of the medieval and the monumental – to get the authorities to conserve them. Furthermore, Vacquer represented the age of amateur archaeologising, which lacked bolstering from professional organisations and publicity campaigns. Only from 1883 was there much of a will to conserve anything Lutetian. By then it was too late – most of the Roman city which the eyes of Théodore Vacquer had seen lay under the remodelled environment of the city of modernity. There were some memories – in this case, Vacquer's memories – which Parisians seemingly did not care to have.

The modernising myth of nineteenth-century Paris was a juggernaut which crushed beneath it the frail and vestigial findings of Théodore Vacquer. It had no time for what the eyes of our failed archaeologist had seen. Furthermore there is evidence that even Vacquer himself fell under the Haussmannian myth which his whole life had seemed to resist.

Vacquer spent the last decades of his life preparing a map of Roman Lutetia, based on archaeological findings across the centuries, and especially those which he had seen with his own eyes. The map was – characteristically – unfinished when he died. But his friend Pachtère subsequently published a map of early Paris based on Vacquer's sketches and drawings.[57] He highlighted all that Vacquer had achieved in revolutionising historical knowledge of the city by also supplying a series of maps based on what earlier *savants* had imagined the early city to be like (Figure 2). In the Middle Ages and for much of the early modern period, reconstruction had been based on Julius Caesar's account of the Gallic Wars plus some mythological imaginings. The nineteenth century had seen more systematic archival research, plus adventitious archaeological finds, which had gradually reshaped contemporaries' sense of the ancient physiognomy of Lutetia. Dulaure – the standard source when Vacquer was a boy – showed a Left-Bank city emerging, with traces of Right-Bank occupation too. Dulaure – as Lenoir, in a later depiction – stressed the

---

[55] Thanks to Simon Ditchfield for this helpful comparison. See e.g. D. Bocquet, 'L'archéologie dans la capitale italienne: Rome 1870–1911', *Mélanges de l'Ecole française de Rome*, 113 (2001); M. Tarpin, 'La Rome antique de Mussolini: actualité des fouilles et restaurations d'avant-guerre', in *L'esprit des lieux*, ed. Grance and Poulot, esp. 97ff.

[56] The Musée National du Moyen-Âge was established by Alexandre Sommerard in 1843, in the *hôtel* of the abbés of Cluny, constructed in and over the Thermes de Julien in the fifteenth century.

[57] F. G. Pachtère, 'Préface: légendes et traditions sur la ville antique: les débuts et les progrès de son histoire. État de la question', in *Paris à l'époque gallo-romaine*, xxv.

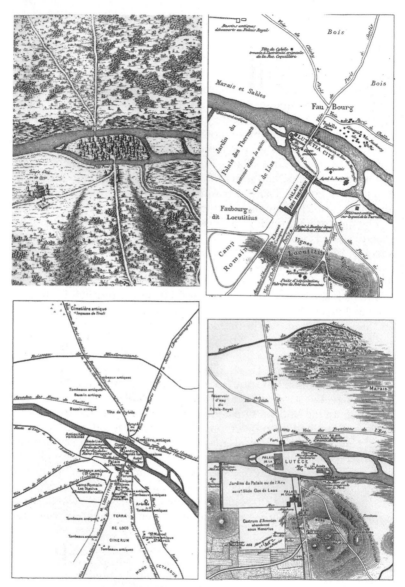

Figure 2 Historical maps of Paris. Top left: according to De La Mare, eighteenth century. Top right: according to Dulaure, early nineteenth century. Bottom left: according to Jollois, mid-nineteenth century. Bottom right: according to Lenoir, second half of nineteenth century. From 'Préface', F. G. de Pachtère, *Paris à l'époque gallo-romaine (Etude faite avec l'aide des papiers et des plans de Th. Vacquer)* (Paris, 1912).

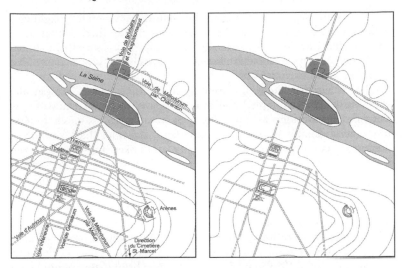

Figure 3 Left: Ancient Paris, according to Vacquer. From F. G. de Pachtère, *Paris à l'époque gallo-romaine (Etude faite avec l'aide des papiers et des plans de Th. Vacquer)* (Paris, 1912), xxv. Right: Vacquer's map, adjusted to take account of archaeological finds.

natural features: the physical relief, the marches, the fields, the vines, the waterways. But Vacquer's map of Lutetia – presented with no natural land features, only contour lines – showed a remarkable transformation.

To a considerable extent, this map is a latter-day triumph for Vacquer's art and science. It presents Lutetia according to the gridiron pattern which late nineteenth-century archaeologists were finding throughout Europe – and in North Africa, in fact, where French colonial archaeologists were revealing geometrically conceived Roman cities which contrasted forcefully with the souk-like intricacy and muddle of the Arabic habitations overlaying them.[58]

Yet this record of all that Théodore Vacquer's eyes had seen was also a record of how much his mind had imagined.

In order to get some purchase on the extent of Vacquer's discoveries, I have taken a highly positivistic step. I have mapped on to Vacquer's gridiron designs the sections of the streetplan which up-to-date archaeological authority shows that we have hard archaeological evidence about (Figure 3, right).[59] This process allows the wheat of proven material

---

[58] Cf. N. Oulebsir, *Les usages du patrimoine. Monuments, musées et politique coloniale en Algérie (1830–1930)* (Paris, 2004). Thanks to Bryan Ward-Perkins for putting me on this track

[59] I have drawn especially on Busson, *Paris, ville antique.*

existence to be separated out from the chaff of Vacquerian imaginings. What is as plain as a pikestaff when we compare the maps is that there exists no hard evidence whatever for the majority of streetplan shown on Vacquer's map. They are streets of his imagining. It is a map of his invention.

What is also strikingly apparent from Vacquer's map – especially when set against the agreed archaeological record – is that unwittingly (we may profoundly assume) Vacquer had made Roman Lutetia into a Haussmannian city. Unconsciously, Vacquer had swallowed Haussmannian notions of Paris, hook, line and sinker. This Don Quixote of Roman Lutetia, who had spent so much time in his life tilting at the windmills of Parisian modernity, was seemingly a Haussmannian through and through, even if it was *sans le savoir*. We may indeed, with a few changes of wording, put into Vacquer's mouth the quotation I cited above of the great architectural restorer, Viollet-le-Duc. 'To *excavate* an edifice' (Viollet-le-Duc had said 'to restore') 'is not to maintain it, repair it or refashion it; it is to reestablish it in its complete state which may never have occurred at any given moment.' [60] What Viollet-le-Duc had been to the monumental record of the Middle Ages, Vacquer had unconsciously reproduced as regards his highly creative, even fantastical imagining of Lutetia. The archaeologist was thus far more than the servile recorder of the minutiae of the past; he was also the inventor, the mythologiser of history and the servant of a Haussmannian myth he spent much of his life resisting.

It is tempting to dismiss Vacquer the archaeologist as a man who failed in all that he attempted on which he set a price. Intriguingly, that judgement – which may well have been his own – is less widely held in our own day. In the last decades of the century which has elapsed since his death in 1898, Vacquer's scholarly reputation has soared. His findings now structure the historical as well as the archaeological record of Parisian Antiquity. Although his techniques were beginning to look archaic by the time of his death, his concern with minute observation, his eye for depiction, his dating through stratigraphy, his sense of the importance of the environment and his marked preference for fieldwork over fireside archaeology are now hailed as having been well ahead of his time. The revival of urban archaeology in the post-Second World War era has led scholars increasingly to highlight his work. In 1998, in his authoritative study of Lutetia, Didier Busson saluted Vacquer as 'the first modern archaeologist of Paris and one of the precursors of urban archaeology'.[61] By then Vacquer's former employer, the Musée Carnavalet, had also finally changed its tune: after bringing out of the warehouses where they had lain, away from public gaze since the First

[60] Cf. above, p. 169.
[61] Busson, *Carte archéologique*, 44.

World War, the Gallo-Roman findings which Vacquer had catalogued (and indeed in a great many cases, actually found), they opened up, in 1991, a new room within their premises for them. They called it the Salle Vacquer – in honour of a Parisian nobody who really was a somebody.

In retrospect it is possible to conclude that, in some senses, the time had not been right for Théodore Vacquer's findings to be incorporated unproblematically into the myths which Parisians and French men and women cultivated about their pasts in the late nineteenth century. They nurtured the idea of *le Vieux Paris* as an undifferentiated but also largely medievo-gothic entity, recalcitrant to Gallo-Roman or Germanic influence. And – especially after the national humiliation of 1870–1 – they established a historiographical caesura in French history with the advent of the Franks, thereby exploding Vacquer's cherished periodisation. If even at the turn of the twenty-first century, moreover, we still, as Bruno Latour has said, 'inhabit the materialised dreams of Haussmann',[62] how much more must this have been the case for someone who had such close personal knowledge of the pre-Haussmannian city – and who had seen the myth of urban modernity growing up round him.

Nonetheless, tracing with care the lineaments of that personal failure, and focusing on the sphynx-like eyes of archaeologist Théodore Vacquer, we can come to grasp and to weigh the force of the ambient myths which structured the reception of his research. Through the eyes and the imagination of the 'permanently rolled-up hedgehog' that was Théodore Vacquer, we can can glimpse, as through a glass darkly, not only the shape and texture of Roman Lutetia but also significant domains of the history of nineteenth-century Paris – its archaeology, its built environment, its developing sense of *patrimoine* and the awesome ideological power of its self-mythologisation, caught midway between past and future, record and imagination, memory and amnesia.

[62] B. Latour and E. Hermant, *Paris ville invisible* (Paris, 1998), 109.

ROYAL HISTORICAL SOCIETY
REPORT OF COUNCIL
SESSION 2006–2007

Officers and Council

- At the Anniversary Meeting on 25 November 2006 Dr V.A. Harding succeeded Dr K.C. Fincham as Honorary Secretary; the remaining Officers of the Society were re-elected.
- Dr M. Smith, Honorary Librarian retired early from post in November 2006, to be replaced by a new Honorary Director of Communications, Professor M. Cragoe with effect from January 2007.
- The Vice-Presidents retiring under By-law XVII were Professor D.R. Bates and Professor W.R. Childs. Professor A. Curry and Dr A. Foster were elected to replace them.
- The Members of Council retiring under By-law XX were Professor G.A. Hosking, Professor R.S. Mackenney and Professor D.M. Palliser. In accordance with By-law XXI, Professor S. Connolly, Professor T Hitchcock, and Professor S. Smith were elected in their place.
- Dr R. Hammersley and Dr H. Barker joined the *Studies in History* Editorial Board, replacing Professor M. Braddick and Dr R. Spang.
- The Society's administrative staff now consists of Sue Carr, Executive Secretary since 25 August 2006 and Melanie Batt, Administrative Assistant.
- haysmacintyre were re-appointed auditors for the year 2006–2007 under By-law XXXIX.
- Heartwood Wealth Management continued to manage the Society's investment funds.

Activities of the Society during the Year

The Annual Report contains individual reports of the activities of the seven Committees which support the work of Council – Research Policy, Teaching Policy, General Purposes, Publications, Finance, Membership and Research Support – and the remarks which now follow are a preface to these more detailed reports.

Throughout the year the Society has maintained its prominent role in defending and advancing the interests of the discipline and the profession.

The President and Honorary Secretary had a useful meeting with Natalie Ceeney, CEO of the The National Archives, David Thomas, and James Strachan, on 15 December 2006. Subjects discussed included TNA's strategy for ensuring preservation of the records of government decisions and actions, its plans for digitisation and searching of existing records, the closure of the Family Records Centre in Clerkenwell, the next Aylmer Seminar, and the ways in which the Society could help TNA achieve its objectives. It was agreed that Natalie Ceeney would speak to the next Research Policy Committee and that David Thomas would be proposed as a member of Council.

Following their meeting with Professor Philip Esler, Chief Executive of the AHRC, on 21 June 2006, the then Honorary Secretary wrote to him to urge the importance of consulting learned societies such as the Society when strategic issues such as the relations between research councils are under review, and received a brief reply. The President has written to AHRC to express the Society's reservations over the proposed introduction of a new 'institutional block grant' system for funding postgraduate students. The Honorary Secretary attended an informal meeting on 13 March 2007 between a group of academics, including past President Dame Janet Nelson and others from different disciplines, and Professor Rick Trainor, a member of the council of AHRC, to make similar points. The President also wrote to AHRC deploring the termination of AHRC funding for the Arts and Humanities Data Service (AHDS) based at the University of Essex, announced in May 2007. The President and the Honorary Secretary had a useful meeting with Professor Tony McEnery, Director of Research at AHRC, on 11 July 2007, at which he outlined the reshaping of AHRC's decision-making structures.

The President and the Honorary Secretary met with Professor Philip Esler, Chief Executive of AHRC, on 13 July 2007. We discussed a number of issues, including the cuts imposed on research council funding and the implications of the Comprehensive Spending Review. It is clear that AHRC does not see itself as funding the Bibliography in the long term, arguing that it should be funded as part of Research Infrastructure, from FEC and QR (RAE) money; this is therefore a matter of high importance for the Society. We also pressed our concerns about AHDS, particularly that the decision had apparently been taken notwithstanding objections from interested parties including the Society, and without a coherent plan for the future sustainability of the electronic resources created with AHRC research funding. Other issues discussed included the future of the RAE, and how it might draw on AHRC's college of advisors, and the question of metrics.

The President and Professor Bates, former Vice-President of the Society, have continued to attend occasional ministerial meetings on the role of history in the school curriculum and its relationship with proposed teaching on 'citizenship'. Regular meetings of the Society, the Institute of Historical Research, History UK (HE) and the Historical Association have continued this year to pool ideas and co-ordinate responses to developments within the discipline. Conferences at the Institute of Historical Research, usually in conjunction with the Society, play an important part in building bridges with schools, the educational establishment, politicians and the wider public.

Over the past year the Society has responded to consultative documents on a wide range of issues, including QAA. It has also made nominations for the AHRC Peer Review College and History Panel.

As usual, the Society made two very successful visits outside London, the first to the University of Hertfordshire on 21 October 2006, and the second to the University of Wales, Bangor on 27 April 2007, as reported in the Spring 2007 Newsletter.

Continuing problems have delayed setting up the Society's new website and simplifying our electronic connections, but it is expected that the new site will go live in autumn 2007. This is a first stage only, and we aim to develop our online presence in future, with the assistance of the new Honorary Director of Communications, Matthew Cragoe.

Council and the Officers record their gratitude to the Society's administrative staff: to Joy McCarthy who returned to hold the fort until the new Executive Secretary Sue Carr took office in August 2006, to Sue herself for a very successful first year in post, and to the Administrative Assistant, Melanie Batt. We thank them for their expert and dedicated work on the Society's many activities. We are very pleased that Melanie is increasing the hours she works for the Society, to help us with our expanding range of activities and responsibilities.

RESEARCH POLICY COMMITTEE, 2006–7

On behalf of the Society, each year the Committee helps to organise the G.E. Aylmer Seminar in honour of one of our past presidents. The next seminar will be hosted by the National Archives at the British Library on 23 October 2007 on the subject of *Digital Horizons: How the Digital Revolution Changes the Relationship between Historians and their Archival Sources.*

The Committee continues to monitor the Bologna Process. Dr Elisabeth van Houts has taken responsibility for this and the Committee is exploring ways in which the Society can collaborate with other learned societies to promote the development of the Process.

The Committee monitors the activities of the AHRC, informed by comments from Fellows and Council members and the Society's representatives on its panels and committees. Aspects of AHRC activity in which it has taken a close interest include: the review of the devolution of selection for doctoral awards to HEIs; its role in the European Science

Foundation project of producing Europe-wide rankings of journals in the arts and humanities; its consultation over its role in relation to museums and archives; its evaluation of its research funding in Modern History; its apparent confusion over its responsibility for funding research in later twentieth century history. In response to representations from the Society and others AHRC proposals for devolution for selection for doctoral awards were largely unchanged; there were minor changes in the ESF proposals for the ranking of journals; definition of the relative responsibilities of AHRC and ESRC for the funding of historical research into the recent past was improved.

The Committee carefully follows RAE arrangements, actual and proposed, present and future, including the contentious issue of metrics. Developments in research support in Wales, Scotland and Northern Ireland are also closely watched and helpfully reported upon by members of the committee. Concern was expressed about possibly detrimental effects on Scottish research performance due to the fact that JISC is not supported by the Scottish Executive and about the merger of Scottish postgraduate funding with the AHRC.

In September 2006 Bill Stockting of the Strategy and Planning Team at the National Archives addressed the Committee on the *Archives UK: Connecting Archives Project*. The Committee expressed support for the project but wished to be assured that 'access for all' would be balanced by due attention to access for scholarly researchers and that the quality of cataloguing of material should be maintained. It was agreed that the Society would be consulted as TNA's action plan progressed; would discuss the implications with other professional bodies; that the Committee would receive a further presentation from representatives of TNA. This was provided at the February 2007 meeting by Natalie Ceeney (CEO of TNA) and her colleague Vanessa Carr. Ms Ceeney very helpfully outlined the challenges being faced by TNA as paper-based government records are replaced by electronic communication, preservation of which is uncertain and problematic. She and Ms Carr explained the strategies being adopted to ensure that records of recent and current government activity survive for the use of future historians. It was agreed that the Society and the TNA would maintain contact on these issues and that the Society would continue to monitor the situation.

TEACHING POLICY COMMITTEE, 2006–7

Ably led since 2003 by Vice-President Professor Wendy Childs, the Teaching Policy Committee has now become firmly established as a recognised part of the role of the Royal Historical Society. In November 2006 Wendy handed over the Chair of the committee to newly elected Vice-President Andrew Foster; although the Honorary Secretary

Kenneth Fincham stood down in this year, he has been unable to escape continued valuable service on this particular committee.

The year has been characterised by continued cooperation with other bodies such as the Institute of Historical Research, the Historical Association, History UK(HE) and the History, Classics and Archaeology Subject Centre. A successful conference on Assessment was held at the IHR in October 2006, while the Society was also represented at conferences on E-learning, History Teaching in Further Education and Dr Foster addressed the annual Subject Centre meeting for departmental heads. The highlight of the year was probably the major conference on 'Why History Matters?' hosted at the IHR in February 2007.

The Society was heavily involved this year in consultation exercises promoted by the QAA and QCA. The big issues included the History Subject Benchmark Statement, new specifications for A-level, a revised QAA code on assessment, discussions about Masters' level work and the Bologna process. On all of these fronts the committee has felt that it has made a positive impact.

The committee has continued to raise concerns abut the need for continuous professional development for teachers of history through secondary, further and higher education. The President has raised these matters at ministerial level, while the Society has been planning even closer cooperation with the Historical Association regarding possible 'badging' of short-courses for teachers as part of their proposed 'Chartered Teacher' scheme.

Progress on the above has perhaps been slower than expected owing to concerns that materialised during the year about the future of the History element of the History, Classics and Archaeology Subject Centre. The History directors, Paul Hyland and Alan Booth resigned in spring 2007 and there have been extensive discussions since on how to maintain their valuable work. Dr Foster has been heavily involved in these discussions as the Society's representative on the History Advisory Panel of the Subject Centre, while the committee has been kept well informed thanks to the involvement of the overall Centre director Dr Colin Brooks as a co-opted member. It is sad that no sooner than the Teaching Policy Committee had drawn together possibly all parties with an interest in pedagogy, than one critical player has experienced problems. Nevertheless, the Society is well placed to ensure that it will take forward all the initiatives noted in this report in the forthcoming year.

GENERAL PURPOSES COMMITTEE, 2006–7

The General Purposes Committee has numerous responsibilities, in particular making arrangements for the card of session, and for conferences, monitoring the representation of the Society on various outside bodies, and arranging for the assessment of the various prizes awarded by the Society. During the year the Committee invites and then considers proposals for speakers for paper readings, and for the Colin Matthew Lecture and the Prothero Lecture. The Committee works hard to try to ensure a balance of papers throughout the year, on different periods, and geographical and subject areas.

This year, the Committee approved two new developments, with the aim of widening participation in our programme of lectures and meetings. Fellows will in future be invited to propose speakers for the London meetings (starting with the 2009 card of session). The present programme of visits to regional Departments of History will shift to a programme of collaborative symposia, to be proposed by Departments of History in association with at least one other local institution and supported and partly funded by the Society. We envisage a maximum of two symposia per annum, as with the present regional visits. The first symposia of this kind will take place in 2009; information on how to make a proposal will be circulated to heads of history departments.

The Committee is also responsible for the appointment of assessors for the various prizes that the Society awards, and, where appropriate, for the reassessment of the terms and conditions under which these awards are made.

Following the reconfiguration of the Alexander Prize in 2005–6, the Committee will consider restructuring the David Berry Prize for Scottish History along similar lines.

Meetings of the Society

5 papers were given in London this year and 2 papers were read at locations outside London. Welcome invitations were extended to the Society to visit the History Departments at the University of Hertfordshire and the University of Wales, Bangor (Future visits are planned to include the University of Essex on 19 October 2007, and Sheffield Hallam University on 25 April 2008.)

At the ordinary meetings of the Society the following papers were read:

o 'The Burden and Conscience of Government in the Fifteenth Century' Dr Jeremy Catto (5 July 2006: Prothero Lecture)
o 'The Archaeology of Modernity in 19th-Century Paris' Professor Colin Jones (20 October 2006 at the University of Hertfordshire)
o 'Text, visualization and politics: London, 1130–1250' Professor Derek Keane (2 February 2007)
o 'The language and symbolism of conquest in early 19th century Ireland' Professor Jackie Hill (27 April 2007 at the University of Wales, Bangor)

o 'The death of consumer society'
Professor Matthew Hilton (11 May 2007)

● At the Anniversary meeting on 25 November 2006, the President, Professor Martin Daunton delivered his second address on 'Britain and Globalization since 1850: The rise of insular capitalism, 1914–39'.

Conferences

i) a joint conference with the National Maritime Museum was held from 13–14 July 2006 on 'The Seven Year's War';
ii) a joint conference was held with the Bibliographical Society on 4 November 2006 on 'Historians and Bibliographers in Conversation', at the IHR;

The Colin Matthew Memorial Lecture for the Public Understanding of History – previously known as the Gresham Lecture – was given on Wednesday 1 November 2006 by Dame Joan Bakewell, CBE on the subject of 'The Curse of the Poke Bonnet: Television's Version of History'. These lectures continue to be given in memory of the late Professor Colin Matthew, a former Literary Director and Vice-President of the Society. The lecture in 2007 will be on Wednesday 31 October when Dr Simon Thurley, Chief Executive of English Heritage and TV historian will present 'The Fabrication of Medieval History. Archaeology and Artifice at the Office of Works'.

Prizes

The Society's annual prizes were awarded as follows:

● The Alexander Prize was awarded in 2007 to Alice Rio, BA, for her essay 'Freedom and Unfreedom in Early Medieval Francia: the Evidence of the Legal Formulae'.
● The David Berry Prize for an essay on Scottish history, was not awarded in 2006.
● The Whitfield Book Prize for a first book on British history attracted 22 entries. The generally high quality of the entries was again commended by the assessors.

The Prize for 2006 was awarded to:

Kate Fisher, *Birth Control, Sex and Marriage in Britain*, 1918–1960 (Oxford University Press)

The judges' citation read:

'Once upon a time historians went to the archives and read documents. Now historical research is undertaken by going round old people's homes in South Wales and talking to the inmates about their experiences of sex. From the wonderfully engaging material that Kate Fisher collected, she has produced a well-written, subtly analysed and skilfully argued book. Beginning with the demographic truism that fertility as measured by birth rates declined sharply in the first half of the twentieth century, Kate Fisher has asked how and why that came about, and, in particular, what part did the practice of birth control play. Her response, insightful and sensitive, is that birth control was indeed significant, but less than might have been supposed, since it was men, rather than women, who continued to be responsible for practising contraception. This study is a fascinating contribution to understanding of relationships within marriage and to gendered attitudes to sexuality more generally. It is also a very humane, even moving, book'.

- Thanks to the continuing generous donation from The Gladstone Memorial Trust, the Gladstone History Book Prize for a first book on a subject outside British history was again awarded. The number of entries this year was 30.

The Prize for 2006 was awarded to:

James Shaw, *The Justice of Venice. Authorities and Liberties in the Urban Economy 1550–1700* (Oxford University Press)

The judges wrote:

'We found this an impressive and original study of 'market justice' in early modern Venice, based on meticulous research in unpublished archives. Dr Shaw analyses his material acutely and imaginatively, examining the social profile of litigants, types of case and judicial outcomes, and drawing on the words of the protagonists themselves in the best manner of micro-history. All of life is there: penalties for builders who did not complete their work by the due date; boatmen overcharging for rides being sentenced to two hours in the *berlina*, a cage at Rialto where criminals were exposed to public ridicule; an apothecary defending his reputation – 'my qualities in dealing and trading are clear to all the world . . . my accuser should wash his accusations out of his mouth'. His book also provides us with a clear account of the institutions of justice and the role of the guilds in regulation and medicine. But Dr Shaw's book is much more than a social or institutional history. It extrapolates on broader issues, with some telling observations on the nature of the early modern economy in this complex and unique city ('bonds of credit overlapped with those of household, workshop and neighbourhood to create a complex web of social ties that cut across social ranks'. . .'a submerged economy of informal relations that lay beneath the structure of guilds and state'. More significantly still, it challenges prevailing and simplistic views of centralisation and the role of the state. Dr Shaw provides a nuanced view of a flexible and responsive judicial system which attempted to regulate society in a practical and humane way. As he himself sums up, 'rather than exercising absolute command, Venice operated according to a pragmatic model of compromise with intermediate authorities'. This book provides an original and thoughtful insight into the realities of the period, and is a significant contribution to early modern history'.

The judges nominated one proxime accesit:

Davide Rodogno, *Fascism's European Empire. Italian Occupation during the Second World War* (Cambridge University Press)

- The Society established a new graduate essay prize in memory of its former President and distinguished medieval scholar, Professor Sir Rees Davies (1938–2005).

The prize for 2006 was awarded to:

Emma Cavell (Wolfson College, Cambridge) for her essay 'Noblewomen and the Medieval Welsh Frontier: the Shropshire evidence'.

The judges wrote:

'This meticulously researched and elegantly written piece reassesses the role of women in the militarised conditions of the Welsh marches, and in a nuanced argument shows the possibilities for and the limitations of female agency. It is fitting that the first winner of this prize should be writing an essay which takes as its starting point Rees Davies' own work'.

The judges nominated one proxime accesit:

Mike Ebester (University of Reading) for his essay 'No Good Reason for the Government to Interfere: Business, the State and Railway Employee Safety in Britain, c. 1900–1939'.

- In order to recognise the high quality of work now being produced at undergraduate level in the form of third-year dissertations, the Society continued, in association with *History Today* magazine, to award an annual prize for the best undergraduate dissertation. Departments are asked to nominate annually their best dissertation and a joint committee of the Society and *History Today* select in the autumn the national prizewinner from among these nominations. The prize also recognizes the Society's close relations with *History Today* and the important role the magazine has played in disseminating scholarly research to a wider audience. 39 submissions were made.

First prize was awarded to:

Edward Swift (University of Durham) for his essay 'Furnishing God's Holy House: John Cosin and Laudian church interiors in Durham'.

Runners up were:

Matthew Neal (University of Cambridge) for his essay 'The Fall of Walpole'.

James Williamson (University College London) for his essay 'To what extent, If at all, did the Marshall Plan impose limits upon Post-War Labour Government's policies of nationalisation and creation of the welfare state'.

Articles by the prize-winners presenting their research will appear shortly in *History Today* editions in 2007. Twelve prize entrants and four of their respective tutors accepted the invitation to visit the National Archives on 10 January 2007, where they were welcomed by Dr David Thomas (Director of Government and Archive Services), and given a guided tour of the Archive facilities.

- The German History Society, in association with the Society, agreed to award a prize to the winner of an essay competition. The essay, on any aspect of German history, including the history of German-speaking people both within and beyond Europe, was open to any postgraduate registered for a degree in a university in either the United Kingdom or the Republic of Ireland.

The winning essay in 2006 was by Anna Menge (University of Oxford) 'The Hindenburgh Myth in Weimar Culture'.

- Frampton and Beazley Prizes for A-level performances were awarded following nominations from the examining bodies:

Frampton Prizes:

AQA: Thomas Allan Smith (Harrogate Grammar School) and Emma J McCarroll (St Bernard's Convent School)
Edexcel Foundation incorporating the London Examination Board: No award
OCR: Thomas Holroyd (Leeds Grammar School)
Welsh Joint Education Committee: No award

Beazley Prizes:

Northern Ireland Council for the Curriculum Examinations and Assessment: No award
SQA: Mark J Scott (George Heriot's School)

- The Director of the Institute of Historical Research announced the winner and runners-up of the Pollard Prize, at the Annual Reception on 4 July 2007. The prize is awarded annually to the best postgraduate student paper presented in a seminar at the IHR.

  The Pollard Prize winner for 2007 was Kathryn Gerry for her paper on 'The Alexis Quire and the cult of saints at St Albans', delivered to the Earlier Middle Ages seminar.

  Second place: David Manning for his paper on 'A mode of wickedness: practical atheism and blasphemy, 1660–1740', delivered to the Religious History of Britain seminar.

Publications

PUBLICATIONS COMMITTEE, 2006–7

One of the most important developments of the year was that the contents of *Transactions* from 1872 up to 2001 went live on JSTOR through their 'Arts and Sciences complement' package (though some fellows may find that their institutions do not currently subscribe to this enhanced supplementary JSTOR package). JSTOR will maintain a five-year moving wall. Current volumes of *Transactions* as well as the Camden volumes are available through the Cambridge University Press website.

The Society's online Bibliography of British History continues to generate a growing traffic, and the project embarked on a new grant from the Arts and Humanities Research Council in January 2007.

The periodic updates of the Bibliography in 2006–7 added nearly 12,000 records from the Society's team; nearly 10,000 more records were added by the partner project Irish History Online. The database now contains 427,000 records overall. Meanwhile the project team has been laying the ground work for the next phase working on a re-engineering of the ADLIB application to improve the functionality of the resource, and exploring the ways of ensuring the increased exposure of the data to search engines. At the end of September 2007 the General Editor will be attending a conference in Berlin bringing together representatives from analogous projects elsewhere in Europe to talk about ways of making the various bibliographic resources cross-searchable.

Late 2006 also saw major developments at the Bibliography's partner project, Irish History Online, based at the National University of Ireland, Maynooth, under the direction of Professor Jacqueline Hill. In September 2006 Irish History Online completed its initial project to digitize the entire contents of the printed and microfiche *Writings on Irish History* and this data was placed online in our October data update. The *Writings* for the period 1934–2001 are now fully available online and the total number of titles relating to Irish history available through the bibliography has reached nearly 60,000. Anyone interested in Irish history must be extremely grateful to the Irish Research Council for the Humanities and Social Sciences Government of Ireland Project Grants scheme for its support, and to Professor Hill and her team (both the editor, Dr Tony McCormack, and the data inputter, Mary Murray) for all their work.

Furthermore, Irish History Online has now embarked on a new project, with funding from the same source, to increase the coverage of material on the Irish diaspora, especially that published outside Britain and Ireland. A new editor, Dr Frank Cullen, started work in October 2006 and titles from his work are already entering the live data. The new project, which will last for three years, will involve research in libraries in Europe and America but, while the prime focus will be on literature about the Irish abroad, it will also seek to add information about new publications on Irish history in general, so that Irish History Online will function as a current bibliography of Irish history.

The Bibliography has also developed co-operation with a new partner in the form of the Scottish Historical Review Trust. A team established by the Trust at the University of Stirling under the direction of Dr Emma McLeod is preparing material on Scottish history for inclusion in the bibliography. The Bibliography's Scottish coverage will be improved, but those who have previously used the *Scottish Historical Review* lists will also have access to a more frequently updated service with more extensive subject indexing that will also be enriched by the wider searching for Scottish material in non-specialist journals that co-operation with the RHS Bibliography will make possible.

Transactions, Sixth Series, Volume 16 was published during the session, and *Transactions*, Sixth Series, Volume 17 went to press, to be published in November 2007.

In the Camden, Fifth Series, *Debating the Hundred Years War: Pur ce que plusieurs (La Loy Salicque) and a declaracion of the trew and dewe title of Henrie VIII*, ed Craig Taylor (vol. 28) and *British Envoys to Germany, 1816–1861 Volume III: 1848–1850* ed. M. Mosslang, S. Freitag and Peter Wende (vol. 29) were published, and '*The Affairs of Others': The Diaries of Francis Place, 1825–1836*, ed. James Jaffe (vol. 30) and *The Correspondence of Henry Cromwell, 1655–1659*, ed. Peter Gaunt (vol. 31) went to press for publication in 2007–8.

The *Studies in History* Editorial Board continued to meet throughout the year. The second series continued to produce exciting volumes. In 2006–7 The Society invested additional funds in the series to ensure that two extra volumes could be published in advance of the RAE deadline. The following volumes were published, or went to press, during the session

o *Gladstone and Dante: Victorian Statesman, Medieval Poet* Anne Isba
o *Gender, Crime and Judicial Discretion, 1780–1830* Deirdre Palk
o *Women in Thirteenth-Century Lincolnshire* Louise Wilkinson
o *Women and Violent Crime in Enlightenment Scotland* Anne-Marie Kilday
o *Scottish Public Opinion and the Union of 1707* Karin Bowie
o *Gender and Space in Early Modern England* Amanda Flather

As in previous subscription years, volumes in the *Studies in History* series were offered to the membership at a favourably discounted price. Many Fellows, Associates and Members accepted the offer for volumes published during the year, and the advance orders for further copies of the volumes to be published in the year 2007–2008 were encouraging.

The Society acknowledges its gratitude for the continuing subventions from the Economic History Society and the Past and Present Society to the *Studies in History* series.

Finance

• The Society welcomed further bequests of £14,450 from the estate of deceased Fellow Miss Vera C. M. London of Shropshire. This was in addition to the legacy of £45,070 already received.

FINANCE COMMITTEE, 2006–7

The Finance Committee approves the Society's accounts each financial year and its estimates for the following year. The accounts were again efficiently audited by haysmacintyre. They are presented elsewhere in *Transactions*.

Expenditure and income in 2006–7 were generally in line with the estimates drawn up last year. The profit-share scheme with Cambridge University Press produced a steady income and continues to work to the satisfaction of the Committee. The Committee also keeps an eye on the costs of the Society's other publishing projects. We are grateful to the Economic History Society and to *Past and Present* for renewing their grants to the *Studies in History* series, which reduce the level of subsidy required by the series. A number of efficiencies have been made within the office with the arrival of a new Executive Secretary, and these have kept spending costs down. The accounts also include income from the sale, at Christie's in June, of part of the Society's library, a project which has been planned for some time.

Council decided last autumn to increase subscriptions from July 2007, as in fact the auditors had recommended in view of the degree of the Society's dependence on investment income to cover necessary expenditure. Currently our income from membership subscriptions amounts to around 40% of the Society's annual expenditure and Council wishes to increase it to 50%. Our finances balance only because of the recent health of the stock market. Subscriptions were last raised in 2002 for 2003.

This increase is being accompanied by a review of the Society's activities, focusing particularly on the task of improving services to the membership. The first fruits of this review are an increase of 50% (to £30,000) in funding for the Research Support scheme for postgraduate historians, to take effect from 2007–8, and an increase in the subsidy to the *Studies in History* series which will enable it to publish seven volumes rather than six in a normal year. Further proposals will follow, as will a revamped website and an improved membership database.

The Committee monitors the performance of the investment portfolio regularly. The managers, Heartwood Wealth Management, produced a satisfactory performance in 2006–7. The value of the main fund increased by 11.8%, somewhat ahead of its benchmark. However the Society's total wealth has still not quite recovered to the level of 2000, when it stood at £2.7 million. The Committee also reviews management charges and transaction levels and continues to be satisfied with Heartwood's approach and conduct.

Unfortunately Lawrence Heasman, who has run our equity-based portfolio at Heartwood for several years, will shortly retire, and Heartwood have taken the decision to move away from direct equity management to a fund-based investment approach. They have therefore asked us whether we wish to accept their new strategy, and the Finance Committee has had to consider whether it suits the Society as well as the old one. Shortly after the year end, it recommended a change of investment manager, to Brewin Dolphin. This change will allow us to continue the emphasis on direct equity management with an income bias, while the culture and charging regime of Brewin seemed congenial to the Committee. Having been approved by Council, the change of management was due to take effect at the end of September 2007. Of course, challenging times for investment may lie ahead, and we cannot expect the same level of gain that we have seen in recent years.

- Council records with gratitude the benefactions made to the Society by:
  - Mr. L.C. Alexander
  - Professor Olive Anderson
  - Professor Roger Bartlett
  - Professor Judith Bennett
  - The Reverend David Berry
  - Professor Andrew Browning
  - Dr Peter Cunich
  - Professor Anne Curry
  - Professor Sir Geoffrey Elton
  - Mr. P.J.C. Firth
  - Mrs. W.M. Frampton
  - Dr James Inglis
  - Mr Martin Jones
  - Professor Sir Ian Kershaw
  - Miss V.C.M. London
  - The widow and family of the late Professor Martin Lynn
  - Professor P.J. Marshall
  - Dr Athol Murray
  - Professor Deborah Oxley
  - The Reverend Nicholas Paxton
  - Professor R. Preston
  - Sir George Prothero
  - Dr. L. Rausing
  - Miss E.M. Robinson
  - Professor Norman Rose
  - Dr Anne Sutton
  - Professor A.S. Whitfield
  - Dr Mark Whittow

Membership

MEMBERSHIP COMMITTEE, 2006–7

The Membership Committee reviews all of the applications the Society receives for fellowship and membership and makes recommendations to Council. We are a committee of three, at present Paul Seaward, Robert Frost and Tim Hitchcock. Over the year 2006–7, 98 applications for fellowship and 17 applications for membership were received, and 97 fellows and 21 members were elected.

Applications are reviewed carefully against the published eligibility criteria: for fellows, the publication of one or more than one book of historical scholarship based on original research; or the publication of a body of scholarly work (for example, learned articles, essays, catalogues, calendars); or a major contribution to historical scholarship in a form other than publication, for instance, the organisation of exhibitions, collections, or conferences, or the editing of local history serials. Membership is more broadly defined, with the aim of attracting a wider group of people who may not necessarily regard themselves as academic historians but are contributing in many and important ways to the study of history: applications will be considered from individuals who are engaged in advanced historical scholarship and research, or teaching history in higher or further education, or who have rendered many years of service to history at national or local level. Applicants may, for example, be in the later stages of, or have completed, their doctoral dissertations; equally they may be active local historians or archivists. They may, but need not, have one or more scholarly publications to their name. Occasionally we propose to applicants for the Fellowship, where we do not feel that their application quite matches our criteria, that they become members of the society instead.

- The following were elected to the Fellowship:

Donald ADAMSON, MA, MLitt, DPhil
Joan ALLEN, BA, PhD
Dana Rebecca ARNOLD, BA, MSc, PhD
Thomas Scott ASBRIDGE, BA, PhD
Brenda ASSAEL, BA, MA, PhD
Stephen BARBER, BA, MA, PhD
Riccardo Beniamino Francesco Luca BAVAJ, MA, PhD
Graham BEBBINGTON
David George BROWN, BA, MA, PhD
Martin David BROWN, BA, MA, PhD

Kevin James Martin CAHILL, BA
Edward Paul de Gruyter CHANEY, BA, MPhil, PhD, Laurea di Dottore
Lloyd Glen CLARK, BA, MA
Alan Edward COATES, MA, DPhil, MA, DipLib
Jonathan CONLIN, BA, MA, PhD
Bruce Edward Christopher COPLESTONE-CROW
Paul Steven CORTHORN, BA, MA, PhD
Krista COWMAN, BA, MA, DPhil
Bernd Markus DAECHSEL, MA, PhD
Waltraud ERNST, MA, PhD
Jeffrey FORGENG, BA, MA, PhD
Charles Francis FOSTER, BA, MA
Mark David FREEMAN, MA, MPhil, PhD
Thomas Sanders FREEMAN, BA, MA, PhD
Marie-Pierre GELIN, BA, MA, MA and MPhil, PhD
Natasha Alice Florence GLAISYER, BA, BA (Hons), PhD
George Francis GOODALL, MA, PhD
Timothy George GRASS, BA, PhD
Emma Alice GRIFFIN, BA, MA, PhD
Nicholas William GROVES, BA, BMus, MA, MA
James Michael HAGERTY, BA, MA, MPhil, PhD
Rachel HAMMERSLEY, BA, MA, DPhil
Michael HEFFERNAN, BSc, PhD
Frances Margaret Stewart HENDERSON, BA, DPhil
David Michael HIGGINS, MA, MPhil, PhD
Fabian HILFRICH, MA, PhD
Violetta HIONIDOU, BSc, MSc, MSc, PhD
Andrew Robert HOLMES, BA, MLitt, PhD
Matt HOULBROOK, BA, PhD
Kathryn Anne HUGHES, BA/MA, MA, PhD
Anne Ingram ISBA, MA, PhD
Alan JAMES, BA, MA, PhD
Norman Walter JAMES, MA, DPhil
Maxwell Hugh JONES, BA, MA, PhD
Nicholas Daniel Alexander KEMP, BA, MA, MSc, DPhil
Simon Keith Andrew KITSON, BA, DPhil
Mark James KNIGHTS, BA, PhD
James LEVY, BA, MA, PhD
Christian Drummond LIDDY, BA, MA, DPhil
Janet Senderowitz LOENGARD, BA, LLB, MA, PhD
John Patrick LOUGHLIN, BA, PhD
Robert George Arnold LUTTON, BA, PhD
Mary Ann LYONS, MA, M. es L., PhD

Richard Gervase MABER, MA, DPhil
John Wesley MARRIOTT, BSc, BA, PhD
Paul Keneth MARTIN, BA, PhD
Rory MCENTEGART, BA, MPhil, PhD
Natalie Ann MEARS, MA, MLitt, PhD
Nicola MILLER, MA, MPhil, DPhil
Adrian Peter MURDOCH, BA, MA
Diana Rosemary NEWTON, BA, PhD
Micheal O'SIOCHRU, BA, MA, PhD
David Owen PAM
Steven Carl Anthony PINCUS, AB, AM, PhD
Helen Elizabeth RAWLINGS, BA, MPhil
Andrew REYNOLDS, BA, PhD
Jeffrey Stephen REZNICK, BA, MA, PhD
Catherine Rosemary RIDER, BA, MA, PhD
Davide RODOGNO, PhD
Douglas John SADLER, BA, MPhil
Dilip SARKAR, MBE
Peter Andrew Vincent SARRIS, BA, MA, DPhil
David Alaric SEARLE, MA, MPhil, DPhil
Robert Charles SELF, BSc, PhD
Peter SHAPELY, BA, PhD
Alexandra Jane SHEPARD, BA, MPhil, PhD
Donald Graham Johnston SHIPLEY, MA, DPhil
Takashi SHOGIMEN, LLB, PhD
Andrew SIMPSON, BA, PhD
Hannah Elizabeth SMITH, BA, MA, MPhil, PhD
Leonard SMITH, MA, PhD, HonDD
Roel STERCKX, BA/MA, MPhil, PhD
Katie STEVENSON, BA, PhD
Rowan Gordon William STRONG, BA, LTh, TheolM, PhD
Bernhard STRUCK, MA, PhD
Peter David Edward SUTCH, BA, MA, PhD
J. Lee THOMPSON, MA, PhD
John Philip TINCEY, BA
Diana Beatrix TYSON, BA, PhD
Keir WADDINGTON, BA, MA, PhD
Andrew Richard WARMINGTON, BA, DPhil
Robin Sinclair WHEELER, BA, MA, MA, PhD
David WILLCOX, BA, MA, PhD
Andrew Nason WILLIAMS, BA, BM, BCh, MSc
Ronald WOODLEY, MusB, DPhil
Russell Neville WYLIE, BA, MPhil, PhD
Benjamin ZIEMANN, MA, PhD

We are delighted to receive new applications for either fellowship or membership, and hope that fellows will encourage others to apply, for both categories. Full details are available on the Society's website. Please remind any applicant to fill in the necessary forms carefully – we receive a number of applications which are not properly completed, and therefore take longer to process – and that they will need a reference from an existing fellow of the Society.

- The following were announced in the Queen's Honours' Lists during the year:

  Professor Chris Bayly, Vere Harmsworth Professor of Imperial and Naval History at the University of Cambridge - Fellow – was made a Knight Bachelor

  Dr David Starkey – Fellow – was appointed C.B.E for services to History

- Council was advised of and recorded with regret the deaths of 13 Fellows, 12 Retired Fellows, 1 Honorary Vice-President, 1 Corresponding Fellow, 1 Associate and 3 Members.

  These included
  Major A. Abela – Fellow
  Professor W.G. Beasley – Retired Fellow
  Dr B.G. Blackwood – Fellow
  Professor A.L. Brown – Fellow
  Dr P.T.V.M. Chaplais – Honorary Vice-President
  Dr R. Cueto – Retired Fellow
  Dr J. Durkan – Fellow
  Dr L. Fox – Retired Fellow
  Professor S. Gopal – Corresponding Fellow and Life Member
  Mr L .Gorton – Retired Fellow
  Dr E.H.H. Green – Fellow
  Dr F. Hebbert – Associate Fellow
  Professor P.M. Holt – Retired Fellow
  Dr C. Knowles – Fellow
  Dr M.E. James – Retired Fellow
  Dr J.D. Jones – Retired Fellow
  Dr P.B. Jones – Retired Fellow
  Mr R.A. Laing of Colyton – Member
  Mr L. Macfarlane – Member
  Miss P.A. McNulty – Fellow
  Dr M.H. Merriman – Fellow
  Mr R. Neillands – Member
  Sir Henry Phillips – Retired Fellow

Professor Emeritus M. Powicke – Retired Fellow
Dr R. Preston – Life Fellow
Professor P.H. Ramsey – Fellow
Mr B.E. Robson – Fellow
Professor M.R. Robinton – Retired Fellow
Dr D. Thomas – Retired Fellow
Professor Sir Glanmor Williams – Retired Fellow
Professor R.W. Winks – Fellow

- The membership of the Society on 30 June 2007 numbered 2932, comprising 1972 Fellows, 578 Retired Fellows, 11 Life Fellows, 13 Honorary Vice-Presidents, 91 Corresponding Fellows, 65 Associates and 202 Members.

- The Society exchanged publications with 15 Societies, British and Foreign.

Representatives of the Society

- The representation of the Society upon other various bodies was as follows:
  - Professor David Ganz on the Anthony Panizzi Foundation;
  - Dr. Julia Crick on the Joint Committee of the Society and the British Academy established to prepare an edition of Anglo-Saxon charters;
  - Professor Nicholas Brooks on a committee to promote the publication of photographic records of the more significant collections of British Coins;
  - Dr Christopher Kitching on the Council of the British Records Association;
  - Mr. Phillip Bell on the Editorial Advisory Board of the *Annual Register*;
  - Professor Christopher Holdsworth on the Court of the University of Exeter; Professor Claire Cross on the Council of the British Association for Local History; and on the British Sub-Commission of the Commission Internationale d'Histoire Ecclesiastique Comparée;
  - Professor Ludmilla Jordanova on the Advisory Council of the Reviewing Committee on the Export of Works of Art;
  - Professor Wendy Davies on the Court of the University of Birmingham;
  - Professor Rosamund McKitterick on a committee to regulate British co-operation in the preparation of a new repertory of medieval sources to replace Potthast's *Bibliotheca Historica Medii Aevi*;
  - Professor Wendy Childs as member of the Court of the University of Sheffield;

- o Dr. Jane Winters on the History Data Service Advisory Committee;
- o Professor Arthur Burns on the user panel of the RSLP Revelation project 'Unlocking research sources for 19th and 20th century church history and Christian theology';
- o Professor Noel Thompson on the Court of Governors of the University of Wales, Swansea;
- o Dr. Richard Mackenney on the University of Stirling Conference;
- o Dr Malcolm Smith on the Court of Governors of the University of Wales, Cardiff;
- o Dr. Christopher Kitching on the National Council on Archives;
- o Professor John Breuilly on the Steering Committee of the British Centre for Historical Research in Germany

- Council received reports from its representatives.

Grants

RESEARCH SUPPORT COMMITTEE, 2006–7

The Committee has, as usual, met six times in the course of the year to carry out the entirely agreeable task of allocating funds to research students needing financial help to carry out specific elements of their research in Britain and overseas, and help others to present papers to sessions of relevant, significant conferences. Under another funding head, the Committee also tries to assist organisers seeking to cushion, by partial subsidy, the costs of student attendance at their conferences. All of this work reflects the Society's enthusiastic commitment to the encouragement of young scholars and their historical research. The Society's funds are however limited and research expenses are increasingly costly; accordingly in the course of the year the Committee must carefully read and then discuss the applications of many more candidates than it can ultimately benefit. Budgetary limits also mean that we must decide how much of a funding request we can meet as we are only rarely able to provide students with the total sum for which they have asked.

The development of the scholarly careers of young historians and the wider dissemination of their research achievements, one of the major concerns of the Royal Historical Society, lay behind the launch in 2005 of a new speakers' programme for which the Committee is responsible. Under this scheme, the Royal Historical Society's Postgraduate Speakers Series, history departments are encouraged to become acquainted with the work of young historians. Past recipients of research awards or conference grants have been, with their consent, listed and their names, along with a description of their research, are circulated to the conveners of history research seminars in the United Kingdom. Conveners may then invite speakers from that list in the knowledge that the Society will pay for the visiting scholars' expenses. The success of the initiative in its one year trial in 2005–6 has led to its continuation for 2006–7.

- The Royal Historical Society Centenary Fellowship was awarded for the academic year 2006–2007 to Catriona Pennell (Trinity College, Dublin) studying 'Responses within the United Kingdom of Britain and Ireland to the Outbreak of the First World War, July to December 1914'.
- The Society's P.J. Marshall Fellowship was awarded in the academic year 2006–2007 jointly to Eyal Poleg (Queen Mary, University of London) studying 'Meditations of the Bible in Late Medieval England' and Suzannah Lipscomb (Balliol College, Oxford) studying 'Maids, wives and mistresses: disciplined women in Reformation Languedoc'. Professor Marshall had confirmed his plans to support a Fellowship every year for the next few years for which the Society wishes to express its grateful acceptance of his generosity.
- Grants during the year were made to the following:

Travel to Conferences (Training Bursaries)

○ Susan Louise ASPINALL, PhD, University of Warwick
American Association for the History of Medicine, 80th Annual Conference, held in Montreal, Canada, 3rd–6th May 2007.
○ Gemma BETROS, University of Cambridge
Social History Society Annual Conference 2007, held at the University of Exeter, 30th March–1st April 2007.
○ Karen Mary BUCKLE, PhD, Wellcome Trust Centre for the History of Medicine at UCL
Visuality and the Other Senses, held at the University of Oslo, Norway, 11th–12th May 2007.
○ Alison CARROL, PhD, University of Exeter
The Society for the Study of French History 21st Annual Conference, to be held at University of St Andrews, 1st–3rd July 2007.
○ Nikolaos CHRISSIS, PhD, Royal Holloway, University of London
International Medieval Congress 2007, to be held in Leeds, 9th–12th July 2007.
○ David CLAMPIN, PhD, University of Wales, Aberystwyth
Conference on Historical Analysis and Research in Marketing, held at The Hartman Center at Duke University, North Carolina, USA, 17th–20th May 2007.
○ Xavier Hernando DURAN, PhD, London School of Economics and Political Science

European School of New Institutional Economics (ESNIE), held 21st–25th May 2007.

o Catherine Lucy FLETCHER, PhD, Royal Holloway, University of London
Renaissance Society of America annual meeting, held in Miami, USA, 22nd–24th March 2007.

o Fiona Anne FRANK, PhD, Strathclyde University
Jewish Journeys, held at Isaac and Jesse Kaplan Centre for Jewish Studies and Research, University of Cape Town, 4th–11th January 2007.

o Miguel GARCIA-SANCHEZ, PhD, Institute of Historical Research
European Association of Urban History Conference 2006, held in Stockholm, 30th August–2nd September 2006.

o Erin Jacquelyn GILL, PhD, University of Wales, Aberystwyth
Fourth Conference of the European Society of Environmental History, held 5th–9th June 2007.

o David Ian HARRISON, PhD, University of Liverpool
33rd Annual International Byron Conference, to be held at Venice International University, 9th–13th July 2007.

o Melissa HOLLANDER, PhD, University of York
North American Conference on British Studies in conjunction with the North East Conference on British Studies, held at the Royal Sonesta Hotel, Boston, USA, 17th–19th November 2006.

o Susanne KRANZ, PhD, University of Leeds
New York Conference on Asian Studies 2006: The Asian Subject: Negotiating Identity, held at St. Laurence University in Canton, New York, USA, 6th–7th October 2006.

o Thomas LAMBERT, PhD, University of Durham
International Congress of Medieval Studies, held in Kalamazoo, Michigan, 9th–13th May 2007.

o Daniel LAQUA, PhD, University College London
Internationalism and the Arts: Anglo-European Cultural Exchange at the Fin-de-Siècle, held at Magdalene College, Cambridge, 3rd–5th July 2006.

o Carlos LOPEZ GALVIZ, MPhil/PhD, Institute of Historical Research
Walter Benjamin and the Architecture of Modernity, held at the Centre for Social Theory and Design, University of Technology Sydney, Sydney, Australia, 17th–19th August 2006.

o Marina MARTIN, PhD, London School of Economics and Political Science
35th Annual Conference on South Asia, held at the University of Wisconsin-Madison, USA, 19th–22nd October 2006.

o Anne Michele MOATT, PhD, Lancaster University
The American Society for Church History Spring Conference, held in Salt Lake City, USA, 12th–14th April 2007.

o Tara Louise MORTON, MPhil/PhD, University of Warwick
IHR Research Training – Visual Sources for Historians, held at the Institute of Historical Research, London, 13th February–13th March 2007.

o Thomas NEUHAUS, PhD, University of Cambridge
Imperial Curiosity: objects, representations, knowledges, held at the University of Tasmania, Hobart, 27th–29th June 2007.

o Matthias NEUMANN, PhD, University of East Anglia
39th National Convention of the American Association for the Advancement of Slavic Studies (AAASS), to be held in New Orleans, USA, 15th–18th November 2007.

o Keiko NOWACKA, PhD, University of Cambridge
International Medieval Congress, held at University of Leeds, 10th–13th July 2006.

o Zsuzsanna PAPP, PhD, University of Leeds
Regional and European Identities in the Medieval Baltic Sea Region, held at Tallinn Centre for Medieval Studies, Estonia, 4th–13th August 2006.

o Iris RAU, MPhil, University of Leeds
Social History Society Annual Conference 2007, held at the University of Exeter, 30th March–1st April 2007.

o Marie SANDELL, PhD, Royal Holloway, University of London
15th Annual Conference of the Women's History Network, Thinking Women: Education, Culture and Society, held at Collingwood College, University of Durham, 1st–3rd September 2006.

o Jonathan SHEA, PhD, University of Birmingham
Sixth Annual Byzantine Greek Summer School, to be held at Queen's University Belfast, 24th June–14th July 2007.

o Julia Margaret SMITH, PhD, University of Warwick
The American Association for the History of Medicine Annual Conference 2007, held in Montreal, Canada, 3rd–6th May 2007.

o Denise SUMPTER, PhD, Imperial College, University of London
CEU Advanced Summer School: Philosophy and Science in the Greco-Roman World, held in Budapest, 16th–29th July 2006.

o Alice TAYLOR, DPhil, University of Oxford
The Haskins Society Conference of Anglo-Saxon, Anglo-Norman, Angevin and Viking Studies, held at Georgetown University, USA, 2nd–5th November 2006.

o Katrina TOWNER, PhD, University of Southampton
Making Global and Local Connections: Historical Perspectives on Port Economics, held in Kotka, Finland, 18th–20th August 2006.

o Natalya VINCE, PhD, Queen Mary, University of London
African Studies Association 2006 Annual Meeting: "(Re) Thinking Africa and the World: Internal Reflections, External Responses," held

at Westin St. Francis Hotel, San Francisco, USA, 16th–19th November 2006.
o Brodie WADDELL, MPhil/PhD, University of Warwick
Social History Society Annual Conference, held at the University of Exeter, 30th March–1st April 2007.

(33)

Research Expenses Within the United Kingdom:

o Andrew ABRAM, PhD, University of Wales, Lampeter
Visits to British Library and National Archives, London, and Bodleian Library, Oxford, 14th–25th August 2006.
o Luke Richard Henry BLAXILL, PhD, King's College London
Visits to various archives in East Anglia, November 2006–July 2007.
o Elizabeth FILBY, PhD, Institute of Historical Research
Visits to Liverpool Records Office, Liverpool and John Rylands Library, Manchester, 4th–22nd September 2006.
o Jayne Louise GIFFORD, PhD, University of the West of England
Visits to archives in Kew, Birmingham, Durham, London, Oxford and Cambridge, Easter and Summer vacations 2007.
o Ryan JOHNSON, DPhil, University of Oxford
Visits to the Wellcome Library, the British Library and the Public Record Office, October 2006–October 2007.
o Simon MILLAR, PhD, Institute of Historical Research
Visits to Gillies Archive, Sidcup, the Wellcome Trust Archive, the Guinea Pig Club Museum, East Grinstead and various locations to conduct interviews, 2006–2009.
o Jennifer RAMPLING, PhD, University of Cambridge
Visits to archives in London, Aberystwyth and Leeds, July 2007.
o William RUPP, PhD, University of Warwick
Visits to various archives in Wiltshire, Bedfordshire, London, Nottingham, Winchester and Wrotham, April–August 2007.
o Koji YAMAMOTO, PhD, University of York
Visits to The National Archives, Chancery, West Sussex Record Office, British Library and Staffordshire Record Office, June–July 2007.

(9)

Research Expenses Outside the United Kingdom:

o Nir ARIELLI, PhD, University of Leeds
Visits to various archives in Rome, 28th May 2007–15th June 2007.
o Robert BARNES, PhD, London School of Economics
Visits to various archives in USA, 1st August–14th September 2007.

o Justin Adam BRUMMER, PhD, University College London
Visit to archives in the USA, 1st May–1st July 2007.
o Emanuel BUTTIGIEG, PhD, University of Cambridge
Visits to archives in Rome, 22nd January–26th February 2007.
o Andrew COHEN, PhD, University of Sheffield
Visit to archives in Lusaka, Zambia, July 2008.
o Lara COOK, PhD, University of Newcastle Upon Tyne
Visits to various archives in Moscow, 26th March–21st April 2007.
o Chiara FORMICHI, PhD, School of Oriental and African Studies,
University of London
Visits to various archives in The Netherlands, June–July 2007.
o Robert HENDERSON, PhD, Queen Mary, University of London
Visits to various archives in Moscow, 1st April–13th May 2007.
o Uriel HEYD, PhD, Royal Holloway, University of London
Visits to Virginia Historical Society, New York Public Library and
Winterthur Library, October–December 2006.
o Melena Denise HOPE, PhD, Courtauld Institute of Art, University of
London
Visit to various archives/locations in France, 25th June–4th July 2007.
o Michelle HOWELL, University of Cambridge
Visits to various archives in Paris, 20th January–20th March 2007.
o Vivian IBRAHIM, PhD, School of Oriental and African Studies,
University of London
Visits to archives in Cairo, 7th December 2006–30th January 2007.
o James KORANYI, PhD, University of Exeter
Visits to archives in Munich and Gundelsheim, 31st August–14th
September 2006.
o Olga KUCHERENKO, PhD, University of Cambridge
Visits to various archives in Russia, Belarus and the Ukraine, October
2006–March 2007.
o Daniel LAQUA, PhD, University College London
Visit to Mons and Brussels, Belgium, 18th June–2nd July 2007.
o James MARSHALL, PhD, University of Newcastle
Visits to various archives and archaeological sites, Greece, September–
October 2006.
o Carlos Albrecht MEISSNER, PhD, University of York
Visit to Costa Rica, 20th November 2006–21st April 2007.
o Josipa Gordana PETRUNIC, PhD, University of Edinburgh
Visit to Archives Henri Poincaré, Nancy, France, 21st–25th May 2007.
o Sian Lliwen ROBERTS, PhD, University of Birmingham
Visits to various archives in the USA, September 2007.
o Ian SUTHERLAND, PhD, University of Exeter
Visits to various archives in Berlin, Munich and Dresden, 5th
September 10th October 2006.

o Paul Arthur Albertus SWANEPOEL, PhD, University of Edinburgh
  Visits to various archives in Uganda, Tanzania and Kenya, 1st April–
  30th September 2007. [Awarded the Vera London Award.]
o Junya TAKIGUCHI, PhD, University of Manchester
  Visits to various archives in Moscow, September 2006–February 2007.
o Mark Jonathan Breedon TILSE, PhD, University College London
  Visit to various archives in Berlin, Germany, 4th–14th June 2007.

(23)

Conference Organisation (Workshop)

o Sarah ANSARI
  Conference, "Beyond Independence: South Asia, 1947–1977," held at
  Royal Holloway, University of London, 11th–12th April 2007.
o Ian ARCHER
  Conference, "London in Text and History, 1400–1700," held at Jesus
  College, Oxford, 13th–15th September 2007.
o Harald BRAUN
  Conference, "Cultures of Political Counsel, c.800–c.1800," held at the
  University of Liverpool, 13th–15th July 2007.
o Thomas CORNS
  Conference, "The Bangor Conference on the Restoration: politics,
  religion and culture in Britain and Ireland in the 1670s," held at the
  University of Wales, Bangor, 25th–27th July 2007.
o Kent FEDOROWICH
  Conference, "The British World Conference 2007: Defining the British
  World," held at the University of Bristol, 11th–14th July 2007.
o Sue NIEBRZYDOWSKI
  Conference, "Medieval Women in their Third Age: Middle Age in
  the Middle Ages," held at the University of Wales, Bangor, 12th–14th
  September 2007.
o Isabel NORONHA-DIVANNA
  Conference, "Historicising the French Revolution," to be held at the
  University of Cambridge, November 2007.
o Andrew PETTEGREE
  Conference, "17th Annual Conference of the European Reformation
  Research Group (ERRG)," held at the University of St Andrews,
  Scotland, 4th–6th September 2007.
o Huw PRYCE
  Conference, "Third Bangor Colloquium on Medieval Wales," held at
  the University of Wales, Bangor, 14th–15th October 2006.
o Aldwin ROES
  Conference, "Second Annual Postgraduate Conference in Imperial

and International History," held at the University of Sheffield, 31st May 2007.

o Frank TALLETT and David TRIM

Conference, "Crossing the Divide: Continuity and Change in Late Medieval and Early Modern Warfare," held at the University of Reading, 11th–12th September 2007.

o Stephen TYRE

Conference, "21st Annual Conference of the Society for the Study of French History," held at the University of St. Andrews, 1st–3rd July 2007.

o Laura UGOLINI

Conference, "Retail Trading in Britain," held at the University of Wolverhampton, 20th September 2006.

o Laura UGOLINI

Conference, "Business Links: trade, distribution and networks," held at the University of Wolverhampton, 29th–30th June 2007.

o Edward VALLANCE

Conference, "Loyalties and Allegiances in Early Modern England," held at Blackburne House, Liverpool, 9th February 2007.

o Bjorn WEILER

Conference, "Thirteenth-Century England 12: Plantagenet Britain and its Neighbours, c.1180–c.1330," held at the University of Wales Conference Centre, 10th-13th September 2007.

Katherine WILSON

Conference, "Tapestries: Producers, Patrons and Purchasers," held at Glasgow University/ Burrell Collection, Glasgow, 24th August 2007.

o Catherine WRIGHT

Conference, "Generations (History Lab Postgraduate Conference 2007)," held at the Institute of Historical Research, London, 25th–26th June 2007.

(18)

Martin Lynn Scholarship

o Busani MPOFU, PhD, University of Edinburgh
Visits to various archives in Zimbabwe, September 2007.

(1)

Royal Historical Society Postgraduate Speakers Series (RHSPSS)

o University of Leeds
o University of Liverpool

- ○ Royal Holloway, University of London
- ○ University of Hull

(4)

Bursaries for Holders of ORS Awards

- ○ Cameron Mitchell SUTT, St. Catharine's College, Cambridge.

(1)

(Total = 89)

29 September 2007

THE ROYAL HISTORICAL SOCIETY
FINANCIAL STATEMENTS
FOR THE YEAR ENDED 30 JUNE 2007

haysmacintyre
Chartered Accountants
Registered Auditors
London

THE ROYAL HISTORICAL SOCIETY REFERENCE AND ADMINISTRATIVE INFORMA-TION

Members of Council:

THE ROYAL HISTORICAL SOCIETY
REPORT OF THE COUNCIL OF TRUSTEES
FOR THE YEAR ENDED 30 JUNE 2007

The members of Council present their report and audited accounts for the year ended 30 June 2007.

STRUCTURE, GOVERNANCE AND MANAGEMENT

The Society was founded on 23 November 1868 and received its Royal Charter in 1889. It is governed by the document 'The By-Laws of the Royal Historical Society', which was last amended in November 2006. The elected Officers of the Society are the President, six Vice-Presidents, the Treasurer, the Secretary, the Director of Communications and not more than two Literary Directors. These officers, together with twelve Councillors constitute the governing body of the Society, and therefore its Trustees. The Society also has two executive officers: an Executive Secretary and an Administrative Assistant.

Appointment of Trustees

The names of the Trustees are shown above. The President shall be *ex-officio* a member of all Committees appointed by the Council; and the Treasurer, the Secretary, the Director of Communications and the Literary Directors shall, unless the Council otherwise determine, also be *ex-officio* members of all such Committees.

In accordance with By-law XVII, the Vice-Presidents shall hold office normally for a term of three years. Two of them shall retire by rotation, in order of seniority in office, at each Anniversary Meeting and shall not be eligible for re-election before the Anniversary Meeting of the next year. In accordance with By-law XX, the Councillors shall hold office normally for a term of four years. Three of them shall retire by rotation, in order of seniority in office, at each Anniversary Meeting and shall not be eligible for re-election before the Anniversary Meeting of the next year.

All Fellows of the Society are able to nominate Councillors; they are elected by a ballot of Fellows. Other Trustees are elected by Council.

At the Anniversary Meeting on 25 November 2006, the Officers of the Society were re-elected, or in the cases of Dr Harding (Hon. Secretary) and Professor Cragoe (Hon. Director of Communications) newly elected. The Officer retiring under By-law XX was Dr K Fincham. The Librarian Dr M Smith retired early from post. The Vice-Presidents retiring under By-law XVII were Professor D Bates and Professor W Childs. Professor A Curry and Dr A Foster were elected to replace them. The Members of Council retiring under By-law XX were Professor G Hosking, Dr R Mackenney and Professor D Palliser. In accordance with By-law XXI, amended, Professor S Connolly, Professor T Hitchcock and Professor S Smith were elected in their place.

Trustee training and induction process

New Trustees are welcomed in writing before their initial meeting, and sent details of the coming year's meeting schedule. They are advised of the Committee structure and receive papers in advance of the appropriate Committee and Council meetings, including minutes of the previous meetings. Trustees are already Fellows of the Society and have received regular information including the annual volume of *Transactions of the Royal Historical Society* which includes the annual report and accounts. They have therefore been kept apprised of any changes in the Society's business. Trustees may have previously served on Council, in which case their knowledge of procedures will assist their understanding of current issues. Details of a Review on the restructuring of the Society in 1993 are available to all Members of Council.

Standing Committees

The Society has operated through the following Committees during the year ended 30 June 2007:

MEMBERSHIP COMMITTEE   Dr P C Seaward – Chair
                             Professor R I Frost (from November 2006)
                             Professor T Hitchcock (from November 2006)
                             Professor G A Hosking (to November 2006)
                             Professor D M Palliser (to November 2006)

RESEARCH SUPPORT COMMITTEE   Professor R J A R Rathbone - Chair
                               Professor S R I Foot
                               Professor D M Palliser (to November 2006)
                               Professor S Smith (from November 2006)

FINANCE COMMITTEE   Professor G W Bernard
                               Professor M Finn (to November 2006)
                               Mr P J C Firth
                               Professor P Mathias
                               The six officers (President – Chair)

PUBLICATIONS COMMITTEE   Professor A Curry – Chair (from November 2006)
                               Professor D R Bates – Chair (to November 2006)
                               Professor G W Bernard (from November 2006)
                               Professor T Hitchcock (from November 2006)
                               Professor R I Frost (to November 2006)
                               Professor G A Hosking (to November 2006)
                               Professor J Ohlmeyer (to November 2006)
                               Professor M E Rubin (from November 2006)
                               The six officers

GENERAL PURPOSES COMMITTEE   Professor J E Burton - Chair
                               Professor S Connolly (from November 2006)
                               Dr R S Mackenney (to November 2006)
                               Professor J Ohlmeyer (from November 2006)
                               Professor M E Rubin (to November 2006)
                               Professor G Stone
                               The six officers

TEACHING POLICY COMMITTEE   Dr A W Foster – Chair
                               Professor W R Childs – Alternate Chair (to November 2006)
                               Professor D R Bates (to November 2006)
                               Dr C Brooks (from November 2006)
                               Professor B Coward
                               Professor E J Evans
                               Dr C A Holmes
                               Professor R O'Day
                               The six officers

RESEARCH POLICY COMMITTEE   Professor P M Thane – Chair
                               Dr C J Kitching – Chair (to November 2006)
                               Professor G W Bernard
                               Professor P G Burgess (from November 2006)
                               Professor R I Frost
                               Professor G A Hosking (to November 2006)
                               Dr P Seaward (to November 2006)
                               Dr E M C van Houts
                               The six officers

STUDIES IN HISTORY
EDITORIAL BOARD   Professor J S Morrill – Convenor
                               Dr H Barker (from January 2007)
                               Professor M J Braddick (to November 2006)
                               Professor A Burns
                               Dr S D Church
                               Dr N Gregor
                               Dr R Hammersley (from January 2007)
                               Professor C C Kidd (to November 2006)
                               Dr J M Lawrence – Literary Director
                               Professor M Overton
                               Dr J P Parry – Honorary Treasurer
                               Professor A M Walsham

OBJECTIVES AND ACTIVITIES

The Society exists for the promotion and support of historical scholarship and its dissemination to historians and a wider public through a programme of publications, papers, sponsorship of lectures, conferences and research and by representations to various official bodies where the interests of historical scholarship are involved. It is Council's intention that these activities should be sustained to the fullest extent in the future.

ACHIEVEMENTS AND PERFORMANCE

Grants, Fellowships and Prizes

The Society awards funds to assist advanced historical research. This year it distributed more than £20,000 in grants to 85 individuals. It operates five separate schemes, for each of which there is an application form. The Society's Research Support Committee considers applications at meetings held regularly throughout the year. In turn the Research Support Committee reports to Council. The Martin Lynn Scholarship, for the support of postgraduate research in African history, was awarded for the first time. This year the Society was able to offer both its Centenary Fellowship and its Marshall Fellowship for postdoctoral study, as well as a range of prizes. Full details and a list of awards made are provided in the Society's Annual Report.

Lectures and other meetings

During the year the Society holds meetings in London and at universities outside London at which papers are delivered. It continues to sponsor the joint lecture for a wider public with Gresham College. It has expanded its involvement in meetings with other bodies relating to teaching and research policy issues. Full details are provided in the Annual Report.

Publications

This year, as in previous years, it has pursued this objective by an ambitious programme of publications. A volume of *Transactions*, two volumes of edited texts in the *Camden* Series and further volumes in the *Studies in History* Series have appeared.

Library

The Society began to act on its decision to sell most of its library holdings, which are held in the Council Room. A first selection was sold at auction in the summer of 2007, realising over £18,000 in incoming resources. It continues to subscribe to a range of record series publications housed in the room immediately across the corridor from the Council room, in the UCL History Library.

Membership services

In accordance with the Society's 'By-laws', the membership is entitled to receive, after payment of subscription, a copy of the Society's *Transactions*, and to buy at a preferential rate copies of volumes published in the *Camden* series, and the *Studies in History* series. Society Newsletters continue to be circulated to the membership twice annually. The membership benefits from many other activities of the Society including the frequent representations to various official bodies where the interests of historical scholarship are involved.

Investment performance

The Society holds an investment portfolio with a market value of about £2.64 million (2006: £2.42 million). It has adopted a "total return" approach to its investment policy. This means that the funds are invested solely on the basis of seeking to secure the best total level of economic return compatible with the duty to make safe investments, but regardless of the form the return takes.

The total return strategy does not make distinctions between income and capital returns. It lumps together all forms of return on investment – dividends, interest, and capital gains etc, to produce a "total return". Some of the total return is then used to meet the needs of present beneficiaries, while the remainder is added to the existing investment portfolios to help meet the needs of future beneficiaries.

The Society's investments are managed by Heartwood Wealth Management, who report all transactions to the Honorary Treasurer and provide six monthly reports on the portfolios, which are considered by the Society's Finance Committee which meets three times a year. In turn the Finance Committee reports to Council.

The Society closely monitors its investments. The portfolios are assessed against the FTSE APCIMS balanced benchmark.

During the year the general fund portfolio generated a total return of 11.8% compared with its benchmark return of 8.9%. The Whitfield and Robinson portfolios generated returns of 11.3% and 9.3% respectively against their benchmark of 10.1%.

FINANCIAL REVIEW

Results

The Society's finances continued to recover with total funds increasing from £2,420,828 to £2,670,200, an increase of £249,372. This was largely due to an improvement in the stock market and the receipt of legacies and donations, together with the receipt of £18,000 from the sale of part of the library collection.

Membership subscriptions increased from £72,782 to £75,980 and investment income amounted to £103,562 compared to £87,202 in 2006.

Income from royalties decreased from £36,247 to £35,460, and grants for awards increased from £2,000 to £16,000. Total costs increased from £215,309 to £220,391 reflecting higher publication costs.

Fixed assets

Information relating to changes in fixed assets is given in notes 5 and 6 to the accounts.

Risk assessment

The trustees are satisfied that they have considered the major risks to which the charity is exposed, that they have taken action to mitigate or manage those risks and that they have systems in place to monitor any change to those risks.

Reserves policy

The Council have reviewed the Society's need for reserves in line with the guidance issued by the Charity Commission. They believe that the Society requires approximately the current level of unrestricted general funds of £2.4m to generate sufficient total return, both income and capital, to cover the Society's expenditure in excess of the members' subscription income on an annual basis to ensure that the Society can run efficiently and meet the needs of beneficiaries.

The Society's restricted funds consist of a number of different funds where the donor has imposed restrictions on the use of the funds which are legally binding. The purposes of these funds are set out in notes 13 to 15.

FUTURE PLANS

Council agreed to raise subscriptions with effect from July 2007. It plans a significant increase in the financial support that it gives to postgraduate and other young historians. It has continued to review the use and functionality of its website and aims to launch a new version which will allow better communication and interaction with the Fellowship. It plans to continue its involvement in public discussions about teaching and research issues. It has approved an expansion in the number of volumes to be produced in the *Studies in History* series each year. It is beginning to consider ways of recasting its lecture programme and its programme of provincial visits.

STATEMENT OF TRUSTEES' RESPONSIBILITIES

Law applicable to charities in England and Wales requires the Council to prepare accounts for each financial year which give a true and fair view of the state of affairs of the Society and of its financial activities for that year. In preparing these accounts, the Trustees are required to:

- select suitable accounting policies and apply them consistently;
- make judgements and estimates that are reasonable and prudent;
- state whether applicable accounting standards have been followed, subject to any material departures disclosed and explained in the accounts;
- prepare the accounts on the going concern basis unless it is inappropriate to presume that the Society will continue in business.

The Council is responsible for ensuring proper accounting records are kept which disclose, with reasonable accuracy at any time, the financial position of the Society and enable them to ensure that the financial statements comply with applicable law. They are also responsible for safeguarding the assets of the Society and hence for taking reasonable steps for the prevention and detection of error, fraud and other irregularities.

In determining how amounts are presented within items in the statement of financial activities and balance sheet, the trustees have had regard to the substance of the reported transaction or arrangement, in accordance with generally accepted accounting policies or practice.

AUDITORS

A resolution proposing the appointment of auditors will be submitted at the Anniversary Meeting.

By Order of the Board

Honorary Secretary

Dr V Harding

21 September 2007

THE ROYAL HISTORICAL SOCIETY
INDEPENDENT REPORT OF THE AUDITORS
FOR THE YEAR ENDED 30 JUNE 2007

We have audited the financial statements of The Royal Historical Society for the year ended 30 June 2007 which comprise the Statement of Financial Activities, the Balance Sheet, and the related notes. These financial statements have been prepared under the accounting policies set out therein.

This report is made solely to the charity's trustees, as a body, in accordance with the regulations made under the Charities Act 1993. Our audit work has been undertaken so that we might state to the charity's trustees those matters we are required to state to them in an auditor's report and for no other purpose. To the fullest extent permitted by law, we do not accept or assume responsibility to anyone other than the charity and the charity's trustees as a body, for our audit work, for this report, or for the opinions we have formed.

Respective responsibilities of trustees and auditors

As described in the Statement of Trustees' Responsibilities the charity's trustees are responsible for the preparation of the financial statements in accordance with applicable law and United Kingdom Accounting Standards (United Kingdom Generally Accepted Accounting Practice).

We have been appointed as auditors under section 43 of the Charities Act 1993 and report in accordance with regulations made under section 44 of that Act. Our responsibility is to audit the financial statements in accordance with relevant legal and regulatory requirements and International Standards on Auditing (UK and Ireland).

We report to you our opinion as to whether the financial statements give a true and fair view and are properly prepared in accordance with the Charities Act 1993. We also report to you if, in our opinion, the Trustees' Report is not consistent with the financial statements, the charity has not kept proper accounting records and if we have not received all the information and explanations we require for our audit.

We read the Trustees' Report and consider the implications for our report if we become aware of any apparent misstatements within it.

Basis of audit opinion

We conducted our audit in accordance with International Standards on Auditing (UK and Ireland) issued by the Auditing Practices Board. An audit includes examination, on a test basis, of evidence relevant to the amounts and disclosures in the financial statements. It also includes an assessment of the significant estimates and judgements made by the trustees in the preparation of the financial statements, and of whether the accounting policies are appropriate to the charity's circumstances, consistently applied and adequately disclosed.

We planned and performed our audit so as to obtain all the information and explanations which we considered necessary in order to provide us with sufficient evidence to give reasonable assurance that the financial statements are free from material misstatement, whether caused by fraud or other irregularity or error. In forming our opinion we also evaluated the overall adequacy of the presentation of information in the financial statements.

Opinion

In our opinion the financial statements:

- give a true and fair view, in accordance with United Kingdom Generally Accepted Accounting Practice, of the state of the charity's affairs as at 30 June 2007 and of its incoming resources and application of resources in the year then ended; and
- have been properly prepared in accordance with the Charities Act 1993.

haysmacintyre
Chartered Accountants
Registered Auditors

Fairfax House
15 Fulwood Place
London
WC1V 6AY

THE ROYAL HISTORICAL SOCIETY

STATEMENT OF FINANCIAL ACTIVITIES
FOR THE YEAR ENDED 30 JUNE 2007

	Notes	Unrestricted Funds £	Endowment Funds £	Restricted Funds £	Total Funds 2007 £	Total Funds 2006 £
INCOMING RESOURCES						
Incoming resources from generated funds						
Donations, legacies and similar incoming resources	2	21,958	–	2,000	23,958	11,444
Investment income	6	101,476	–	2,086	103,562	87,202
Incoming resources from charitable activities						
Grants for awards		6,000	–	10,000	16,000	2,000
Conferences		399	–	–	399	259
Subscriptions		72,980	–	–	75,980	72,782
Royalties		35,460	–	–	35,460	36,247
Other incoming resources		18,996	–	–	18,996	750
TOTAL INCOMING RESOURCES		260,269	–	14,086	274,355	210,684
RESOURCES EXPENDED						
Cost of generating funds						
Investment manager's fee		15,684	303	–	15,987	14,078
Charitable activities						
Grants for awards	3	40,411	–	12,956	53,367	49,934
Lectures and other meetings		12,004	–	–	12,004	18,467
Publications		67,918	–	–	67,918	60,564
Library		4,716	–	–	4,716	4,577
Membership services		45,209	–	–	45,209	47,056
Governance		21,190	–	–	21,190	20,633
TOTAL RESOURCES EXPENDED	4	207,132	303	12,956	220,391	215,309
NET INCOMING/(OUTGOING) RESOURCES		53,137	(303)	1,130	53,964	(4,625)
Transfers		(790)	–	790	–	–
Other recognised gains and losses						
Net gain on investments	6	189,454	5,954		195,408	172,592
NET MOVEMENT IN FUNDS		241,801	5,651	1,920	249,372	167,967
Balance at 1 July 2006		2,350,453	68,138	2,237	2,420,828	2,252,861
Balance at 30 June 2007		£2,592,254	£73,789	£4,157	£2,670,200	£2,420,828

The notes on pages 223 to 227 form part of these financial statements.

THE ROYAL HISTORICAL SOCIETY

BALANCE SHEET AS AT 30 JUNE 2007

	Notes	2007 £	2007 £	2006 £	2006 £
FIXED ASSETS					
Tangible assets	5		1,187		1,903
Investments	6		2,638,551		2,419,077
			2,639,738		2,420,980
CURRENT ASSETS					
Stocks	7	2,925		3,595	
Debtors	8	6,598		19,991	
Cash at bank and in hand		46,140		13,114	
		55,663		36,700	
LESS: CREDITORS					
Amounts due within one year	9	(25,201)		(36,852)	
NET CURRENT ASSETS/ (LIABILITIES)			30,462		(152)
NET ASSETS			£2,670,200		£2,252,861
REPRESENTED BY:					
Endowment Funds	13				
A S Whitfield Prize Fund			49,833		46,770
The David Berry Essay Trust			23,956		21,368
Restricted Funds	14				
A S Whitfield Prize Fund – Income			1,983		1,608
P J Marshall Fellowship			–		–
The David Berry Essay Trust – Income			1,174		629
The Martin Lynn Bequest			1,000		–
Unrestricted Funds					
Designated – E M Robinson Bequest	15		150,210		134,437
General Fund	16		2,442,044		2,216,016
			£2,670,200		£2,420,828

The financial statements were approved and authorised for issue by the Council on 21st September 2007 and were signed below on its behalf by:

President . . . .
Professor M Daunton

Honorary Treasurer . . . .
Dr J Parry

The notes on pages 223 to 227 form part of these financial statements.

THE ROYAL HISTORICAL SOCIETY

NOTES TO THE ACCOUNTS FOR THE YEAR ENDED 30 JUNE 2007

1. ACCOUNTING POLICIES

a) *Basis of Preparation*
   The financial statements have been prepared in accordance with the Statement of Recommended Practice "Accounting and Reporting by Charities" (SORP 2005) and with applicable accounting standards issued by UK accountancy bodies. They are prepared on the historical cost basis of accounting as modified to include the revaluation of fixed assets including investments which are carried at market value.

b) *Depreciation*
   Depreciation is calculated by reference to the cost of fixed assets using a straight line basis at rates considered appropriate having regard to the expected lives of the fixed assets. The annual rates of depreciation in use are:
   Furniture and equipment   10%
   Computer equipment   25%

c) *Stock*
   Stock is valued at the lower of cost and net realisable value.

d) *Library and archives*
   The cost of additions to the library and archives is written off in the year of purchase.

e) *Subscription income*
   Subscription income is recognised in the year it became receivable with a provision against any subscription not received.

f) *Investments*
   Investments are stated at market value. Any surplus/deficit arising on revaluation is included in the Statement of Financial Activities. Dividend income is accounted for when the Society becomes entitled to such monies.

g) *Publication costs*
   Publication costs are transferred in stock and released to the Statement of Financial Activities as stocks are depleted.

h) *Donations and other voluntary income*
   Donations and other voluntary income is recognised when the Society becomes legally entitled to such monies.

i) *Grants payable*
   Grants payable are recognised in the year in which they are approved and notified to recipients.

j) *Funds*
   Unrestricted: these are funds which can be used in accordance with the charitable objects at the discretion of the trustees.
   Designated: these are unrestricted funds which have been set aside by the trustees for specific purposes.
   Restricted: these are funds that can only be used for particular restricted purposes defined by the benefactor and within the objects of the charity.
   Endowment: permanent endowment funds must be held permanently by the trustees and income arising is separately included in restricted funds for specific use as defined by the donors.

   The purpose and use of endowment, restricted and designated funds are disclosed in the notes to the accounts.

k) *Allocations*
   Wages, salary costs and office expenditure are allocated on the basis of the work done by the Executive Secretary and the Administrative Secretary.

l) *Pensions*
   Pension costs are charged to the SOFA when payments fall due. The Society contributed 10% of gross salary to the personal pension plan of one of the employees.

2. DONATIONS AND LEGACIES	2007 £	2006 £
Martin Lynn Bequest	2,000	–
G R Elton Bequest	438	1,696
Donations via membership	1,007	555
Gladstone Memorial Trust	600	600
Browning Bequest	1,263	93
Vera London Bequest	14,450	6,000
Sundry income	500	2,500
Gift Aid reclaimed	3,670	–
	£23,958	£11,444

3. GRANTS FOR AWARDS

	Unrestricted Funds £	Restricted Funds £	Total 2007 £	Total 2006 £
RHS Centenary Fellowship	10,622	–	10,622	2,500
Alexander Prize	250	–	250	252
Sundry Grants	300	–	300	200
Research support grants (see below)	19,615	1,000	20,615	20,342
A–Level prizes	300	–	300	520
A. S. Whitfield prize	–	1,144	1,144	1,111
E. M. Robinson Bequest				
– Grant to Dulwich Picture Library	–	–	–	2,500
Gladstone history book prize	1,690	–	1,690	1,111
P. J. Marshall Fellowship	–	10,790	10,790	9,624
British History Bibliography project grant	–	–	–	4,380
David Berry Prize	–	22	22	426
History Today Prize	–	–	–	16
Staff and support costs	7,634	–	7,634	6,952
	£40,411	£12,956	£53,367	£49,934

During the year Society awarded grants to a value of £20,615 (2006: £20,342) to 85 (2006: 85) individuals.

GRANTS PAYABLE

	2007 £	2006 £
Commitments at 1 July 2006	2,500	1,650
Commitments made in the year	45,733	42,982
Grants paid during the year	(48,233)	(42,132)
Commitments at 30 June 2007	£–	£2,500

Commitments at 30 June 2007 and 2006 are included in creditors.

4. TOTAL RESOURCES EXPENDED

	Staff costs £	Support costs £	Direct costs £	Total £
Cost of generating funds				
Investment manager's fee	–	–	15,987	15,987
Charitable activities				
Grants for awards (Note 3)	4,913	2,720	45,734	53,367
Conferences	4,602	1,360	6,042	12,004
Publications	9,203	5,441	53,274	67,918
Library	2,301	1,360	1,055	4,716
Membership services	27,922	13,602	3,685	45,209
Governance	6,902	2,720	11,568	21,190
Total resources expended	£55,843	£27,203	£137,345	£220,391

STAFF COSTS

	2007 £	2006 £
Wages and salaries	43,958	43,346
Social Security costs	7,895	7,013
Other pension costs	3,990	235
	£55,843	£50,594

SUPPORT COSTS

	2007 £	2006 £
Stationery, photocopying and postage	13,065	14,097
Computer support	559	1,792
Insurance	1,520	1,670
Telephone	119	659
Depreciation	716	715
Bad debts	8,324	7,064
Other	2,900	2,309
	£27,203	£28,306

The average number of employees in the year was 2 (2006: 2). There were no employees whose emoluments exceeded £60,000 in the year.

During the year travel expenses were reimbursed to 20 Councillors attending Council meetings at a cost of £3,536 (2006: £4,449). No Councillor received any remuneration during the year (2006 nil).

Included in governance is the following:

	2007 £	2006 £
Audit and accountancy	8,031	7,931
Other services	–	558

5. TANGIBLE FIXED ASSETS

	Computer Equipment £	Furniture And Equipment £	Total £
COST			
At 1 July 2006 and 30 June 2007	33,224	1,173	34,397
DEPRECIATION			
At 1 July 2006	31,321	1,173	32,494
Charge for the year	716	–	716
At 30 June 2007	32,037	1,173	33,210
NET BOOK VALUE			
At 30 June 2007	£1,187	£	£1,187
At 30 June 2006	£1,903	£ –	£1,903

All tangible fixed assets are used in the furtherance of the Society's objects.

6. INVESTMENTS

	General Fund £	Robinson Bequest £	Whitfield Prize Fund £	David Berry Essay Trust £	Total £
Market value at 1 July 2006	2,217,037	130,459	49,354	22,227	2,419,077
Additions	378,297	16,590	15,730	2,142	412,759
Disposals	(355,922)	(16,957)	(15,814)	–	(388,693)
Net gain on investments	178,753	10,701	3,366	2,588	195,408
Market value at 30 June 2007	£2,418,165	£140,793	£52,636	£26,957	£2,638,551
Cost at 30 June 2007	£1,930,831	£87,409	£43,062	£12,872	£2,074,174

	2007 £	2006 £
U K Equities	1,675,378	1,604,958
U K Government Stock and Bonds	472,181	561,321
Overseas equities	219,897	141,827
Uninvested Cash	278,096	110,971
	£2,638,551	£2,419,077
Dividends and interest on listed investments	102,873	86,203
Interest on cash deposits	689	999
	£103,562	£87,202

7. STOCK

	2007 £	2006 £
Transactions Sixth Series	847	731
Camden Fifth Series	2,078	1,957
Camden Classics Reprints	–	907
	£2,925	£3,595

8. DEBTORS

	2007 £	2006 £
Other debtors	4,820	14,603
Prepayments	1,778	5,388
	£6,598	£19,991

9. CREDITORS: Amounts due within one year

	2007 £	2006 £
Sundry creditors	2,786	2,873
Subscriptions received in advance	3,128	3,935
Accruals and deferred income	19,287	30,044
	25,201	£36,852

10. LEASE COMMITMETS

The Society has the following annual commitments under non-cancellable operating leases which expire:

	2006 £	2005 £
Within 1–2 years	£25,140	£–
Within 2–5 years	£–	£15,272

11. LIFE MEMBERS

The Society has ongoing commitments to provide membership services to 16 Life Members at a cost of approximately £50 each per year.

12. UNCAPITALISED ASSETS

The Society owns a library the cost of which is written off to the Statement of Financial Activities at the time of purchase. This library is insured for £82,000 and is used for reference purposes by the membership of the Society.

13. ENDOWMENT FUNDS

	Balance at 1 July 06 £	Incoming resources £	Outgoing resources £	Investment gain £	Balance at 30 June 07 £
A. S. Whitfield Prize Fund	46,770	–	(303)	3,366	49,833
The David Berry Essay Trust	21,368	–	–	2,588	23,956
	£68,138	£–	£(303)	£5,954	£73,789

A. S. Whitfield Prize Fund

The A. S. Whitfield Prize Fund is an endowment used to provide income for an annual prize for the best first monograph for British history published in the calendar year.

The David Berry Essay Trust

The David Berry Essay Trust is an endowment to provide income for annual prizes for essays on subjects dealing with Scottish history.

14. RESTRICTED FUNDS	Balance at 1 July 06 £	Incoming resources £	Outgoing resources £	Transfers £	Balance at 30 June 07 £
A. S. Whitfield Prize Fund Income	1,608	1,519	(1,144)	–	1,983
P. J. Marshall Fellowship	–	10,000	(10,790)	790	–
The David Berry Essay Trust Income	629	567	(22)	–	1,174
Martin Lynn Bequest	–	2,000	(1,000)	–	1,000
	£2,237	£14,086	£(12,956)	£(790)	£4,157

A. S. Whitfield Prize Fund Income

Income from the A. S. Whitfield Prize Fund is used to provide an annual prize for the best first monograph for British history published in the calendar year.

P. J. Marshall Fellowship

The P. J. Marshall Fellowship is used to provide a sum sufficient to cover the stipend for a one-year doctoral research fellowship alongside the existing Royal Historical Society Centenary Fellowship at the Institute of Historical Research.

The David Berry Essay Trust Income

Income from the David Berry Trust is to provide annual prizes for essays on subjects dealing with Scottish history

The Martin Lynn Bequest

This annual bequest is used by the Society to give financial assistance to postgraduates researching topics in African history.

15. DESIGNATED FUND	Balance at 1 July 06 £	Incoming resources £	Outgoing resources £	Investment gain £	Transfers £	Balance at 30 June 07 £
E. M. Robinson Bequest	£134,437	£5,072	£–	£10,701	£–	£150,210

E. M. Robinson Bequest

Income from the E. M. Robinson bequest is to further the study of history and to date has been used to provide grants to the Dulwich Picture Gallery.

16. GENERAL FUND	Balance at 1 July 06 £	Incoming resources £	Outgoing resources £	Investment gain £	Transfers £	Balance at 30 June 07 £
	£2,216,016	£255,197	£(207,132)	£178,753	£(790)	£2,442,044

17. ANALYSIS OF NET ASSETS BETWEEN FUNDS

	General Fund £	Designated Fund £	Restricted Funds £	Endowment Funds £	Total £
Fixed assets	1,187	–	–	–	1,187
Investments	2,414,552	150,212	–	73,789	2,638,551
	2,415,739	150,212	–	73,789	2,639,738
Current assets	51,506	–	4,157	–	55,663
Less: Creditors	(25,201)	–	–	–	(25,201)
Net current (liabilities)/assets	26,305	–	4,157	–	30,462
Net assets	£2,442,044	£150,212	£4,157	£73,789	£2,670,202